MAN INCORPORATE

CARL B. KAUFMANN is manager of the Publications Division, Public Relations Department, at E. I. du Pont de Nemours and Company in Wilmington, Delaware. He has studied at Dartmouth, MIT, the University of Michigan, and the University of Delaware, where he did his graduate work.

"Business is the principal social service."
—CLEMENT OF ALEXANDRIA

"Business is for the birds."
—STANFORD UNIVERSITY SENIOR

Man Incorporate

THE INDIVIDUAL AND HIS WORK
IN AN ORGANIZED SOCIETY

Carl B. Kaufmann

REVISED EDITION

Anchor Books

DOUBLEDAY & COMPANY, INC.
GARDEN CITY, NEW YORK

1969

For my wife

Man Incorporate was originally published by
Doubleday & Company, Inc., in 1967.
The revised Anchor Books edition is published by
arrangement with Doubleday & Company, Inc.

Anchor Books edition: 1969.

CONTENTS

CONTENTS

ACKNOWLEDGMENTS

Asked how much time a writer invests in a book, someone once said, "His total age, plus one year—the year it takes off at the end of his life." If in practice the investment is a bit smaller, the saving is due to the assistance of others. This book could not have been written without the comfort and support of a patient family, and the aid of numerous friends and colleagues, notably Charles M. Hackett, Glen Perry, and Thomas W. Stephenson, who thought well of the idea at the start, and encouraged me to persist in it; several members of the history department of the University of Delaware, principally Professors John Beer, Evelyn Clift, Walther Kirchner, and George Windell, whose stimulus was greater than they know; and Mrs. Charles Downing and Miss Helen Logan, who exhausted reams of paper on my behalf. I hold them blameless for inadequacies and errors in this volume, but remain greatly in their debt.

CARL B. KAUFMANN

1

INTRODUCTION

This is a book about man and his work, with special reference to work in organizations. It deals in part with the tools and techniques man has turned to his service, and in part with his ideas about himself and his labor. It is concerned with the relationship between the individual and the organization, and with the preservation of man's sense of identity in a society that is increasingly institutionalized.

In a way, this book is intended as a general commentary on our times, for work is an inseparable feature of life. Most of us work, have worked, or will work. That plain fact provides reason enough to explore the subject.

In a similarly practical vein, it is in order to examine the organizations in which work is focused. Conventionally, as a measure of our respect for the individual, we talk about work in terms of independent effort, but in point of fact few of us today are occupied in singular fashion. For better or worse we work in groups, often very large ones. That being the case, it is appropriate to look at organizations, and to scrutinize with particular care the ones that employ a majority of the work force, the profit-oriented corporations. What they do for society, or to it, has distinct relevance to each of us, however employed.

There is also good reason, and perhaps a need, to examine work on a looser time scale and a broader base, to ask how society arrived at its present arrangement, what alternatives have been tried, and what better solutions there might be to man's future economic and social needs.

It would be wrong to expect too much of history, but foolish to expect too little. If the record of the past holds no magic answers, it at least suggests that the questions are not new, and in quest of current answers it may pay to explore previous solutions.

This book is in part a history, probing the chronology of organizations, the technology of work, and the ideas that surround both, in the hope that these may shed light on organizations and technology and ideas today. It exalts no heroes except Everyman, and marks no military conquests, although it notes some other kinds of triumphs. It invokes the past only to provide context for the present, and to trace the origins, insofar as they can be traced, of the dedications, experiments, sacrifices, and ideals that man has brought to his work.

"Work" is taken here in the most general sense and in all its forms, intellectual and manual. As such, it is as much a part of our heritage as the Magna Charta and the Declaration of Independence, and it has equal relevance to current generations. Impelled by the cane or more temperate persuasions, many of us as youngsters committed to memory the dates of the Monroe Doctrine and the firing on Fort Sumter. Here, we mark other milestones—the technical advances by which man added leverage to his labor, his victories in the war against want, his trials and errors in sculpting organizations to his needs.

In the interest of simplicity, these are discussed as though they were separate topics. This is but a convenient fiction, adopted to reduce segments of history to digestible size. Civilization is not like an engine bolted together in pieces. It is like an organism so arranged that its parts derive shape as well as support from each other. There is no way to dissociate tools from organizations, or to consider these apart from society's broadest objectives. Work is in no way intelligible as an isolated function, to be acknowledged (on the present schedule) for forty hours a week. Man is what he thinks and does; his work is implicit in both, a cause as much as an effect, and it has been a primary force shaping the character of society.

This is an inquiry, then, into men, work, and organizations. If it can be said to have a premise, the premise is this: Whatever work man has done, however noble or shabby the effort, the sweat of brow has been a major factor in the construction of civilization and the evolution of human values. Failing to find purpose in his work, it seems reasonable to conclude, man is not likely to find purpose anywhere else.

The Paradox of Prosperity

The premise is subject to challenge and, in fact, is being challenged on several counts in many quarters. In the eyes of some, technology now appears not as a humane and benevolent genie, but as a specter of tragedy, a shadowy thief of man's dignity and probably his livelihood. The institutions which today provide a focal point for so much of man's work are viewed in some quarters with fear and suspicion, as though they are out of step with society and hostile to its best interest. Work itself, once lauded on moral as well as economic grounds, today is considered by many to be irrelevant to "the good life." It is taken as a sentence, a task devoid of virtue, and perhaps even indecent or antisocial in its meaning. It is to be endured in payment for time off, during which time each of us will be able to "do his own thing," and thus redress the moral balance. Allegedly, we have now attained such material abundance that large numbers of us are threatened with a surplus of involuntary leisure. In sum, man incorporate, *homo technicas*, beneficiary of five thousand years of increasing social organization and technical proficiency, has come to doubt the contributions of his organizations, to fear the results of his technology, and above all to question the basic purpose of labor.

This seems a paradox. The United States and Western Europe constitute the most highly organized and technically-minded civilization ever constructed. The material wealth of this economic unit is staggering by the standards of any previous century. The freedom and economic mobility offered the individual, while far from complete, nonetheless are at a level that was hardly imaginable in earlier civilizations. Why bite the hand that feeds you?

But what is at issue here is not take-home pay or purchasing power or working conditions, although these are problems of moment. Automation, unemployment, and labor-management relations also are involved, but they are not primary either. The mood of alienation reflects a problem transcending the immediate. What does man seek in his work, and what are the consequences of that search, both to himself and his civilization? That problem has not come up before, at least not in quite the present form. In all previous centuries and societies, the moral issue was buried by economics: man worked to survive. Why look for other reasons?

Some people looked anyway—those who had the leisure to do so. In every society since Homeric Greece, the aristocracy and intelligentsia have debated the relationship of man to his work. At times the mood of doubt and rejection has been far stronger than it is today.

The consequences are worth noting, for there appears to be a fundamental link between man's outlook on work and his prospects for the future. If history is any guide, the current ground swell of despair should be a matter of great concern. For what history seems to say is that man has progressed toward his highest accomplishment when he has looked upon enterprise with favor, and sought individual fulfillment through his work. Where work has been held in disrespect, and other pursuits have been interjected as substitutes, civilization has faltered and declined.[1]

Significantly, the problem of rejection is strongly manifest today in the United States. This is understandable, in one sense. Here more than anywhere else, there is the wealth to eliminate raw economic need, enough wealth, in fact, to provoke a suggestion that at some future date not too distant, many of us will be paid for not working.

One provocative proposal, originated several years ago by the Ad Hoc Committee on the Triple Revolution, and since modified by others, recommends that each head of a household in the United States be guaranteed a minimum $3000 per annum, by gift if necessary. That idea has provoked outrage in some quarters, but it has gained considerable support as a quick way of lifting the "have nots" at least to a subsistence level. Among the advocates of a negative income tax are men of such diverse persuasions as Milton Friedman of the University of Chicago, Joseph Block of Inland Steel, Albert Nicholson of Mobil, and Robert Theobald, socio-economist and writer who has worked closely with the center for the Study of Democratic Institutions. They argue that a properly administered system of income support would be less expensive than existing welfare programs, and less degrading to the recipients.[2]

Whatever the merits and political prospects of this proposal, it is intriguing in part for what it does not say. Work is not scorned, but neither is it seen as socially indispensable. The objective is to make people less poor, and that is commendable. But a parallel objective must be to provide them a chance for dignity, and it is debatable that this can be done without reference to an ethic of work. Psychic poverty is debilitating too, and may remain untouched by the negative income tax.

This is undeniably a rich nation, the first in all of history rich enough to pose ethical questions about work not only to a small elite, but also to the broader civic body. The bottom layer of that polity, the least educated slice of society, has found its own answer to the ethical question, and a way to articulate its feelings. One of the messages the poor have been sending middle-class America, with bricks as well as words, is that they want jobs. They want dignity, not the dole.

In a historical sense, America is perhaps the least likely nation to alienate itself from work, and to levy charges against its economic institutions. For this is the outstanding modern example of a society that deliberately and knowingly has identified work as a central community function. In the course of building this nation, the people gave great encouragement to enterprise and perspiration. We organized technology, and we made it pay. Our unmatched wealth, for which some of us now seem apologetic, is abundant evidence of the efficacy of that course.

The United States certainly did not invent the organized life, but it has been the principal protagonist, and the urge to consolidate has appeared as strongly in cultural and political realms as in economics. The units of participation are larger and more numerous here, more specialized in function, more technical in focus, and more dependent upon one another, than in any other nation.

It has been this way from the beginning. In 1835, when America had only begun to show its zeal, the perceptive and indefatigable French visitor, Alexis de Tocqueville, entered this observation in his commentary *Democracy in America:*[3]

> Americans of all ages, all conditions, and all dispositions constantly form associations. They have not only commercial and manufacturing companies, in which all take part, but associations of a thousand other kinds, religious, moral, serious, futile, general or restricted, enormous or diminutive. The Americans make associations to give entertainments, to found seminaries, to build inns, to construct churches, to diffuse books, to send missionaries to the antipodes; in this manner they found hospitals, prisons, and schools. If it is proposed to inculcate some truth . . . they form a society. Wherever at the head of some new undertaking you see the government in France, or a man of rank in England, in the United States you will be sure to find an association.

Tocqueville should see us now. The nation is even more gregarious than it was in the 1830s, it is fourteen times as populous, and it is infinitely more organized. There are groups to aid travelers, save the minor leagues, unite lonely hearts, preserve barbershop quartet singing, and explore space. We have colleges and universities (2000 of them), philanthropic organizations (6000), Boy Scout troops (65,000), symphony orchestras (1100), labor unions (17 million pay them dues), and Legion posts (16,000).

This nation operates the most highly organized scientific and engineering establishment ever fashioned. About 1.5 million people, in a work force of about 70 million, are scientists, engineers, or teachers working in this area of education. Under the sponsorship of private foundations, universities, industrial corporations, and government agencies (in ascending order of expenditure), outlays for research and development have grown at a rate of 10 per cent a year since 1910. Spending has passed the rate of $25 billion a year, with no peak yet in sight.

There are more than 100,000 units of state, local, and federal government in existence, operating on budgets that account for about one-fourth of the value of everything the United States produces.

The business community is divided into about five million units. Three million of these commercial institutions occupy their owners and not more than one or two employees each. However, dozens among them count their employees in the tens of thousands, and the largest offers sustenance and fringe benefits to 760,000 citizens. As it works out, the labor force is split about 50–50 between firms with more than 500 employees and firms with less.

On the periphery of the business community, there are 13,000 trade associations and 5000 local Chambers of Commerce or community development agencies. There are associations for makers of lawn mowers and leaf springs, button molds and business forms, oak flooring and olive oil, peat moss and pencils. There is even an association of executives of associations, claiming 2000 members. Lumping all these together, it develops that more than 45 million people participate directly in the business of business.[4]

It would be almost impossible to keep an accurate census of America's organizations. They come and go so fast that all catalogs are obsolete on completion. In a free society, organizations survive only as long as they can muster support, and the public can be whimsical, or at any rate unpredictable, in dispensing it. We lack a fixed code for rendering judgments, choosing instead to let the process of consensus take care of the missteps.

Organizations range in purpose from the sacred to the ridiculous, without unanimity as to which is which; one man's frivolity is another man's crusade. That being the case, and in keeping with the principle that the public ought to make the decisions, the nation constantly reviews its institutions and modifies its judgments about them. It is a necessary and healthy process.

We are now reassessing our economic organizations, not because they have failed us, but because in some ways they have succeeded too well. Within this century, largely because of these institutions, man has gained a level of productive efficiency and a command of nature that dwarfs his previous performance. This has provoked the question, which is entirely in order, of what man has lost in the bargain. Through technical legerdemain, also largely developed in these organizations, our vision has been extended outward to the far reaches of the cosmos, and inward to the tiniest recesses of the atom. This excites us, but it forces us to ask what price we pay to tamper with nature. Is Technology now in the saddle, riding Man?

Texas style, we boast of the bigness of organizations, yet underneath, people are clearly troubled by the size of our economic units and by their imputed penetration into human affairs. There is uneasiness about the power and ethics of the business community, based largely on the belief that the largest members of the club have somehow imposed their own set of standards on society, different from those of the public in general. Has a pall of conformity settled over our affluent society? Have we created, in the modern corporation, a power without suitable checks and balances?

The View of Work

One of the problems here stems from the fact that our vision of work is out of step with reality. We cling to one view of labor, and see another before our eyes.

Throughout most of history the environment in which man worked was well defined and relatively stable. The object of man's effort was a finished product or service, usually handcrafted. There were convenient yardsticks by which man and society could judge the personal contribution. The field was plowed, the ship was piloted into harbor, the shoe was taken from the cobbler's bench, finished. A man could say, "I did that," secure in the knowledge that no one could deny his claim.

In many fields today, such tangible measures are lacking. The individual contribution is diffuse, indirect, and sometimes invisible. The hours expended and the thickness of calluses may or may not be meaningful, and the finished product, which would stand as its own symbol of worth, may or may not be exposed to public view.

Tens of millions of people work in industries where, for the sake of efficiency, the total effort is subdivided into minute specialties. Many rarely touch an end product and, very often, only men with specialized training can tell whether a task has been done skillfully or ineptly.

Removed from the final product, contributing but a fraction to its completion, people naturally have come to question the significance of their work. Surrounded by hydra-handed machines stronger than man—tireless machines which function more quickly than eye and hand and are capable of self-adjustment to meet changing conditions—people understandably ask whether man is now master or slave.

A second cause of uneasiness is the impersonality of large organizations. Increasingly, work is focused in institutions with a membership beyond the circle of family and acquaintance, and with a tenure beyond the individual life span. The typical organization has become the lengthened shadow not of one man, but of hosts of men working in concert and succession.

This has long been the pattern with respect to political affairs, and is accepted without comment. It is taken for granted that units of government will outlast their mortal sponsors. Sometimes this is deplored: Organizations, like men, struggle to survive whether they are doing anything worthwhile or not, and it is all too easy, as C. Northcote Parkinson has observed, to spawn bureaucracy in inverse proportion to accomplishment. Nonetheless, the permanent political institution is one of man's finest inventions. As has long been apparent, groups of people failing to devise an enduring structure of leadership do not climb the staircase of civilization; they huddle in caves.

The same pattern of permanence is found in other fields. In manufacture and commerce, education, culture, and even in recreation, most groups today operate on the premise that they will survive indefinitely. If they fail, it is usually by reason of bad planning and execution, not by intent. Again, the logical rationale for an enduring structure is not really in question. Society could hardly survive if every organization expired with its proprietor, and every generation had to build its own economic structure from scratch. Still, questions arise. How *do* people keep from getting lost in an organization comprising tens of thousands of people? What of all our lofty phrases about the priceless value of the individual? Are they but fine words to be chiseled on the tombstone of man's lost dignity?

In the minds of many, we have made Faust's bargain: Man is swapping his soul for a summer cottage and a second car. To cap the bargain, he has tossed in the well-being of his own society. Our vaunted wealth is overstated, for in buying the cars and cottages, we never paid the attendant social costs.

There are no statistics to measure this conviction, but no poll of the public psyche is needed to show its existence. It appears as rejection among young people appalled at the blight and human decay and injustice that still exist in this land of material riches, and willing to condemn the system that permits this. It appears as limp resignation among older people obsessed by personal rewards, but unconcerned with their own investment of talent. There is a clamor for higher pay and more generous fringes—an appeal that is logical enough, but that frequently is unrelated to any increase in personal contribution.

It appears, too, in the guise of the plumber who forgets his tools, and the mason who refuses to set more than a specified number of bricks a day, regardless of the number his talent could command. It is implicit in the "standby" arrangement, a remarkable contract device by which musicians receive pay not for playing, but for being present while someone else plays. It is the hidden ethic of the office worker with a near genius for appearing busy while producing at the minimum level of strain, and of the manager untroubled by elementary conscience, who permits defective merchandise to be shipped to a customer. It is the unwritten clause in contracts stipulating that typographers shall be paid to set useless type. This "junk" duplicates material already prepared for publication in another form; the type is broken up as soon as it is set.

These and other examples of nonwork are furiously protested (and, it must be acknowledged, frequently exaggerated), but for some reason the most important problem is rarely stated. The problem is not principally economic. It is not alone a problem of ethics, although nonwork does violate our professed and somewhat puritanical code. The main problem is the effect on the people involved in it. How can any man deliberately limit his contribution, or accept the anonymity of The Establishment, and retain a sense of usefulness or dignity?

The Process of Substitution

The answer, as some would have it, is that there is no dignity in most types of work anyway. Critics charge that work is so fragmented, and the institutions of work so de-personalized as to require no talents worthy of a man. They point to technology and mass production as the culprits, and argue that much of the nation's productive machinery could be run by children (as, indeed, it once was).

How much justification there is for this view is a matter for later review. Now, it is enough to note that many people undoubtedly accept such a gloomy interpretation, and look elsewhere for compensation. They may look fairly far afield. Psychological studies suggest that this problem may be vital as an underlying factor in serious juvenile crime and promiscuity. If they see nothing beyond material rewards awaiting them in a career,[5] youngsters are likely to look elsewhere for what they may call "kicks," but which may really be their search for identity.

We have to proceed carefully here. Poverty, prejudice, lack of education, and other forces are involved in juvenile misbehavior, and the usual disclaimer about "the younger generation" must be entered. One of the few advantages of growing up is that one gains the right to complain about the decline and fall of the young. The privilege is more than most of us adults can resist. Moreover, the deficiencies of American youth can perhaps be traced to the example their parents have set.

The process of substitution, of seeking values outside the work atmosphere that are presumed not to exist within, is by no means limited to minors. It is adult voices, by and large, that have been loudest in protesting the "face-less" toils of the industrial age, and in singing the merits of a "leisure society" in which life will be made bountiful and creative via off-the-job pursuits. In communities throughout the land, adults have led in the almost frantic pursuit of "outside" activities. The word itself signifies a quest tangential to work.

Witness, for example, the spectacle of amateurs who have never learned to draw struggling with the elusive substance of water-color painting. (Amateur painters number ten million.) Note the men who lay in a stock of power tools and, being all thumbs, proceed to hammer or saw off one or both of them. (The do-it-yourself urge sustains a $6-billion industry.) Count the ladies embarking on community projects for which the need is debatable and the qualification of the group invisible. Observe the Little (If Any) Theater, as it has been aptly called, doing annual battle with the works of Shaw and Shakespeare. (Community theaters number more than a thousand.)

There is no use extending the list. Such pastimes are not always absurd, and the jokes about them have a hollow ring.

The pursuit of culture is not always a mark of neurosis. It can be a sign of curiosity or intelligence. Most hobbyists are simply enjoying themselves; until they put a price on their craftwork or otherwise ask to be judged by professional standards, they deserve no criticism. The ladies who sally forth to reform the community may well be meddling, but they also may be on the way to impressive accomplishments. There are schools, hospitals, and libraries all over this country built by "militant do-gooders." One would be bold indeed to say them nay, for they are following a do-it-yourself tradition that began in this country at Jamestown.

Moreover, male or female, young or old, if they seek in diversions something they cannot find in their work, they are almost certainly doomed to failure. If they cannot draw a sense of creativity and purpose from their jobs, are they not (with the lady in the immortal song) more to be pitied than censured?

The tragedy lies in disillusionment. There never has been a "leisure society," and there is no reason to suppose that there ever can be one. The examples invoked in defense of this approach prove just the opposite point, as is demonstrated in a later chapter. Those societies which have accomplished the most have been dedicated not to idle pleasures, but to the rigorous work of hand and mind.

Presumably, those who now seek the salvation of man in the "leisure society" have something more in mind than fishing and softball. They advocate a "meaningful" use of off-work hours. But this leaves insurmountable barriers.

For one thing, who is to say what is meaningful? Pericles, the Athenian statesman, suggested one approach nearly 2500 years ago. "The individual can be trusted," he said; "Let him alone."[6] Opposite Pericles is the equally old, and ominous view that man needs to be prevented from "debasing" himself. He needs a cultural keeper. To use the words of sociologist Georges Friedmann, there seems to be a need for some "intermediate zone of planned intervention, centralized at State level." In some remarkable fashion, unexplained, this planning is to be kept free from "totalitarian tendencies."[7]

A good many banners have been nailed to each of these flagpoles, but no one has yet resolved the basic difficulty of the leisure society. Whether we make a mockery of freedom by stuffing the purposeful life down the public throat, or let people "waste" their hours pursuing trivia, man's off-the-job activities are often a dubious substitute for more conventional ways of earning self-respect. As psychiatrists from Freud to Fromm have pointed out, men need a realistic standard to which they can repair. Work is one of the few things in life, if not the only thing, that makes inflexible demands. Far from creating neuroses, the day-to-day requirements of a job serve quite literally as occupational therapy (and are used as such by psychiatrists with patients who need emotional first aid). As Erich Fromm suggests in *The Sane Society*, man's mode of work is an essential element in forming his character. The most commendable of leisure activities can serve as no more than a pathetic substitute.

A suggested alternative, that we reduce the pace of change and return to a more pastoral, craft-centered life, is as unrealistic as the "leisure society." It has a certain innocent appeal, but unfortunately it fails to address the problem. We have made our compact with the organized life, and cannot renege.

More or less from habit, America preserves the imagery of its once agrarian life. Perhaps there is something of Henry Thoreau in all of us, or Fletcher Christian. At any rate, we all but revere (in theory) a life next to nature.

Were we polytheists, we would doubtless include among our gods one to guarantee each man a sanctuary, his own patch of ground in the country, far from the city with its high living and low virtue.

The agrarian ethic leads to some striking contradictions. One lady I know, the wife of an heir to a major fortune, is vexed by the fact that highway planners may slice a corner off the family land holdings to widen a badly over-crowded road. She happens to live 200 miles from the homestead, but the principle of the thing bothers her. Her soul cringes at the thought of bulldozers in the placid glens. She has lots of company. What she fails to note is why the road in question is so crowded. It carries increasing numbers of employees to their jobs in the family corporation, where they help make increasing profits for this selfsame family. I have called this fact to her attention, but it leaves her unimpressed. She still wants an eighteenth-century life—with twentieth-century dividends. Even her millions cannot buy that. (America, incidentally, has no monopoly on such sentiment, as is demonstrated by the British schoolboy who wrote that agriculture once was widespread in England, adding glumly, "Today it is confined to the rural areas."[8])

When we school our children in rocks and rills, woods and templed hills, we give them passable history and good conservation, but a poor reflection of present conditions. A number of trends, irreversible, have turned the agrarian society into an urban one. Like it or not, large numbers of people will continue to live and work in an industrial, technically facile society with crowds and traffic problems, offices and factories, noise and commotion.

The plain facts of population (quite apart from the cold war and our own economic ambitions) are enough to sweep away at a stroke all talk of escape for most of us. There are three billion people on this planet, and not enough sylvan retreats to hold more than a fraction of that number. Barring nuclear catastrophe or a wholly unexpected reversal of trends, the population could reach seven billion by A.D. 2000, with the United States at that date

holding 400 million. If people are to remain civilized, or
even fed, they will have to stay organized.

This is not the disaster it might seem, even though it
offends some of our legends. It could be a good thing,
depending upon the kinds of organizations involved and
the opportunities people find in and around them. Whatever the conventional view, the agrarian life is not an un-
mixed blessing. It has its share of horrors, as many rocks
as rills, and even in its most appealing features it lacks
much of the flavor and stimulus of urban life, with the
concomitant attractions of universities, hospitals, art gal-
leries, and the company of many different people. It is
nice to live in the country, but civilization happens to be
a product of cities (and vice versa).

Civilized man has always had to settle for an uneasy
compromise between the individual and the group, and
the increasing scale of group activity requires some sacrifice or subordination of personal volition. To this conflict
there can be no final resolution. The objective is not to
abolish such problems, or ignore them, but to gain the
most from the compromises.

The central question is whether the organized life, in its
present and potential forms, offers man the opportunity to
establish a sense of commitment and dignity in his life;
whether, in effect, the sacrifices he makes extend or limit
the freedoms he values most.

How satisfactory is the quid pro quo? In quest of an
answer, there follow some observations about technology
and economic organization through history, an examination of the attitudes that have surrounded work in various
times and places, an inquiry into the remarkable social and
economic record of the United States, and finally a report
on what it is like to work in large organizations, from the
vantage point of one who has.

THE INSTITUTIONAL HERITAGE

Historians have long searched for a key to progress, a simple way to explain why one society endures while another crumbles. They have not found it, for the subject will not admit to simplification. Edward Gibbon dedicated twenty-seven years and three volumes to the decline of Rome, but his account, instead of settling the matter, only touched off almost two hundred years of further debate and elaboration. It still cannot be said with finality what brought that civilization to its knees, and one explanation that would encompass all societies is even more remote.

Some civilizations have survived over extended periods, to the point where they appeared unassailable. Egypt existed for more than two thousand years as a political entity and much longer as a distinct culture. Yet it succumbed at last. Other civilizations have thrived only a few centuries, yet have left us monuments and masterworks as enduring as any produced over the millennia. Hellenic Greece is the prime example. The world has never recovered all that it lost when the Athenian democracy fell to Sparta. Yet Athens flourished but two hundred years, and its highest cultural accomplishments were concentrated in an even shorter span of time.

Still other societies have earned no place at all in the chronology of progress. They have survived without reference to time, recording little gain or decline. The Berbers of northern Africa are such a people; the Australian aborigines, a still more primitive example. Both have begun only in this century to emerge from the Neolithic period, a stage of development through which others of their contemporaries passed six thousand years ago.

The search for explanations to cover such polar examples brings forth all manner of propositions. Hospitality of climate and availability of natural resources have been investigated. Genetic and cultural difference among races and ethnic groups have been explored. Societies have been poor, it has been said, because of inferior soil, oppression by colonial powers, overpopulation or underpopulation, lack of educational facilities, shortage of venture capital, or because the people were lazy. Other societies have prospered, it is maintained, because they possessed the opposite advantages, because they are God's chosen people, or because they are plain lucky. It has even been suggested that the human feature characteristic of high performance is a long, narrow head, that being the shape found among certain Europeans.

Some historians have tried to restate the past in the form of laws. Oswald Spengler, dean of this school, proposed the existence of an unseen hand guiding civilization along a path of birth, growth, and death. Other Europeans, extending the thoughts of the German *Naturphilosophen,* have envisioned the destiny of society in the rule of superman and superstate, a dream that nearly found a frightening reality in the Third Reich. Some, with Karl Marx, have reduced history to class conflict based on economic power. Others have expressed the belief (as much from faith as from scholarship) that all events will someday find a place in the comprehensive history of liberty, while still others have ruefully submitted that the record, if anyone lives to write it, will turn out to be the chronicle of tyranny. The law of history, to restate Lord Acton's familiar conclusion, may be that "power corrupts, and absolute power corrupts absolutely."

It may be, as philosophers point out, that we are tilting at windmills. There may be no laws of history of a sort to satisfy mathematicians or physicists. The search for universal statements is futile unless civilization happens to be "law abiding," and we lack resolute proof that it is.

What we can profitably seek in history, if not a simplistic doctrine or "final answer," is some record of order with significance to our own time. Our world becomes more intelligible, perhaps, if we know something of past patterns and departures from patterns, continuities and discontinuities, and forces that provoke change and forces that solidify the status quo.

With this as the objective, it is intriguing to examine the institutional heritage of the Western world. It proves to be a rich chronicle, and the sector of it that deals with economic life is especially pertinent, for all of it can be discussed in the modern idiom. Whether people are pushed by an unseen hand or left by a disinterested Providence to fend for themselves, whether their skulls are appropriately oblong or are as round as cannon balls, they are confronted in every generation by economic requirements. The idea of meeting these in an organized way, rather than leaving every man to himself, was a premise and prerequisite of early Mesopotamian civilization, and the structure that surrounds work today can be traced to that ancient point of origin.

Modern economic institutions are not products of the Industrial Revolution or of the birth of capitalism, but of a succession of experiments in organization that began in prehistory. The market-centered economy is not a contemporary invention, but an outgrowth of trends well established by the end of the Middle Ages. The imperfections and impositions of the organized life, together with the advantages, have been topics of discussion from a time long predating the birth of Christ.

Moreover, the economic element has a broader bearing. It is implicit in the history of organizations of all forms and purposes, and in the evolution of the energetic, multifaceted political and social structure of the Western world today. Economically even more than politically, there has been a turbulent but a decided flow from autocracy to freedom. Decisions imposed by the few have given way to

a dissemination of authority among the many. We regard
this, properly, as one of humanity's greatest triumphs; one
of the responsible agencies, very notable in its contributions, is the institution man has devised for the accomplishment of work.[1]

Subdivide and Conquer

One of man's first steps into the organized life—his first
major compromise with his savage independence, and at
the same time one of his most intelligent decisions—was
to subdivide his work. We retain the notion, perpetuated
in countless schoolbooks, that the Industrial Revolution
brought this about by assigning individuals to narrow
specialties. This is a fiction which obscures an important
fact. The division of work into specialties is not an event
identified with one time or place; it is part of the civilizing
process. It is a function of urbanization, which is another
way of saying the same thing. Regardless of the period of
history, in populous areas, work has been fragmented.

Early in his tribal experience, man learned that the jack-
of-all-trades masters few. At least seven thousand years ago,
and more probably ten thousand, community organizations
existed with men and women assigned to particular tasks
according to age, strength, and dexterity. By 3500 B.C., in
the civilization created in Sumer, life was well enough organized to permit city planning, farm irrigation, and experiments with elaborate structures of government, all of
which suggests a high degree of specialization and some
administrative skill. By 1400 B.C., division had reached
such refinement that guilds of craftsmen had been organized, and were important enough to warrant listing in
clay tablets, the vital records of the time.

Division prompted subdivision. Several hundred years
before Christ's birth, Xenophon, in his biography of Cyrus
the Persian, noted the link between the ways of work and
the size of a community:[2]

. . . in small towns the same workman makes chairs and doors and plows and tables, and often this same artisan builds houses, and even so he is thankful if he can find employment enough to support him. And it is of course impossible for a man of many trades to be proficient in all of them. In the large cities, on the other hand, inasmuch as many people have demands to make upon each branch of industry, one trade alone, and very often even less than a whole trade is enough to support a man; one man for instance makes shoes for men and another for women; and there are places even where one man earns a living by only stitching shoes, another by cutting them out, another by sewing the uppers together, while there is another who performs none of these operations but only assembles the parts. It follows therefore as a matter of course that he who devotes himself to a very highly specialized line of work is bound to do it in the best possible manner.

A unique instance? Herodotus, grandfather of historians, found a similar subdivision of labor among doctors in Egypt. "There are . . . innumerable doctors," he wrote in the fifth century B.C., "some specializing in diseases of the eyes, others of the head, others of the teeth, others of the stomach, and so on."[3]

And some, one would suppose, were general practitioners, though this too entails subdivision, for it makes a specialty of not specializing.

Throughout Greek and Roman history most jobs in the cities were compartmentalized and interdependent to a degree that would be quite acceptable in a modern industrial economy. Technology has added many new types of work (the U. S. Department of Labor's current occupational catalog includes more than 700 job categories), but the crafts that have survived from antiquity, such as carpentry and masonry, are hardly more subdivided today than in Rome.

What the ancient economic order did not require—and this is particularly true of industrial tasks, although it applies as well to trade and finance—was the establishment of large, factory-like organizations with many employees. In either Greece or Rome, a business with fifty or one hundred employees would have been gigantic.

A capitalism similar to the present form did not exist in the ancient world. Banks operated with the capital of their owners alone. They had no stockholders and few depositors in the modern sense. Only a few manufacturing industries attained substantial size, and these were the ones producing widely used, inexpensive products. Glassware, bricks, and furniture were mass produced, and pottery was turned out in such volume that in one Roman plant there was a 10,000-gallon vat for mixing clay. Most often, though, even widespread needs were filled by small firms crowded together into one quarter of the city, each occupying its proprietor and at most a handful of assistants. In sum, work was fragmented and not consolidated.

This was not an oversight. In the ancient world there was no advantage to size. Output rose on an arithmetic scale, in proportion to the number of workers. The great multiplier of productive efficiency, and the principal justification for large-scale production units, was the joint development of machine tools and the mass market, both of which were far in the future.

The closest approach to capitalism, at least until the Middle Ages, was a tripartite arrangement popular in Greece. A moneylender, a merchant, and a shipowner joined forces to undertake ventures larger than they could tackle individually. The financier advanced the necessary funds—at interest rates up to 25 per cent or more, depending on the (usually considerable) risks involved—the shipowner supplied the vessel and crew, and the merchant traveled as supercargo, buying and selling to the account of the triumvirate. At the end of the voyage, if there was a profit, the three partners divided the gains at dockside, and went their separate ways looking for other opportunities.

The Idea of Organization

The idea of commerce is nearly as venerable as the subdivision of work, and is equally a part of civilization. Isolationists to the contrary notwithstanding, few societies have ever stood alone economically. As Isocrates, a Greek teacher of about 400 B.C., put it, speaking some time before the Common Market, "There is no country sufficient to itself, but in all there is a shortage of one product and a surplus of another."

Early societies dealt with the problem in the most natural way possible. They bartered. (They also pirated and looted, another of man's inventions for the redistribution of property.) The Minoans and Phoenicians turned this into nearly a full-time career, supporting themselves more by hauling goods than by making them. The Greeks built themselves a mixed economy, heavily dependent upon sea trade. The port of Piraeus, near Athens, became a world emporium, "a store where everything abounds." From Piraeus went oil, wine, woolen products, lead and silver from the mines at Laurium, marble, pottery, and arms. To Piraeus came grain, preserved fish and meat, cheese, fruit, iron and copper, timber (by this time the woodlands around Athens had been stripped, and the Greeks were paying the price for nonconservation), raw wool and flax, tile, bronze, and such luxury items as perfume which were unavailable locally.

The Romans, "prime borrowers of the ages," combined the commercial system of their neighbors with the most highly consolidated political and administrative system known until then. The synthesis produced a flourishing economy, at least for a time, within a political domain encompassing all of the Mediterranean coastline, Britain, all of what are now France and Spain together with part of Germany, and most of the land surrounding the Aegean and Black seas.

Both Romans and Greeks saw their economies collapse,

the Romans in part because they were too eager to organize, the Greeks largely because they were not eager enough. Greek civilization was composed of a loose-knit and quarrelsome collection of city-states. Unwilling or unable to band together into more rational political units, they were too small to survive indefinitely on their own resources or by conquest.

The Romans erred in the opposite direction, swallowing more than they could digest. It may well be that the fall of Rome was "inevitable," not in the sense that such an economy is inherently too cumbersome to be operated by a centralized dictatorship (consider the USSR today) but in terms of other limitations. The crudities of communication and the absence of effective control and production mechanisms might have spelled Rome's doom even if she had always had the wisest of rulers, which she did not. What Rome needed was an aristocracy less squanderous of her resources, a better way of matching goods and services to the needs of her people, and what is now called more output per man-hour. The process of distribution was guided from a central command post months out-of-date in its information, and often captained by patronage and cupidity.

Meaning no frivolity, a centralized economy on the scale of Rome, if it was to endure, would have benefited by telephones, a supply of Jeeps, and some bright supply officers. The great advantage of a dictatorship—its ability to force change and progress, sometimes to the good of the people—is at the same time its crippling disadvantage. It is bound to err some of the time, and the cruder its communications and information processing system, the more serious its misjudgments are likely to be. As Plato noted, in the hands of fallible and ambitious men communal utopias degenerate into despotism. Benevolent dictatorship, he concluded, would not work even on the small scale of the city-state. On the scale of the Roman Empire, which was much vaster than anything Plato had in mind for his philosopher-kings, such a utopian state becomes all the more precarious.

It is, of course, pure speculation to say that no centralized society could survive without modern technology, but until the present era no large, centralized civilization has sustained itself. Rome, the Macedonian empire of Alexander, Byzantium, and Islam are the four societies of the past that attained the broadest physical dimensions, and none was able to consolidate and hold its position of power.

The alternative way of organizing economic life, which none of these four tried, is to center the power of decision in the marketplace instead of the palace. Such a system looks implausible. It often lacks the ability to shift direction on short notice. It is difficult to police, and it has a tendency to wander off on "uneconomic" tangents. But it can be applied in all but the smallest societies, it contains its own mechanism for correcting mistakes and imbalances, and in the long run it is more flexible and amenable than any centrally controlled structure.

The open economy implies a climate of political freedom, a widespread spirit of enterprise, and a diversity of outlets for man's energies. The development of these came as part of a pattern of economic change throughout the Middle Ages. During this period of more than one thousand years, there was a realignment of manufacture, trade, finance, and agriculture which altered all facets of life, and brought capitalism into existence.

Towns and cities expanded, new measures of wealth developed, and new kinds of men rose to commanding positions in economic affairs. Finance and manufacture were coupled to trade, establishing an integrated economy of the type Rome needed but never attained. The factory system was inaugurated, providing new locations and methods of work. To the prevailing authority vested in the Church and monarchy, there was added a third institution, the middle class; that is, the businessman. There were gains in personal mobility and opportunity, and an erratic but nonetheless pronounced rise in living standards. There were also created new sets of problems, some of which society is still trying to resolve.

Feudal Trial and Failure

Feudalism was a preliminary step. It consolidated work in a new way, and brought a measure of stability to a civilization that had been chaotic and fractionated. In many ways it failed as an economic system, but it kept society going, and in the tenth through twelfth centuries, this was no small accomplishment.

Europe in the tenth century was almost totally lacking in economic and political cohesion. Local wars and petty quarrels swept the land. A lord's domain was whatever territory he could occupy and defend, and for this he had only such protection as he could recruit to his personal pennant. The peasant, bottom man on life's totem pole, lacked even that protection.

Man abhors anarchy the way nature abhors a vacuum, and with painful experience as their teacher, the people of the early Middle Ages fashioned the hierarchy of feudalism. The knight swore allegiance to a noble; the noble pledged himself to defend the lord; the lord, the prince. The oath of fealty, weak as it was, was better than nothing. It brought the king an army, a company of dubious fighting skill, to be sure, but nonetheless a more effective force (he hoped) than any lesser noble could assemble. The oath also conveyed upon the king the power to tax; in exchange for this license the king's vassals were given land and the right to administer it. This was the feudal fief, to be parceled out or sublet among lesser men as the landholder saw fit, and to be taxed for his own support. As for the serf, if land had ever belonged to him, title to it had now been transferred to his seigneur, the lord of the manor, in exchange for protection and a mild degree of economic security. Though not legally a slave, the serf and his children were bound generation after generation to a hereditary calling. Unless they were called to military service, or found careers as servants of the Church, they saw nothing of life beyond their manor and village. Their only legal recourse, as transgressors or petitioners, lay with the seigneur, who conducted his own court and dispensed whatever brand of justice he liked, with conscience and tradition his only jurors.

The feudal system was hardly a voluntary economic arrangement. Both peasant and seigneur were driven into it by an absence of known alternatives. However, it was not the unqualified horror it is sometimes pictured to be. There was a give-and-take to it, and a measure of comfort. Even at the lowest stratum of society, people received something in return for their obeisance, which is more than could be said for the darker days that had gone before. Inefficient as the feudal economy was, it represented a more productive alignment of manpower and natural resources than the haphazard, chaotic economy it replaced, and for more than three hundred years it lent a sense of order to the lives of more than 90 per cent of the people of Europe. Its major failing and final undoing was its insularity and inequity; it contained no provision for growth, either of human possibilities or economic organization.

It is a commonplace of history that the Catholic Church, the dominant organization of the Middle Ages, held Europe together through the centuries of feudalism. This overstates the case, but the Church is too important to be left unmentioned in any survey of the history of organizations. It was a nearly universal institution, and the only one with any claim to such a title. Specific points of its authority were repeatedly (and sometimes successfully) disputed, but with the exception of the Jews, who were a minority, everyone in Europe came under its general ecclesiastical jurisdiction.

The Church played an important role in the preservation of the knowledge of past ages and the maintenance of a moral code. It ran the schools and universities. It recovered the documents of antiquity, translated and copied them, and taught people to read them. It was the agency of public charity, and the principal arbiter of personal behavior.

During the Middle Ages the Church permitted, and in some cases encouraged, a freedom of expression and a spirit of inquiry that are wholly out of character with its later reputation for censorship and inquisition. Within the Church and community of scholars, the Middle Ages was a period of surprisingly vigorous intellectual exchange.

In the economic arena, the Church never attained the authority it sought. The idea of a unified, corporate Church, supreme in temporal as well as spiritual affairs, was accepted only at particular times and places, never everywhere; and as a leader, the Church was unable to offer daringly imaginative schemes for increasing the public wealth or security. It did, however, offer two approaches to the management of organizations which later centuries were to emulate. The Church pioneered in decentralized management, dispersing authority among subordinate bishops removed from daily contact with the Holy See; and it developed the idea—which today we usually credit to the military—of supplementing line organization with extensive staff and liaison services. It would be hard to overestimate the significance of either of these developments. They are accepted as second nature in modern organizations.

The third economic contribution of the Church was unintentional. It came about indirectly, through the medium of the Crusades. There were eight Crusades, beginning late in the eleventh century and extending through A.D. 1270. At least initially, the objective was to promote Christianity in the Near East and protect Christians there from Moslem infidels. The first Crusade met with some success, returning Jerusalem to the Christian fold; all but one of the others failed, and most of them turned into fiascos. However, apart from any significance as religious missions, the Crusades had another effect: They stimulated trade, and awakened the Western world to possibilities that the parochial, feudal society could never attain. Ironically, this helped create an economy in which the avowed sponsors of the Crusades, political rulers and churchmen alike, found their own power waning.

The Dusty Merchants

Following the fall of Rome and until the Crusades, the ancient trade routes to the East were used very little, and most "domestic" trade was carried on by small though colorful groups of traveling merchants, discontented sons of the soil who were called *pieds poudreux*—dusty feet. A ragtag and restless caravan of humanity, the "pie powers," as their name came to be Anglicized, lived as gypsies, traveling together for protection from highwaymen, stopping only long enough to offer their wares and replenish supplies.

Their visits to the small, isolated communities of feudal Europe gradually developed into fairs. Held annually or more often, these soon became the highlights of an otherwise monotonous rural life. Peasants who knew only drab homespun saw gay, glittering merchandise dangled before their eyes, and heard tales of distant cities and curious lands. Understandably popular, the town fairs became so numerous that merchants could make a living by touring from one fairground to another. From there it was a step to permanent town markets where merchants stayed year-round.

Trade and towns grew together, enhancing each other's prosperity. The ideal locations for markets were towns strategically located along trade routes, and capable of defending themselves against attack and siege. Where these conditions were met, and where the community also was inclined to give merchants the freedom to set up shop, and buy and sell as they wished, the towns rapidly grew—into London, Paris, Cologne.

It was still a long step, though, from a trading economy to a market society. Most merchants of the eleventh and twelfth centuries, transient or resident, sold only products made by others, and traded for coin or other products delivered immediately. There was no widely used credit system, and no integration of production and distribution.

These came in the thirteenth through sixteenth centuries, with the development of large-scale commercial organizations and the rise of a new class of men, the merchant capitalists. Unable singlehandedly to finance extended voyages of trade, merchants combined resources and talents as they had in Greece. However, if the earlier traders intended to support but a single voyage, others later saw the opportunities in enduring alliances and continuing investments.

Because the supply of manufactured goods was uncertain and the price unpredictable, financiers began developing their own sources of supply. For the most part, they did this through the "putting out" system, with the merchants providing raw materials and tools to a number of individual craftsmen who made goods on subcontract, working in their own shops.

Occasionally, the size of the market and the prosperity of merchants encouraged construction of "factories," buildings where tools, workers, and materials were brought together. Such institutions were common, though, only in communities identified both with high finance and widely salable (and usually machine-made) products.

The city of Florence is one example. Today it is revered for its stunning collections of painting, sculpture, and architecture—as someone has aptly said, the whole city is a museum—but its reputation was built on more humble grounds. Florence was a mill town and banking center, one of the first. By the middle of the fourteenth century, there were 200 or more textile plants in Florence, with a work force estimated at 30,000. Machines did most of the work, though in the absence of steam power it often happened that men had to provide the motive force.

Venice was a city without a classical heritage. A direct product of commerce, she was built by trade (in slaves, basic goods, and luxury products), and through much devious manipulation of men and money, she managed to gain as much from the Crusades as the Church lost. By the end of the thirteenth century, Venice was a living legend of wealth, the Golden City risen out of a swamp,

whose Grand Canal is as impressive an avenue of beauty
as any in the Western world.

Again, elegance reflects the economics of careful organization. In the industrial center of Venice, thousands
labored in textile shops, glassworks, and other facilities.
At the height of her prosperity, Venice harbored 36,000
seamen; her municipal shipyard employed 10,000 and was
organized for mass production. Marco Polo and the Polo
brothers, his father and uncle, represented but one of the
hundreds of banking and trading families headquartered
in Venice.

Throughout Europe, the consolidation of enterprise fell
under the aegis of such family dynasties, or of the leading
merchant and craft guilds. The "capitalist bourgeoisie"
which so incensed Marx and Lenin was no product of the
nineteenth-century industrial world. Not only did it exist
in the late Middle Ages, but also it thrived then as it has
never thrived since. Kings as well as paupers fell under
the domain of such businessmen as the Medici in Florence
and the Fuggers of Augsburg. Only the popes, and not all
of them, had as much power as the doge of Venice.

Jacques Coeur, a fifteenth-century Frenchman, began
his business career selling luxury goods to the court, and
ended by controlling mines, mills, factories, and the French
treasury. Francesco Datini, an orphan, amassed enough
of a fortune in trade and textile production to operate a
string of companies throughout most of Europe.

The Medici, bankers and traders, ruled the city of
Florence and had branch banks in dozens of cities. They
were the fiscal agents for the papacy and at one point,
when the pope was deposed and imprisoned in one of the
innumerable quarrels between crown and cross, the Medici
put up the money to ransom him. On a number of other
occasions, popes were obliged to borrow money from the
Medici or other banking clans.

The guilds were no less powerful in the aggregate, although their individual members were usually far less
wealthy. In southern Europe, where production and trade
were not controlled by independent families, they usually

operated under the direction of a council of prominent merchants. In northern Europe, control was more diffuse but no less effective. Here, formally organized guilds held sway. The guilds arose from a natural effort on the part of craftsmen and traders to protect themselves and spread the risks of enterprise. They were partly mutual aid societies, offering assistance to members in need; partly associations designed to preserve order in the marketplace, setting wages, prices, working conditions, and rules of apprenticeship; and partly instruments of monopoly. They offered society a guarantee of good workmanship and reasonable prices, and more often than not they honored that pledge. In return they sought exclusive privilege to all business in their territory.

Because the merchant guilds controlled the markets, they held effective control of the entire economic process. The most powerful of these guilds was the Hanseatic League. Organized in the thirteenth century, the Hansa ultimately extended its control to about seventy towns and cities along the north coast of Europe. The Hansa ruthlessly enforced the price scales it set. Its navy (which it financed by levying taxes on league towns) drove all commercial rivals as well as pirates out of the North Sea and Baltic. Its governing body—and the Hansa was a government in everything but name—adjudicated disputes within the ranks, filed suits against kings whose troops had damaged or taken its goods, and punished its own recalcitrants, forcing more than one misbehaving town to come to the headquarters city of Lübeck, hat in hand, to beg forgiveness. The Hansa even waged war, defeating Denmark and imposing on her king a treaty guaranteeing liberal trade rights to the Hansa.

As rulers, the financiers and guildsmen were a match for the worst examples in the ranks of royalty or the papacy. Theirs was an unpretty code in which cheating, exploitation, and murder each found a place. The idea of an open, competitive market was definitely not part of the credo. The guildsmen were against monopoly only if it was someone else's. However, it was very largely through their efforts that the market-centered economy developed.

The market economy, as mentioned earlier, thrives in societies that are diversified and progressive. The merchant capitalists, in the process of lining their own vaults, were instrumental in transforming feudal Europe into such a society. They standardized coinage and financial exchange, built organizations large enough to think in terms of mass production, and developed a system of credit and merchandising that could cater to the needs of millions. While some of their ventures were directed toward luxury markets—the Florentine textile houses, for example, specialized in silk brocades or fine woolens—for the most part commerce revolved around low-cost products for wider markets—salt fish, timber for shipbuilding, inexpensive yard goods, leather, powder and shot, glass, and ceramic ware.

Similarly, if the famous merchants were men of staggering wealth and power, most of their compatriots were modest in means, and constituted an important economic force only in combination. They lived by numerous small transactions, rather than a few big ones. One historian, Werner Sombart, poring over the records of fifteenth-century Lübeck, found few entries in the ledgers for amounts that would represent thousands of dollars today. Most sales and purchases were of a few hundred dollars or less.

The Dispersal of Decision

It was the multiplicity of small businessmen, in fact, that helped break the power of the financial dynasts. As these lesser-known businessmen gained in prosperity and independence, they became increasingly more difficult to control. In the Hanseatic League, for example, Lübeck's power was not swept away by assault; that city's power corroded. Bit by bit the Hansa disappeared as merchants in one town after another found their interests diverging from the League's, and as competition began to rise from England, France, and the Low Countries. The outcome was the same in central and southern Europe, with the power of the oligarchs dispersed among a rising number of middle-class entrepreneurs.

The seventeenth and eighteenth centuries brought an extension of these changes in economic life. The bourgeoisie continued to grow in numbers and importance. Trade and manufacturing, though still far below agriculture on the economic scale, occupied increasing numbers of men. National governments, considerably more powerful as forces in economic life than they had been in the Middle Ages, lent encouragement to the rise of commerce, providing bounties, patent rights, and protective tariffs to stimulate enterprise. Joint stock companies, pooling the capital of hundreds of people instead of a handful, came into popularity, sometimes bringing disastrous speculation and ruin to imprudent investors (witness the South Sea bubble, for example), but at the same time launching some enduring and profitable ventures.

The doctrine of *laissez faire*, insisting that business should be left strictly unregulated and untrammeled, was proposed and widely championed. Though it was always more an objective than an actuality, it represented a liberation of energy and enterprise. There were countless injustices perpetrated in its name, for what many people really wanted, in their pious proclamations about the virtues of *laissez faire*, was the right to do as they pleased without giving competitors the chance to strike back. Moreover, in this quasi-free economy, the entrepreneur enjoyed a number of special privileges he had no intention of giving up.

Colbert, finance minister to Louis XIV, accurately reflected the spirit of the times in a remark made in a letter in 1671. "Anything which tends to restrict the freedom and number of merchants is worthless," he said, by way of voicing opposition to regional monopolies, apprenticeship restrictions, and other codes imposed by medieval guilds to restrict competition. He did not happen to mention the fact that, while the merchants could combine and barter as they wished, the craftsmen and laborers who worked for them were specifically forbidden to join forces for self-protection. Nor did Colbert note that the principal restrictions then placed on business were imposed by him.

Despite its inconsistencies, this economy was more competitive and more nearly attuned to consumer wishes than any known before. It was both a mirror and a cause of the forces moving society toward the modern concept of freedom, and it was already clear, to some farsighted men, that a still broader measure of economic freedom held exciting prospects.

Pierre Samuel du Pont, a leading figure of eighteenth-century France, was one who saw the implications:

> A few men who have capital, and who as a result of their exclusive privileges encroach on their brothers' livelihood, think that they are doing well; they do not realize that freedom, which would double the activity of every worker, would greatly increase the profits of capitalists.[4]

To the Medici or the merchants of Hamburg, such a step would have seemed insane, but by the end of the eighteenth century it was a prophecy already being fulfilled three thousand miles away, for a majority of the families who had emigrated to the New World. (Among those who decided to put Pierre du Pont's advice to the test was his son, who emigrated to the United States, borrowed $36,000, and founded the chemical company of this name.)

The acceptance of an economic system based on an open market was still some decades away in Europe. Many still clung stubbornly to the ancient notion that the public ought to take whatever it was offered, and it took generations and revolutions to break their grip. But a new kind of market was clearly taking shape, a market in which abundance instead of scarcity would be the norm, with the consumer rather than the vendor holding the power of decision. New manufacturing centers were emerging, and they were no longer principalities to be run at the whim of a merchant prince. They were centers for the production of the goods wanted by an aspiring population.

The process of consolidation and organization, spreading through all facets of economic life, had changed forever the social as well as economic base of European civilization. The penchant for organization brought a wave of new associations. Universities expanded. Professional associations were born, with men of law, medicine, and science banding into groups to pursue common interests, and thereby gaining a leverage they lacked as individuals. The principal scientific organizations of Europe, including the Royal Society of London and the French Academy of Sciences, all are products of the seventeenth and eighteenth centuries.

As the population of Europe increased, there was a steady flow toward the cities. From the beginning of the fourteenth century to the early 1800s, the overall population of Europe doubled. In England, Wales, Scotland, The Netherlands, and Scandinavia, the figures tripled. In Germany it nearly doubled. Only in France and Italy was the growth notably slower, and this observation is somewhat tempered by the fact that by the beginning of the fourteenth century, both already had large populations: Italy about 10 million; France, 22 million.

The major centers of commerce grew most of all. London, Amsterdam, Hamburg, and Vienna multiplied their populations tenfold or more. Antwerp, Manchester, Birmingham, and Madrid grew by factors of 20 or more. Paris, already a city of 80,000 in the fourteenth century, passed the half-million mark before 1800. Cologne, Bruges, Rouen, Milan, Vienna, and Prague all had populations exceeding 35,000 as early as the fifteenth century.[5]

In this increasingly urban, more interdependent economy, traditional stratifications of society broke down. There was a saying in the Middle Ages that "city air makes men free," and indeed it did. For the peasants who somehow freed themselves from the land, town life offered new opportunities and new careers. From the thirteenth century on, men could hope for a life of comfort and comparative security, and perhaps wealth and a political voice, gained through trade or manufacture. For those who remained on the land, the growth of cities and trade created an expanded market for food, a market that paid in cash. This gave the farm population a new form of purchasing power, more flexible than barter, and served as a stimulus to agricultural production. With the increasing technical efficiency of farming, new land could be turned to crops, and the sale of those crops gave farmers the means to buy the products made or sold in the cities.

The hereditary aristocracy, fast becoming an anachronism, found its power challenged by the rising bourgeoisie. The upper class owned the land, but the merchants and bankers had the money and the trade goods, and in the mercantile economy these counted for more than acreage. From this rivalry for power had come a new division of personal rights. As Walter Lippmann has put it, authority had been assigned to kings, and property to private persons. Out of this grew the "main bulwark" of freedom, the idea that any man, whatever his stratum of society, holds indefeasible property rights as long as he can demonstrate a just and clear title.

There was a new mobility in occupations. Many people still held to the work of their fathers, but the bonds were of tradition rather than law. In the eighteenth century, lending the stamp of official approval to a right long since claimed by the people, it was proclaimed that

> all persons, of whatever sort and condition they be, (may) embrace and exercise . . . any profession or craft they choose, or even . . . exercise several together.[6]

How remote this is from the hereditary structure that had prevailed through the ages, in which every man was admonished, as St. Paul counseled the Corinthians, to "abide in the same calling in which he was called."

It is difficult to make detailed statements about changes

in living standards and working conditions through this long span of centuries. Wage scales for various periods can be only partly reconstructed and are not altogether meaningful. It is now apparent, though, that for almost all men there was an increase in living standards through the Middle Ages and into the modern period. Urban workers fared at least as well as agricultural laborers, and usually better.

At the time, the gains were hard to see, and for most people life continued to be, as Thomas Hobbes once described it, "solitary, poor, nasty, brutish, and short." The reorganization of work through capitalism and the factory system meant exploitation and crushing misery for many, and the lot of others, outside of industry, was hardly any better. As one on-the-scene observer wrote of early nineteenth-century England,

> The great cities and towns . . . contain a vast population which lives, one hardly knows how, on mean and precarious wages, in dismal and unwholesome dens. Some of this poverty is merely miserable . . . some is criminal . . .[7]

One can substitute "farms and hamlets" for "cities and towns," and come out with a description of rural life in the same period, as the above author conceded.

This is an essential point. The "happy peasant," secure in pastoral plenitude, is as much a myth as the scrubbed and eager factory worker, striding energetically toward the mill in the morning sun. In truth, both workers were incredibly poor by modern standards, and went to their graves uncomforted by the knowledge that life for their ancestors had been even more penurious. Whether people lived an urban or a rural life, they were participants in a ground swell of economic reorganization that was providing the wealth to underwrite higher living standards for all. The attendant benefits are far more visible now than they were then.

They have been most dramatic in the United States.

Before turning to that locale, though, it is necessary to backtrack twice, once to examine the technical framework that surrounds history, and once to consider the attitudes that have surrounded man's work. Each is essential to the modern condition.

In leaving this account of the consolidation of work, it is to be remembered that change came sporadically, with considerable overlap of different economic systems. Vestiges of the Greek or Roman economy were still to be found long after the Middle Ages had begun. The manor system survived in some parts of Europe after feudalism had died as a political force. Small, traveling markets were to be found long after Venice had built its tremendous merchant fleet and Florence its textile factories, and can still be found to this day.

3

THE ROLE OF TECHNOLOGY

Whatever else civilization is, it is something that people make, and technology is a key to the construction. It is not the means by which man decides what he wants to build, but it sets the parameters of what can be built and, to a significant degree, it is a determinant in the cultural and political aspects of life.

Technology means here, not simply handcrafts or nuts-and-bolts mechanics, but the whole matrix of physical and biological science. It includes countless small and un-sung advances together with major inventions and discoveries that have taken civilization apart by the seams to rebuild it anew. My use of technology comprises all stages of development from the tom-tom to Telstar, from Egyptian astronomy to quantum physics. It is, in sum, the tools man has fashioned to turn nature to his material service.

Thinking of technology as a relatively new force in the world is pleasant self-flattery, as though what existed before the Industrial Revolution was so crude and infantile as to deserve little respect. But technology is far from modern. It is not a stepchild of modern science (although it has progressed most rapidly under such tutelage), and it is neither European nor American in origin. It is not a singular creation but a cumulative force, very old, which first appeared in the Middle East and Orient some five thousand years before the European Industrial Revolution.

Slow to accelerate, subject to reversals, capable of being deterred by opposition or neglect, technology moved through most centuries with as little visible progress as a glacier, but with equal persistence.

Politically, aesthetically, and spiritually, modern man is hardly in a position to boast. The trends toward human advancement have been erratic at best, and reversals have been almost as numerous as gains. The twentieth century, for instance, presumes itself the most enlightened in history, yet it has so far produced the *fasces* of Italy, the Swastika of Nazi Germany, the Rising Sun of Imperial Japan, the Red Star of the Soviet, and the battle flags of sundry other dictatorships, together with the continued growth of democracy.

The history of technology is far less inconsistent—which may be the main reason why man's material gains seem more impressive than his political attainments. Despite a painfully slow start, technology moves forward in almost every century. Even in periods of depression, it usually records more gains than losses, and its early pace, if hesitant and measured, at least was in a forward direction.

Less visible but equally important is the link between technical advance and social organization. Technology has flourished best in those societies which have been the most institutionalized (or, if you will, the best organized). The corollary also seems to hold: Society has advanced most notably, in aesthetic and humanistic terms as well as by economic measures, when it has made optimum use of technology.

One has to avoid deterministic statements here. If there is a linear relationship to be argued, it belongs to theologians, and someone else will have to deal with the chicken-egg question that goes along with it. In *A Man for All Seasons*, the bishop makes a graceful but important distinction in discussing a job aspirant.

"Do I recommend him? No sir, I only wish to point him out."

The distinction applies here. I cannot "explain," à la Spengler, the relationship of technology and culture: I merely wish to point out that there is one.[1]

The Mother (?) of Invention

According to the familiar epigram, in circulation at least since Plato's time, it is necessity that mothers invention. If this is the law, she should be arrested for child neglect. There has been no shortage of problems in this world, and man would have advanced at a gallop had the existence of needs sufficed to produce solutions. Man has existed as a distinct species for more than one-half million years, but only in the most recent 2 per cent of that time did he invent the wheel, domesticate animals, develop pottery, take up weaving, and devise written language. The need for any of these is beyond argument, but remained unfilled for tens of thousands of years.

The Pharaoh Cheops, building the pyramid that became his tomb, could easily have seen the limitations of the tools and techniques available in 2700 B.C. More than two million stone blocks, averaging two and one-half tons each in weight, were quarried, moved down the Nile by boat, dragged to the construction site, trimmed, and raised into position. For this work, there were only hand tools made of copper, the inclined plane, rollers—and men. Improved tools to speed and ease the work were not forthcoming. As has so often been the case, necessity was the worst of parents to invention.

Minoans, Phoenicians, Greeks, and Romans sailed the Mediterranean for two thousand years, needing on every voyage a rig that would permit them to sail well to windward, a compass, a proper rudder, and hulls of superior stability and sail-carrying power. They had abundant time for creative thinking, sitting in port waiting for favorable weather, but the inventions were slower to arrive than the ships.

At times invention and need appear to be total strangers. In Europe, for example, there were obvious applications for sturdy axes to clear the forests, moldboard plows to cut and turn the heavy northern soil, and suitable collars to harness draft animals without choking them. Each device was centuries in coming. Yet with little advance warning, movable type and modern printing were developed, and as several authors have pointed out, it would be difficult to point to the "need" for these. At the time movable type was invented, only an infinitesimal fraction of the population knew how to read.

Invention, then, often manufactures its own needs, and man's advance may be less a response to visible challenges than a reflection of persistent opportunities. Man, so often obtuse, has survived by occasionally being clever.

There have been plenty of lapses of technology, even in those centuries most inclined toward progress. Five hundred years after iron was introduced to the peninsula of Greece, it was still the "stranger from across the sea," and second in favor to the softer metal, bronze. Galileo, on the eve of modern history, was forced by the Inquisition to recant the heresy that the earth is not the center of the universe, but is only a fellow traveler in orbit around the sun. His predecessor Bruno was burned at the stake for similar unorthodoxy. Farmers in quite modern times have refused to use steel plows, convinced that such tools poison the soil. The medical practice of bloodletting, which has cost no one knows how many lives in history, was still in vogue into the nineteenth century. Victims of their own traditions, doctors consulted their tomes, stroked their chin whiskers, and went on bleeding people to death.

During the Middle Ages, despite major advances in agriculture, road building, hydraulic engineering, mining, machine design, and metallurgy, the grandest of nobles lived in palaces that were cold, damp, and bereft of plumbing. Clothes mildewed. Food rotted, if not first eaten by rats. Spices and perfumes arriving by caravan were rightly to be prized; they made the food palatable and human company tolerable.

It was not always thus; one thousand years earlier the Romans had central heating plants in their town houses and running water in the rooms, not to mention public "baths" which amounted to indoor swimming pools. Although no cosmetic joy, the ordinary Roman freeman probably was less redolent than a medieval prince. (As for the peasant, in both societies his state would have been the same; he lived with the livestock and smelled accordingly.)

In the palace at Knossos on the island of Crete, there were private toilets and a central sewage system in use between 1800 and 1500 B.C. Yet Louis XIV had neither of these in Versailles, the most elegant home ever built. His lavish robes and furs were more than decorative; they kept his regal hide warm, for the more than two thousand rooms of Versailles were heated only by fireplaces. Nobility had lost none of its taste for comfort, but the technology to provide it had somehow been misplaced.

These, though, are departures from the norm. In net result if not in every detail, almost every century has recorded some technical gain over the one before. At least from the ninth century A.D., there has been no visible break in the continuum of technical progress.

The limiting factor in most periods has not been the direction technology has taken, but the slowness of its pace and the inefficiency of its applications. Consider, for example, the conditions at the beginning of the Christian era and those that prevailed many centuries later, when the modern era began. Before the time of Christ, man had developed a splendid capacity for adorning and nourishing his mind; philosophy, literature, and statecraft had long since reached a high intellectual plane. In terms of his ability to fill his belly and clothe his nakedness, though, man was still a woeful ignoramus.

The plow was an assemblage of crooked sticks, more efficient than its Bronze Age predecessors but no masterpiece. The growing of crops remained a race between man and predators. After the birds had foraged and insects and weeds had taken their toll, the grain that was left was harvested with a short-handled sickle and winnowed with a flail.

Spinning and weaving were done entirely by hand. While experience had taught the need for an uncontaminated water supply, plague, once started, ran its course through the cities, for the mechanisms of contagion were undiscovered. Chemistry as a science did not exist, and only trial, error, and alchemy guided the preservation of food, the tanning of leather and dyeing of fabrics, and the production of glass and metals.

Most important, it was taken for granted that technical problems would remain unsolved. As Aristotle had said, humanity was doomed to relentless toil until that impossible day when "the shuttles fly back and forth of themselves and the plectrum, untouched by human hands, shall make the strings of the lyre resound."[2]

Aristotle's analysis was impeccable, and for his stature as a prophet he still deserved honor 2050 years later. Despite monumental changes in other facets of life, man's work in A.D. 1700 was much the same as in Christ's lifetime. Most craft chores remained noxious, exhausting, and repetitive, except for those of senior artisans. Although shops made masterpieces of silverware and resplendent robes for royalty, the apprentice and journeyman still spent hours at bellows and forge, while the weaver lived by the ageless rhythm of his loom. The workman still lived according to the equation that had governed all ancestral periods: by sweat of brow, laboring from sunup to dark, he was able to stay alive.

Born to poverty, most men died in its grip. Restricted by the limitations of human endurance, isolated by the crudities of transportation, and insulated even more by the blanket of ignorance, most people knew little of the amenities of culture or of the pleasures of the life beyond their reach. If for a fortunate few life held rare creative excitement, for many more it remained an agony of subsistence.

To Make the Shuttle Fly

The break in the inexorable equation of toil came when man literally found the way to make the shuttle fly under its own steam. The conventional label for this is the Industrial Revolution, but that term hardly does justice to the events. It was not one revolution but several, and the most important point about it is that it was not restricted to industry. It involved every facet of economic life, trade, agriculture, and finance included, and its greatest leverage came from its catholicity.

The tools and techniques of the factory system, which gee-whiz books immortalize, had in many cases been anticipated in earlier centuries, and in almost every instance were less than revolutionary. Men such as Hargreaves, Kay, Maudslay, McAdam, Napier, Savery, Trevithick, and Watt made ingenious and useful contributions. They multiplied the power and precision of human effort, and some of their inventions—most notably Watt's condensing steam engine—were of monumental importance. But it is worth noting that social conditions, as much as mechanical inventiveness, were instrumental in promoting change. The Industrial Revolution took hold most strongly in England, in a period of relative peace and quiet; it came more slowly in areas such as France, then caught up in the turmoil of Continental wars and disorganization.

Most important of all was the change in man's outlook and approach. In the increasingly liberal mood of the late sixteenth through eighteenth centuries, the notion of human perfectability spread to science as much as politics. There developed an open eagerness to study man and nature experimentally, and to the venturesome and curious, science offered both the excitement of discovery and the opportunity to make knowledge the servant and teacher of mankind. It brought a new style to the process of learning, a method by which man could combine imagination and empirical facts and give both discipline and direction to his assault on the physical unknown. This, more than any individual discovery or invention, was the principal instrument of technical progress, and it is in this sense that the technical revolution constitutes a major turning point in history.

(Interestingly, much the same point is being made with reference to science today. Philosopher David Hawkins has argued that the art of scientific inquiry is educationally more basic than any of the theories or facts that scientists uncover. Caryl Haskins, president of Carnegie Institution of Washington, has said that fifty years from now, we may find the main social significance of science not in the products or physical prowess it has given us, but in its guiding philosophy.[3])

Modern science did not arise overnight, nor did it spring full-blown from the marvelous minds of its early practitioners. The data and theory on which it was predicated came, for the most part, from earlier sources, from the work done by Thales of Miletus, whom many call the first true man of science of the Western world; from Aristotle and Galen in their investigations of the characteristics of plants and animals; from Eratosthenes, who knew the world was round 1700 years before Columbus and who calculated its diameter with an error of less than 1 per cent; from Archimedes, Pythagoras, and Euclid; from Empedocles with his theory that everything is made of air, water, earth, and fire, and from Democritus with his belief, strangely modern, that all matter is composed of tiny atoms, identical in substance but varying in size and shape; from the alchemists of Alexandria, mingling astrology and Eastern mysticism to explain the transformation of substances; from the Ptolemaic astronomers and the medieval encyclopedists Alexander Neckham, Bartholomew the Englishman, Albertus Magnus, and Vincent de Beauvais, jumbling fact and ancient fancy in collections that were finally to be given order, intelligibility, and application in the modern era.

This was the legacy of science, a tissue of fact and supposition, riddled with error but priceless, to which the Scientific Revolution brought its new approach. The new science was objective and orderly to a degree surpassing anything known in previous technology, and it brought together as remarkable an aggregation of talent as the world has known.

Within a span of not much more than three hundred years came Copernicus, Tycho Brahe, Galileo, Kepler, Descartes, Leibniz, and Newton in astronomy, mathematics, and physics; Paracelsus, Vesalius, Hieronymus Fabricius, Harvey, Haller, and Bernard in anatomy, physiology, and chemotherapy; Hooke, Swammerdam, Leeuwenhoek, Linnaeus, Lamarck, and Cuvier, in optics, microscopy, and taxonomy; Hutton, James Hall, Smith, and Lyell in geology; and Boyle, Black, Cavendish, Scheele, Priestley, and Lavoisier in chemistry. The population of Europe, at the time it generated this pyrotechnic display, ranged from 70 million to a little more than 100 million.

The Impact of Change

It is hardly necessary to describe the basic changes technology has generated in the common forms of labor. The elaboration of the factory system, the replacement of hand tools by power equipment, and the evolution of mass production are familiar developments, needing no introduction here. The direct effects of science, in extending both comprehension and control of the physical universe, are similarly familiar.

What should be considered here, in an attempt to find a suitable context for technology, is the further consequences of technology in history. Not only has it altered man's jobs; it also has changed the mold of economic organization, shifted the focus of social life toward urbanization, and given life to aspirations which for centuries man had to regard as unattainable dreams.

Champions of technology at times are carried away by its wondrous powers, and claim all sorts of miracles. This is foolish. Mechanics, for all its utility, is not exactly the highest attainment of man, and attempts to elevate it to that throne are embarrassing and at times frightening. However, it offends no sense of balance to observe that what man has sought materially, and what technology has enabled him to earn, are functions of one another. It profanes no sense of art to say that cultural achievements customarily come from societies that have technical endowments. It need disgrace no feeling of humanitarianism to suggest that economic possibilities as well as moral aspirations color the public attitude toward pain, poverty, and human subjection. (For a modern example, one need look no further than the so-called Negro Revolution, now reshaping the social structure and mores of America. It is a revolution born of hope and rising expectations—expectations that the nation has the economic means to fill.) And it outrages none of the hallowed traditions of law to recall that ideas of the attainable, as well as ideas of the just, play a part in the rule of society. Man must live with present conditions even as he seeks to improve them; and technology and economic advance are as much the instrument of that improvement as art, education, or jurisprudence.

Until the nineteenth century, 90 per cent or more of the people in the world were assigned by necessity to agriculture. Facilities and techniques were such that a family could provide only enough for its own subsistence needs, with a small remainder. This "surplus," when it existed at all, was the energizing margin of civilization's advance. To the extent that some members of the community engaged in government, art, manufacture, teaching, and other nonfarm pursuits, they were permitted to do so because there was a sufficient surplus to sustain them. The smaller that margin, the less the attention of society to nonessentials, and the larger the portion of the population living at the marginal level of the peasant farmer.

Customarily, despite ages of agriculture, history focuses on the urban life. Babylon, Athens, Alexandria, Rome, Venice, and London are given bigger billing than the surrounding countryside. This is only natural, for it is in the cities that man has focused his artistic efforts, pursued politics most avidly, plotted if not always fought his wars, planned expeditions and voyages of exploration, and carried on most of his other noble, base, or mischievous projects. Yet it must be remembered that, until very recently, urban societies derived their support directly and almost entirely from agriculture.

There are ways to skirt the economics of the agrarian life, but none of them—with the single exception of an increase in productivity—changes the essential arithmetic of subsistence. Some societies have substituted war and plunder for the more tedious business of farming. But war pays Peter only by killing Paul, and the cost of collection rises as the circle of conquest expands. Even the gold of the Aztecs had a limit, as the Spaniards, now among the least wealthy people in Europe, eventually discovered. Some ancient societies devoted themselves chiefly or exclusively to trade and manufacture. The civilizations of Crete and Phoenicia, for example, lived by sea trade. But again, agriculture was the commanding activity of their times, if not within the borders of these societies, then in the lands with which they traded. In effect, the merchants of Knossos and Tyre were part of a larger economic organization, encompassing all of the countries with which they traded. In this economic unit, at least nine-tenths of all the people found sustenance from the soil.

The civilization of Greece was founded on farming and fishing, and even at the peak of the Hellenic period, when the ships of Athens treated the Aegean as a private pond, most of the population remained in agriculture. This was true despite the fact that Athens had two supplementary sources of income, tribute and taxes forcibly taken from neighbors, and silver extracted from a highly beneficent mine at Laurium, operated by private contractors on behalf of the government. It was problems in agricultural economics that drove the Greeks to trade. The population overpowered the land. Forests were leveled for their timber, and to clear the way for the plow. However, the need grew faster than the resources, and the land, worked too hard, lost fertility. Attica was forced to turn to commerce and colonization for survival.

The colonies helped rid the mother country of its surplus population, and provided overseas sources of food as well as a market for export products. Olives and grapes, which thrive in soil that would starve other crops, provided oil and wine for export;[4] grain was the vital import.

By the fifth century B.C., Athens was the trading center of the civilized world, but was a wholly dependent city. With this very much in mind, the Athenians maintained a powerful navy, and decreed death for anyone caught speculating in the grain trade. The courts did not hesitate to invoke that penalty, for gross disruption of the export-import business could have meant starvation for a population of 200,000 to 300,000.[5]

Much the same set of conditions applied in Rome in the halcyon days of Empire. Life in the Eternal City was comfortable and cultured, at least for those who had picked their parents wisely. The city was also a major trade center, but was basically dependent on agriculture. Like Athens, Rome drew its wealth partly from the spoils of war, and mostly from the endless toil of peasants. Their life was a far cry from the pastoral, blissful frolic idealized in mezzotints of rural life. Often, the peasant owned no land. Literally or figuratively a slave, he lived on the precipice of hunger, and landlords and tax collectors took enough of each year's crop to assure that he stayed close to the edge. Often, he was pushed over. Life expectancy at birth in the Roman Empire was not more than twenty-five years; malnutrition and a frightening infant mortality rate were primarily responsible.

At Rome's peak, the city population was about one million (only a tiny portion of them rich, of course). To sustain Rome and themselves, nearly 50 million labored in the provinces.

As much as any single factor, the failure of the Romans to improve farm technology brought the downfall of the Empire. Masters of construction and civil engineering, skilled in government and facile in the arts of combat, the Romans failed to find ways to expand by any dramatic margin the output of the soil. As city life grew more lavish, and the army and civil service expanded, the demands placed on agriculture increased, and the burden proved to be more than could be carried on the bent backs of the peasants. Long before Rome was sacked by invaders, the Empire was crumbling economically.

While its impact is most clearly demonstrated in agriculture, technology has had a similarly profound effect upon other segments of the economy. In trade and transport, to select but one example, the improvement of ships directly affected the development of urban centers. During the Homeric period, according to the account left us by the poet Hesiod, the wise trader limited his voyages to favorable weather in the summer. When the Aegean was in an angry mood, the prudent man hung the steering oar by the fireside. Inasmuch as the sailing speed of merchantmen was two to three knots, and the Aegean is tempestuous much of the year, the sailing season was short and voyages few. Rowing ships could travel much faster, but traders had no money to support large crews: oars were for warships; merchantmen sailed. Direct passages across open waters were possible, and hundreds were made, but the as yet poorly developed arts of cartography and navigation made the landfall uncertain, and captains had the unhappy choice of hugging the coast, with its rocks and shoals, or risking an outside passage.[6]

By the sixth century B.C., two hundred years later, sailing speeds had more than doubled. Ships had become more seaworthy and larger. This made possible a longer sailing season and a far greater volume of trade, and it was feasible within these bounds, as it would not have been possible otherwise, to sustain an Athenian population of several hundred thousand. Improvements in the following centuries in hull shapes and rigging, the addition of the hinged rudder, and the development of the compass and celestial navigation, were important elements in the exploration, colonization, and urbanization of the Western world.

Three Herring and a Loaf

Just as technology has exercised control over the assignment of labor, it has fixed the range of living standards. In terms of a single group or individual, there may be no rigid or direct parallels between prosperity and technical progress, but in rough measure they move in tandem. As a general rule, the more sophisticated the technology, the higher the income and purchasing power of the people.

This may state the obvious, for all it says is that people who produce little are likely to have little: but it is a truism worth repeating. All too often, poverty and prosperity are discussed as though the only problem were one of distribution. If only the riches of the world could be apportioned equitably, man might be spared the misery of being poor. So it has been assumed. The problem, though, is one of production as well as allocation. Despite gross examples of greed and exploitation, despite lurid disparities between rich and poor in most centuries, it was the limitations of technology and not just the avarice of man that condemned the majority to hardship.

This is no apologia for the rich, but only an exercise in arithmetic. Had all the wealth of the popes and Medici and Borgias been given away, had the legendary gold horde of King Midas and the treasure troves of the Spanish nobles been parceled out among the people—"to each according to his need"—the typical citizen would have been almost as bitterly poor as ever.

Without the technical means of multiplying each man's production capacity, living standards are inevitably low, and this is true whether wages are tendered in money or in kind, to freeman or slave, to city worker or farm laborer, in the first century or the twentieth. The problem, as Dean Swift so neatly put it in *Gulliver's Travels,* is to make two blades of grass grow where one grew before, and the man who can do that deserves mankind's eternal blessing. Given the technology, the job is easy; without it, one must look for miracles, as with Christ multiplying the loaves and fishes.

Statistics in economics and living standards are not precise. Records are fragmentary and the extant data from various centuries cannot easily be put on a common base for comparison. A few figures are worth mentioning, though. In Rome during one of the more equable periods of economic history, bricklayers were paid the equivalent of 22 cents a day, carpenters and shipbuilders about the same, and common laborers about half as much. Slaves, offered for hire by their masters to work in the mines or at the docks, brought about 15 cents a day. Clerks commanded 20 cents. Interestingly, architects, stone carvers, and others who would today be distinguished as professional or semiprofessional workers, drew little more than clerical pay.

How much would these wages buy? At this time in Rome, 8 cents a day would feed a man, and a few cents more would supply raw wool for his tunics, a roof over his head, and sandals for his feet, though the last item was often dismissed as extravagance. The price of a bushel of wheat ranged from 40 cents to $1.20 (fluctuating in response to gluts and shortages). Cheese cost 7 cents a pound, and a day's supply of olive oil sold for about one penny. While more comfortably situated than most of their rural brothers, urban workers had only a small margin for luxuries. Survival consumed 80 to 90 per cent of income in most families.

This was the general condition for most people through the next sixteen centuries. During the Middle Ages in Europe, when rural workers were frequently paid in kind instead of coin, a day's labor was rewarded with three herring and a loaf of bread. In pre-industrial England, a few shillings a week would hire a craft worker, and even less would employ a farm laborer. Living costs remained about as they had been in the Roman world, and a rudimentary diet and the crudest sort of wardrobe absorbed all but a remnant of a man's income.[7]

Similar examples could be cited for other locales and times, but the point is already clear. Whatever the type of work involved or the date in history, living standards are confined in part by the boundaries of technology. The bottom limit is always the same—starvation—and the upper limit, if there is one, has not yet been located.

The Hallmark in Culture

Technology's hallmark is struck just as deeply into the nonmaterial facets of life. Technology is not itself an agency of the human spirit (it is not an agency at all, but a process), but it has provided the increased means and added leisure which Disraeli called "the two civilizers of man." It also has enriched the intellectual climate in which man has made his most notable excursions into theology and natural philosophy.

Much art thrives on a full stomach. Despite the standard assertion of geniuses producing best when starving in garrets, the greatest accomplishments of civilization have come in prosperous, well-fed surroundings. There is always an exception to the rule, but the principal cultural monuments belong to societies in which a substantial minority, if not all people, enjoyed prosperity. This was true of Rome and Greece, of Italy during the Renaissance and of the rest of Europe thereafter. To a smaller degree, it was true of classical Egypt and Crete.

As the late Arthur Compton once put it, "Where technology has been used for the service of man, there is in broad total a healthy growth not only in man's biological life but also in his intellectual life."

Wealth has often been channeled into ostentation and diversion, but it also has provided support for the performing arts, founded universities, built churches and museums, and liberated an important if small number of men for contemplation and creative thought. Moreover, some of the more glaring examples of ostentation contain fine art. The churches and statuary of Renaissance Italy are prime examples, financed by the patrons of Leonardo da Vinci, Michelangelo, Raphael, and Titian.

Had the social and cultural effects of technology always been restricted to a wealthy or intellectual minority, one might well debate the net worth of its contribution to civilization. In the modern ethic, there is something very wrong with an approach which refines a small segment of the populace at the expense of the rest. As a source for reform and progress, though, technology has made itself felt throughout society, lifting the expectations of all. In the ancient and medieval world, men of every station accepted poverty, pain, and servitude as inescapable. Even such introspective and moral men as Plato, Aristotle, and Cicero saw nothing remarkable in the ownership of one man by another. This was the way of life, and, as Plato once suggested only half jokingly, when a poor and humble worker succumbed to life's miseries and went to an early grave, it was probably all the better for him, for he was then "freed from all his troubles."[8]

Slavery. Infanticide. Child labor. These we think of as bestial and savage. Yet the Thracians sold some of their children into slavery, and infanticide was practiced by the Spartans, Slavs, and others. Child labor was universal in the Western world, in rich countries and poor, and in all centuries through the nineteenth.

We think of Greek and Roman law as the fount of free government and jurisprudence, yet the code of Athens encouraged slave recruiting, and permitted a father to expose his infant children, leaving them beside the road to be adopted by another, or to die. Personal liberty was subordinated everywhere in Greece except in Athens, and even there the noncitizen residents were subject to a code more harsh and strict than that imposed on the citizens. Under Roman law, a citizen anywhere in the Empire could plead "civis Romanus sum"—I am a citizen of Rome—thereby demanding the protection of his rights in the courts; but for those who were not citizens, the idea of equal rights simply did not apply. Torture, maiming, and death were punishments for crimes that would be regarded far more lightly today, or would not be considered criminal acts at all. Both Christ and Socrates died because their thoughts were held impious; the man on the cross next to Christ died for stealing.

The extent of human subjugation, even in the most advanced societies, is staggering to comprehend. Gangs of slaves, captured in war or by raiding expeditions, were traded like so much cordwood. Caesar recorded a single instance when 53,000 captives were sold on the spot to slave dealers. He is said to have taken 400,000 captives in Gaul in a ten-year period. In Italy, shortly before Christ's birth, there were 1.5 million slaves in the galleys, mines, workshops, and farms; and in Rome the slaves reportedly equaled plebeians in number (by one estimate, 650,000). Seneca said that the Senate rejected the idea of requiring slaves to dress alike, fearing that they might then realize the strength of their numbers and revolt.

In Athens, estimates of the slave population range from one slave per household to as many as four. Some notion of what this means is given by the fact that in the United States in 1860, far less than half the population of slave-holding states was enslaved, and nearly three-fourths of southern families owned no slaves. Both Greece and Rome were far more committed to slavery than the American South (though it must be added that the manumission of slaves was common to both ancient societies, that slaves held highly placed as well as menial positions, and that many slaves, after buying or being given their liberty, became respected, leading residents of the community, as was not the case in the United States).

It is easy to make value judgments about man's inhumanity to man, but they have to be applied within the context of the times. The harshness of life, the apparent disregard for pain and suffering, do not necessarily mean that ancestral societies were wholly callous and unconcerned. This may indicate only that people could see no alternative.

With inefficient tools and no realistic possibility of significantly increasing output, society could only regard as expendable those whom it could not sustain. The young, the old, the crippled and handicapped, whom today we try to bring under a sheltering canopy in prosperous societies, were of necessity left to a harsher fate in the limited economy of earlier centuries. (And, it is worth adding, this remains the case in some parts of the world to this day;

slavery is not yet completely abolished, and infanticide is still practiced.)

Until man has the technical means of multiplying his output, most jobs remain menial and tedious. Most men remain hewers of wood and drawers of water, and it is hardly remarkable that for so much of history, the impoverished and uneducated were regarded as impersonally as pieces of machinery.

Comparing the past to the present, we must add an equalizer—technology—as well as a dose of humility. The wonder is not that the world in past centuries held human life lightly, but that it progressed as far as it did with the ideas of freedom, equality at law, and humanitarianism. We can fairly ask whether our own society, with its vastly greater technical gifts and economic abundance, has done proportionately better.

4

THE ETHIC OF WORK

Over the centuries the economic value of labor has more or less been taken for granted. The result speaks for itself, especially to a hungry man. The role of work as a stabilizing force in society also has been noted, though the subject deserves more attention than it has received. Beyond these, there has been a search for a further rationale, a search for some justification after material need and civic survival. Put bluntly, if you don't have to work, why bother? The question has often lacked sharp definition, and the answers have been contradictory, but the age-old search for "the good life" has always included a search for a satisfactory ethic of work.

This quest dates from classical history. It became an element in Christian theology, and in the emergence of medieval monasticism. During the Reformation and afterward, when man insisted on examining the possibility of perfectability, the rationale for work became an issue in secular philosophy. In each of these periods, dramatists, poets, novelists, scientists, and political leaders, all of whom pressed their view on society, either debated directly the question of work's purpose, or suggested by word and deed their own resolution of it.

Man's search for an ethic of work, like the broader search for a philosophy of life, has not been noted for harmony or clarity. There have been periods when work was regarded as honorable and worthwhile, and other periods when it was scorned. Separate groups in a single society have held conflicting views, according to social hierarchy or economic stratification. To confuse the matter more, the idea of work has sometimes been applauded while the workman himself has been ridiculed; or, alternatively, the worker has been lauded while the organizations surrounding him have been damned. (This last point —man's attitude toward organizations—releases a whole swarm of bees. I will try to deal with them later, only noting for the moment that man's outlook on commerce and industry—and the technology that goes along with them—is hopelessly entangled with his opinion of work in general. We can unsnarl them a lot easier in print than man can in practice.)

There is a pattern to be found in these inconstant views, a relationship that seems to hold regardless of century or locale. It suggests that the attitude toward work is a mirror of civilization, and has certain predictive value. What people think of their labor reflects what they think of themselves, and when these views are taken in sum, one approaches what some would call the "national goals." The consensus of society, with reference to work and worker, serves as an important indicator of community values and priorities; it also offers a measure of society's prospects for the future.

Our own society, lacking some of the elemental incentive that has always driven man to labor, is more at liberty than any earlier society both to question its ethic of work and to act on its decisions. We are singularly blessed, if that is the word, with the chance to make or break our own future.

Stark necessity, for all the misery attending it, has backstopped man's decision in the past, and helped hold society together. The schoolboy of ancient Egypt, learning the work of a scribe, was counseled to apply himself in earnest to his tasks; his compatriot many centuries later was so implored by McGuffey's *Reader*, for the same fundamental reason. The farmer of 800 B.C. was told to fill his barns "by working with work and more work," just as the farmer of colonial America was admonished from the pulpit to bend his back to toil.

In the folklore of France there is a saying that the best fertilizer is "the eye of the owner." In the Peripatetic literature of Greece, dated at about Aristotle's time, there is this quotation:

> We may commend also a pair of sayings, one attributed to a Persian and the other to a Libyan. The former on being asked what best conditions a horse, replied, "His master's eye."
>
> The Libyan, when asked what kind of manure is best, answered, "The master's footprints."

From Plato and Homer, Hesiod, and Xenophon came advice which, with modest rephrasing, appeared more than two thousand years later in *Poor Richard's Almanac:* "It is from work that men grow rich and own flocks and herds"; "Do not put off until tomorrow and the day after . . . it is keeping at it that gets the work done"; "What a burden it is to support even one idle man"; "Work is no disgrace, the disgrace is in not working"; "The beginning is more than half the work."[1]

The homely maxims go on endlessly, scarcely differentiated by century or locale, acknowledging individual need and, indirectly, man's yearning for social stability. Through centuries of war, flood, and plague, through successive reigns of conquerors and tyrants, ordinary men and women have gone about their chores out of habit as well as hunger. When government has decayed, when learned counselors have abandoned hope for mankind, when further struggle seems pathetic and pointless, when enemy troops have advanced to the city wall, people have gone forth with the morning sun, clinging to the only surviving remnant of order and tradition, their work.

They have planted a new crop in the wake of the locust, rebuilt market stalls in the rubble of ravaged cities, set sail on new voyages after their families have been put to the sword and their villages leveled by fire. *Business as usual* has been a cry of faith as well as commerce, a sign hung in the window of every civilization retaining the flicker of life.

It is easy to dismiss this as materialistic, to brand it as crass and cold-blooded. Moreover, it is difficult to keep invocations about work from sounding smug and pompous. Still, there is a factor to be reckoned with here. Man has found a deep significance in work, bearing upon his ingrained need to keep his sanity and civilization intact. Whatever reversals man has suffered, however deep his despair, he has gone on working, and if this is a measure of cupidity or simple habit, it is also a testament to persistence of will.

The Sanctity of Work

This leaves the further question, the one of special pertinence now. What is the purpose of work, if any, beyond economic expediency and social stability? Is work but an anchor to windward in times of storm, and no more than a means to material ends? Does it, in effect, have some moral or exclusively human content?

"Why work?" The question has always been there, touching the life of every man who has a shred of introspection. It has troubled man for thousands of years, appearing in societies only modestly blessed with affluence, demanding an answer even of men but a step removed from animalistic need. What sort of response has been forthcoming?

Here, we have to exorcise a myth. History is the most tractable of sciences; it will suffer all manner of abuse. Frequently, what everybody "knows" to be true proves only to be a distortion of the record, sanctified by endless repetition. Such is the case here, in reference to man's views on work.

It has been said more times than can be counted that the greatest of societies despised labor, scorned technology, and frowned upon commerce. Presumably, history teaches that only the efforts of the independent mind, and those uncontaminated by material ends, are truly worthy of mankind. This may be what some would like history to say, but it is not what the record shows. To defend the point at all, one has to proceed from carefully selected sources. It is far closer to the truth, if yet an oversimplification, to say that most earlier civilizations respected both labor and laborer, received technology charitably, and were favorably inclined to commerce. Not only does this contradict the legend; it helps account for the progress that these societies recorded. In Greece and Rome, in Western Europe and Great Britain through the Renaissance and into the modern period, the attitude toward work and its institutions was far more favorable than the conventional interpretations would allow.

The distortion lies in the eye of the beholder. They say that history is written by the winning side. It is also written by a select minority, often representing an aristocratic segment of society, and frequently given to curious notions about the popular sentiment. Rulers and scholars, recording their thoughts, have held rude work ignoble; but their many contemporaries in business and trade, not to mention their still more numerous brethren of lesser note, have left fewer records for posterity. Most of them could not read or write.

The aristocratic view is nonetheless worth observing. It follows a cycle. In one society after another, the aristocracy has first committed itself to a life of diligent application, then progressively grown more aloof, and finally turned with contempt from any involvement that would soil the hands or interrupt the hours of pleasure. It is important to note that, soon after the leading group in society has lost its respect for work, the society itself has weakened or disintegrated. Perhaps there is a moral in this as to the wisdom of letting aristocrats run society.

In the Homeric legends, gods and goddesses worked with their hands at ordinary tasks, and became the patrons and guardians of human craftsmen. Odysseus boasted of his skill as a plowman, and claimed he could outwork any rival at the harvest. Later, Aristotle and Xenophon praised the agrarian life, and Xenophon records the pride of a gentleman who personally supervised the work of his gardens and cropland. But by Aristotle's century, enthusiasm for labor was waning. Wealthy Greeks no longer lived on their estates. The amusements of the city held them, and they would condescend only to pay occasional visits to their farm holdings, where hired managers and slaves did all the work. By this time, not by coincidence, the Athenian civilization had passed its zenith.

Roman legend duplicates the Greek. Recall the tale of Cincinnatus, called from his plow to assume the throne at the beginning of the Republic. A few centuries later, no patrician would have demeaned himself with manual labor, Cato, Cicero, Virgil, and Horace continued to heap praise on the agrarian life (interestingly, the only occupations that have been held acceptable by the aristocracy in almost every century are estate management and military service). But the Roman Empire did not intend for a gentleman to strain his back or mind by working. Its idealization of rural living had nothing to do with the ethic of work. It was a reaction against the debauchery of city life which, by Cicero's day, was nearly as decadent as claimed, and which was followed in the next century by political disorganization and decline.

During the Middle Ages and Renaissance, the well-born at first saw personally to the lordly work of the manor and the administration of enterprise. As the trappings and pleasures of courtly life increased, work became a remote concern for the aristocracy. In *The Book of the Courtier*, written in the sixteenth century, Castiglione describes in minute detail the qualifications of a perfect gentleman—acquaintance with art, music, and literature; the social grace to remain at ease in any gathering; and skill in the use of arms. Nothing whatever is said about the courtier troubling himself with peaceful labor. And, as later scholars have ungenerously pointed out, few contributions except negative ones can be attributed to the graduates of the schools for courtiers. They were a singularly vacuous and unimpressive crowd, and were soon supplanted in economic power by the rising middle class, a group with energy to offset inferior pedigree.

The aristocratic view of work may be a useful measure of a society's potential, but it is a notoriously poor guide to popular sentiment. The record of Greece offers a pointed example, though by no means the only one. In Greece, while aristocratic plowboys were turning into playboys, a fierce pride of craftsmanship distinguished more humble efforts. Stone reliefs show craftsmen at work with their tools nearby; the very fact that such carvings were made, in defiance of the aristocratic view, is significant. Epitaphs and tomb carvings carry the proud cries of the artisan. One woodsman, killed in the Peloponnesian War, left these words behind: "Mannes . . . the best of the Phrygians in the broad lands of Athens, lies in this fine tomb; and by Zeus I never saw a better woodman . . ." There was a fellow who believed in his work.

Ordinary pottery and sculpture, as well as work intended for artistic competition, bore the signature of the designer and often of the sponsoring house. One amphora, signed with the name Euthymides, offered an editorial fillip: "Euphranios will never do as well."

This was no Greek-born Cellini speaking. Euthymides was a plain son of Syntrips the Smasher and Asbestos the Sooty One. His pottery was everyday ware and, by art critics' analysis, distinctly second-rate.

Others born to low estate were equally unapologetic about their talents or heritage. Socrates was a stone carver, and not ashamed to admit it. By preference, he spent most of his time with shopkeepers and craftsmen. The orator Lysias was the son of an armorer whom the ruler Pericles counted among his close friends. Demosthenes was the son of a craftshop owner, and shrewd enough to know that popular opinion favored the humble workman against an arrogant upper class. In one trial, defending a client against the jibes of a tormentor, Demosthenes had his witness concede that hard times had befallen him, forcing him to sell ribbons to remain alive. He defied anyone to "take that in bad part."

"Be careful not to speak hardly of the poor," he said. "It is bad enough already to be poor, especially to those who have a trade and earn their living honestly."

Demosthenes had coached his witness well, and such tactics unquestionably worked, for at about this time in Greek history, a law was passed making it slanderous to criticize a man on the basis of his occupation.

There was always some sniping from intellectuals. Plato, Xenophon, Aristotle, and others professed a lofty disgust for labor, and the comic playwrights, most notably Aristophanes, delighted in barbs aimed at the low-born poor. But the words lack sting. Though Aristophanes was a blue-blood himself, he found more virtue among dockworkers and fishwives than among his own kind. Common workers attended the plays, laughed at the jokes about themselves, and realized that most of the jesting hid a dead-serious attack on the corruption and affectation of Athenian upper class.

Reading the Greek writers, one eventually discovers what really bothered them. They shared with the Hebrews the conviction that work is a sentence imposed on errant humanity. In the original creation of Greek legend, as in Eden, man had no need to work. After man's sins exhausted the patience of the deities, work (as Xenophon put it) was made the painful price the gods demand for the necessities of life.

Such toil, the Hebrews lamented, does not "satisfy the soul." Nor does it satisfy the earthly aspirations of the intellect or the requirements of good citizenship, added the Greeks. A life spent in the dust of the pottery shop or the darkness of the mine left a man ignorant, base in his appetites, and incapable of the pursuit of reason.

The problem, then, became one of priorities. As was said by Epictetus, a Greek who had once known slavery at first hand, "Only the educated are free." Endless manual toil left no time for labors of the mind, and thus was taken as a poor route to the good life. For the worker himself, and for his contribution, there was not scorn but sympathy, which shines through even the most biting passages in the classics.

The same sense of honor and dignity is found through the Roman period and into the early Christian era, fortified by the example of Christ and the Disciples. John Chrysostom, a fourth-century saint who lived near Antioch, reminded his followers that Peter was a fisherman, and Paul . . . "standing in a tentmaker's shop, sewed hides together while angels were reverencing him and demons quaking with fear. Nor was he ashamed to say, 'These hands of mine have provided for my needs and those of my companions.' Did I say he was not ashamed. Rather, he gloried in this very fact."

There is an important shift in thought here, a break with a defensive posture and an affirmation of the dignity of work. This found its full statement, a century after John Chrysostom, in the words of St. Benedict, founder of the monastic order bearing his name.

Laborare est orare—To work is to pray.

Here, with poetic economy, a positive ethic of work is set forth, as far as I know for the first time. The sanctification of labor proved to be one of the most powerful ideas of all time. Amended and elaborated, it penetrated theology and temporal thought throughout the Middle Ages, brought important shifts in Catholicism and helped produce the Reformation, and evolved into what is today called the Protestant ethic (a curious title in some respects; Benedict and his followers for a thousand years were Roman Catholics).

In the sixth century, when Benedict founded his monastery at Monte Cassino, monasticism was in a state of torpor. Monks wandered the countryside with little discipline, living by begging. Benedict found such disorder an anathema. He imposed a strict set of rules and procedures, marking off each part of the day to some appointed task. Uniquely, his monastery required every able-bodied man to share in manual labor.

Encouraged by Pope Gregory, who thought so highly of

Benedict that he wrote a biography of him, the order spread throughout Western Europe and England. There followed a succession of sects and orders built on the Benedictine model of hard labor. The Cistercians (the "white monks," so called because of the garb worn to distinguish them from the black-robed Benedictines) became famous as the best farmers in Europe. Willing to tackle unpromising tracts of land, they cleared forests and drained swamps, upgraded marginal soil through skillful crop rotation, and introduced advances in animal husbandry, always subjecting themselves to the domination of toil.

The monks of Clairvaux, an order founded by St. Bernard, hewed to the same discipline, as did the Poor Lollards, the Waldenses, the Cluniacs, and other sects or splinter groups.

William of Ockham, a Franciscan philosopher of the fourteenth century, departed from the monastic view to argue that, before God as well as man, a life of action counted for more than insular reflection. This concept had a formidable influence on the rise of Protestantism. To Martin Luther, leader of the German Reformation, it meant that the scullery maid who did her chores well was as near to God as any priest in the pulpit. To John Calvin, divine will dictated that all men, rich or poor, apply themselves to a rigorous and unindulgent life. Calvin's stern and unforgiving religion denied any superiority in deeds of service to God as compared to work that served man, for he held the two to be indistinguishable.

The Puritan morality went a step further. Wealth was taken as a measure of success in serving God. The accumulation of profit—not for display or idleness, but to be reinvested in productive enterprise—was seen as a mark that one's work had found favor. To be rich but not flaunt it was ideal. To be poor was not merely a misfortune; it was to fail in one's mission, and mock God. This last elaboration of Calvinism, carried to the New World by the Puritans and Quakers, strongly colored the moral code of colonial America, and is still to be seen today, only partly diluted by time, as a form of reverse snobbishness found among the gentry in such watering spots as the North Shore of Long Island. There, in an Episcopal church in which I spent many a Sunday as an acolyte among the WASPS, it was a simple matter to catalog the members of the congregation by their trappings and transportation. New furs and Cadillacs spelled *nouveau riche;* the *ancien riche,* heirs to some of America's largest fortunes, wore Brooks Brothers' jackets patched at the elbows, and drove aging Chevrolets.

Is the ethic of work still of significance? Is it as necessary to this century as to previous ones? No one knows. The most that can be said on the strength of history is that the ethic has had a seminal and profound bearing on the past performance of civilization. Before discarding it, we would do well to inquire as to the alternatives, and of this score history offers no appealing substitute. In the past, alienation from work—the condition so much discussed today—has proved disastrous.[2]

THE ETHIC OF COMMERCE

What is true of men individually holds for men incorporate. Attitudes toward the institutions and forms of work, as much as toward the individuals involved, have influenced the performance and prospects of society. Community economic gains have been most notable where commerce, consolidation, and innovation have been most warmly welcomed. A stigma against any of the three usually has penalized society.

Here, too, polar views stretch as far back in history as one cares to look. Four centuries before Christ's birth, Plato spoke of commerce as the calling of thieves ready for the jailers. Two centuries after Christ, Clement of Alexandria warmly defended manufacture and trade, noting that commerce could not be distinguished from community service, for "as a matter of fact, business is the chief social service." By and large, with exceptions that are very much worth noting, the prevailing attitude has been closer to Plato than Clement. The hostility to business has been costly to society, if often well earned by the businessman. Unlike agriculture, which traditionally has held a favored spot in public reputation, commerce has had to earn its place in society, and live down an abominable reputation. This has happened not once but repeatedly, as part of the process that turns simple, agrarian economies into elaborate, interdependent ones.

The pioneers of commerce were an unlovely lot, and gave ancient societies every reason to look askance at the whole process of buying and selling. The early Mediterranean was not so much an avenue for legitimate trade as an alley of piracy. Most merchants were transients, bent only on fleecing the customer, stealing his household goods and perhaps his wife, and stepping nimbly to the next port of call. The jokes about traveling salesmen applied in full force to these men. Under the circumstances, it was small wonder that Greeks despised men who "traffic with ships," protested "greedy profits," and insisted that every contract, however small in value, be executed in the presence of witnesses.

The process of urbanization produced another breed of merchant. Under the Athenian democracy, as an example, commerce deserved and was usually shown a high degree of respect. Widespread piracy was a thing of the past, long since made unprofitable by the navy of Athens. A body of law had developed to adjudicate commercial differences. Businessmen were permanent residents of the community, and dependent on what is now called repeat business. In self-interest, most of them would not have continued the wayward traditions of the Homeric traders even if the law had allowed.

It was still the practice to witness each contract (except with one's banker, who was usually trusted implicitly; the banking fraternity has rarely enjoyed a reputation as high as it held in Hellenic Greece), but commerce wore the mantle of respectability, and businessmen were counted among the leaders of the community. One financier, Pasion, was so widely known and respected that his son was extended large sums on credit everywhere he went in the Hellenic world. Hermias, another entrepreneur, rose to govern part of Greece. Both Pasion and Hermias, incidentally, began life as slaves, which tells something about the possibilities of social mobility as well as the commercial consciousness of the times.

Some of the centuries-old prejudice survived. Unoccupied aristocrats looked down their noses at ordinary men in business. So did philosophers. Yet one questions the hostile comments. The aristocracy continued to profit from what it claimed to despise. Aristotle, for all his scornful words, managed to exempt from criticism the men of commerce whom he happened to know, and delivered a eulogy at the death of his friend Hermias. Plato, in his construction of an ideal civilization, spoke in terms of a consolidated city-state complete with all the trimmings of commerce. A utopia without a smooth-running business sector appears nowhere in his writings.

An opposite example is found in the Middle Ages, when a low respect for commerce and an inability to perceive the value of its organizations, slowed the economic advance. Remembering that Christ had driven the money-changers from the temple, and mindful of the absence of ethics in numerous bazaars of trade, the medieval Church banned all lending of money at interest. "Usury," which we now think of as interest at exorbitant rates, was used in the Middle Ages to signify any interest at all.

Thomas Aquinas, reverting to the pattern of antiquity (and influenced by the classical revival that took place in the late Middle Ages), assigned agriculture the highest status in his hierarchy of occupations. Handicrafts came second; commerce, a poor third. Aquinas and the Church imposed on commerce the doctrine of "just price," by which a man was permitted to charge only for the materials and labor invested in a job, and was allowed no profit.

That approach to economics was anachronistic and stifling. The "just price" deprived enterprise of incentive at the very time when trade and manufacturing were expanding. It failed to acknowledge any positive contribution of venture capital, even though the need for investment funds was rising and the economy was increasingly turning toward capitalism. It offered no compensation for risk, despite the fact that the perils of enterprise were high, and could be assumed only if offset by the promise of gain. The pressure of the times was toward enduring economic organizations, and in that climate the "just price" was as unenforceable as Prohibition. It suffered the same fate.

The general enmity toward commerce eased only gradually, however. Conveniently ignoring the fact that popes occasionally had to borrow money, and that the Church itself was the biggest business institution in existence, the Church remained suspicious of business and finance, and maintained its belief that commerce and the merchant could "scarcely or never be pleasing to God."

Artists of the late Middle Ages portrayed the money-changer with a face contorted by greed and hands bent into claws. English playwrights as late as the seventeenth century offered audiences a stereotype of the business-man. Though middle-class men of commerce had by then become the key to national wealth, playwrights hewed to the aristocratic contempt for merchants and financiers, giving them such stage names as Gripe, Addle, Cholerick, and Feeble Dotard. And, as is often the case with stereotypes, there remained in the business community more than enough examples to give priests, painters, and playwrights the ammunition they needed.

Not to be overlooked is a further factor. The ethic of work, equating diligence with piety, seemed contradicted by the lives of the more successful merchants and financiers. They labored less to gain more. Given a basic accumulation of funds, skillful lieutenants, and perhaps a patent or trade monopoly (for at the time these were dispensed by royalty to court favorites), the capitalist could compound his profits without visible effort. The same argument could of course be applied to the landed gentry, whose capital was held in the form of land. Their privileges were numerous, and their personal involvement in the work of the soil, negligible. A society in which subsistence was yet an open question found it easy to protest the uselessness of such men, and to find inequity in their gains.

By the eighteenth and nineteenth centuries, commerce had changed, and the mood changed with it. If merchant capitalists of giant wealth continued to prosper, an increasing share of the total economic effort had found its way to the hands of middle-class businessmen who ran their own stores and factories. Their wealth, in those cases where there was wealth, at least appeared to be earned.

The entrepreneur was visibly useful, especially by comparison with the aristocracy, and found a measure of favor in society.

Such dramatists as Steele and Gay, for example, were appalled at the decadence of the landed gentry and still more disgusted by the gap between society's professed code and its actual behavior. In *The Conscious Lovers,* Steele spoke of the merchant as a man "as honourable, and almost as useful, as . . . landed Folks that have always thought yourselves so much above us." Samuel Johnson, acerb critic and wit of the eighteenth century, remarked, "There are few ways in which a man can be more innocently employed than in getting money."

We should not take Dr. Johnson too seriously—the man of commerce was scarcely a lovable public figure, and would continue to be criticized for his narrowness, cupidity, and arrogant materialism. But after five hundred years of expanding business activity, with most of the notorious misadventures of early capitalism in the background, society had begun to see businessmen for what they were— not as saints, but as necessary and useful contributors to society's economic objectives. There was a new appreciation of the virtues of organization, and a new measure of admiration for those who had expanded the world through trade and exploration. There remained the image of the mercantile dynasties, but there was little fear that a commercial minority would ever regain unchecked power. That power had been distributed and superseded, partly by dispersing decisions into the marketplace and partly by the strengthening of political institutions. The social structure was becoming pluralistic, and the climate for enterprise more favorable. It was at this point that Europe began the period of its most rapid progress.

The Welcome to Technology

Something needs to be said now about the reception given to technology. As a predominant force for change, it has served as an indicator of society's mood. If technology is particularly well received, presumably society is of a mind to welcome change, or at least accept change as the price of progress. If it is strongly opposed, one would look for signs of stagnation.

Once again, we must take exception to a popular thesis, and make note of the fact that ancient and medieval societies for the most part welcomed technology. Their major problem was not that they scorned or feared it, but that they could not assemble enough of it.

In classical literature, much is made of the fact that philosophers were enthralled by theory but were contemptuous of its applications. In other words, to draw a perilous line, they thought well of science but not much of engineering. In his biography of the Roman ruler Marcellus, for example, Plutarch maintained that the mechanical arts were repudiated by philosophers. Plato is reported to have hurled invective at two mathematicians who built mechanical models to demonstrate a geometric proof, and Archimedes is said to have needed persuasion to devote his hours to the design of engines of war.

However, this does not establish an "either-or" rule. Plato's point was that models can only approximate a mathematical idea, and that perfection lies in the abstract form. The idea of triangularity, then, is intellectually superior to any particular triangle. This is true (if one agrees with Plato that intangible ideas exist by and of themselves), but surely it cannot be taken to mean that Plato expected man to adorn himself only in the idea of clothing, or to protect himself in battle with the theory of a shield.

Archimedes was similarly intrigued by theory, and to a mind as original as his the construction of catapults and arrow launchers admittedly was a small challenge. Yet he did lend his talents to the defense of Syracuse, and Marcellus, laying siege to that stronghold, found Archimedes' weapons diabolically clever and enormously destructive. The Roman troops, showered with stones and arrows from launchers hidden from view, with their ships lifted bodily out of the sea by levers and grapples, concluded that they had joined battle not with ordinary mortals but with the gods themselves.

In most periods and places, within the societies that developed some forward momentum, technology was taken as a welcome relief to toil. Antipater, a poet of Cicero's time, offered this acclaim to a waterwheel that liberated female slaves from the drudgery of turning a millstone:[1]

> Cease from grinding . . . sleep late even if the crowing cocks announce the dawn . . . the Nymphs perform the work of your hands . . . (and) turn the heavy Nisyrian millstones.

Technology was acknowledged, as well, as an instrument to liberate the mind. Even in monasteries, where manual labor was regarded as a necessary scourge of the flesh, labor-saving devices found favor. One sixth-century abbot, reflecting upon the time his monks spent grinding grain by hand, built a water-driven mill and thus increased their hours for meditation.

The warmest reception for technology came after the Middle Ages, when man began to appreciate the leverage he could gain by turning scientific theory into practical application. His eagerness to better his lot was a central fact of the scientific revolution. Theory and practice were brought together under a common canopy, and the scientist, shedding his hauteur, began to look for ideas anywhere he could find them. Often, he found the company of tinkers and amateurs more inspiring than the learned but sterile lectures of academicians. (Interestingly, the universities contributed comparatively little to the emerging physical and biological sciences. They were more an instrument to preserve the status quo than a force for change.) He also found that manufacturers, mine owners, and merchants were almost desperate in their eagerness to try new tools and re-examine old problems.

Notably, every important technical organization formed during the seventeenth and eighteenth centuries had a declared interest in the utilization as well as expansion of scientific theory. Almost all of them, as well, included in their membership architects, businessmen, and others not formally trained in science. This is true of the Accademia del Cimento, which flourished briefly but brightly in seventeenth-century Florence, and showed the way to a host of followers; of the Royal Society of London, which proved permanent, and of the Lunar Society of Birmingham, which did not; of several societies in Germany, including the famed Berlin Academy found by Leibniz; and of the best-known entrant from the New World, the American Philosophical Society, whose full and correct title includes "for promoting useful knowledge."

Whatever else they might be, science and its attendant technical discoveries were meant to be useful, and it was this characteristic, as much as any, that drew men of practical affairs to the societies. Among the fellows of the Royal Society, together with scientists as Robert Boyle and Robert Hooke, were the renowned architect Christopher Wren; the manufacturer Matthew Boulton, who was James Watt's partner; Watt himself, an instrument maker by trade; John Wilkinson, an armaments manufacturer; and Josiah Wedgwood, owner of the pottery works, a stickler for quality workmanship (the slightest imperfection on a product brought a scrawled, "This won't do for Jos. Wedgwood") and an accomplished amateur scientist in a time when amateurs were at no particular disadvantage.

A similar mingling of theory and practice was found in the Lunar Society of Birmingham, which took its name from the fact that meetings were held on a night close to the full moon, so that members could see their way home. Its founders included Boulton; Erasmus Darwin, a practicing physician, one of the better speculative minds of his century, and grandfather of Charles Darwin; and William Small, a Scotch-born professor who lived in Virginia from 1758 to 1764, and numbered among his admiring students Thomas Jefferson. It was Small who brought together Boulton and Watt and another "lunatic," Wilkinson, whose mastery of ironwork produced the accurately bored cylinders that made Watt's steam engines possible.

Another indispensable man in this network was Joseph Black. A chemistry professor at the University of Glasgow, Black discovered the theory of latent heat and explained it to Watt. This proved to be the scientific key Watt needed; soon afterward, Watt later reported, the idea of a condensing steam engine worked itself out in his mind.

Again and again, the enthusiasm for application appears in this flourishing period of the history of science. The French chemist Antoine Lavoisier, one of mankind's least likable but most useful members, distributed his abundant talents across many fields. He helped manage the government gunpowder plants, and more than doubled their output in three years. (Powder from these plants helped America win the Revolutionary War.) He encouraged the application of science to agriculture, wrote the basic textbook in chemistry, helped straighten out chemical nomenclature, prepared an atlas of the minerals of France, served as a bank president, produced some sterling reports on the political economy and financial structure of France, and worked to improve the Paris water supply and street lighting system. It was partly his familiarity with industrial and municipal problems that led to his theoretical studies of oxidation, combustion, respiration, and the composition of water.

Michael Faraday, though primarily interested in fundamental questions and not their practical consequences, served for a time as a consultant to the Admiralty and was a member of a committee striving to improve the quality of optical glass. Humphry Davy took time from his theoretical labors to answer the plea of a mine-safety committee, and helped solve the problem of explosions. He invented the miner's safety lamp, a straightforward piece of engineering application, and thereby saved no one knows how many lives. Davy and Faraday had laboratories at the Royal Institution in London, an establishment founded for the express purpose of "bringing forward into general use new inventions and improvements . . ."

The progress of technology was immensely fascinating to laymen. An event such as a balloon launching was guaranteed to draw a crowd of thousands, and was dutifully reported by the press as a major event of the social season. However, the appeal of the new science lay not only in circus spectaculars. There was equal fervor, at least among the educated public, for lectures and journals describing the work of distinguished scientists. A public appearance by Davy meant a packed hall, and tickets to his lectures even found their way to scalpers, a public compliment bestowed on few scientists before or since.

This widespread activity in science, together with the cross-fertilization that took place because scientists and laymen respected each other's ideas, largely explains the acceleration of technology in the seventeenth and eighteenth centuries, and goes a long way toward explaining the economic surge of the eighteenth and nineteenth centuries. Science, liberated from the double bond of antiquity and alchemy, striving to follow reason rather than dogma, progressed as it never had before, and became an inseparable part of the revolution that has fashioned the modern world.

Protests and Problems

Revolution, beneficent or not, brings problems in its wake. This one was no exception. Changes in technology, in the institutions of work, and above all in the human outlook forever changed the course of history. The economic expansion of the late eighteenth and nineteenth centuries brought a rising tide of expectations which technology and the economic structure of the time could only partly fulfill. New prosperity and mobility were offered to many, but to others change meant hardship, or desperation. Frustration and discontent spread through Europe, generating necessary reforms, but also providing a seedbed for socialism and the Marxist movement.

The idea of progress is a potent force. Unleashed in this period, it produced new standards and demands. If, by economic measures, living conditions in Europe were better than in earlier centuries, this was no longer considered good enough, or even tolerable. Conditions a medieval peasant might have accepted fatalistically, in the hope of finding redress in the next world, were now protested as unjust and demanding of correction. The unprivileged had received half a loaf; as is the way in these matters, they wanted the other half, and not posthumously.

There was a utopian mood, particularly strong in the early nineteenth century, promising to make earth a heaven. Few expected delivery on the contract, but many did expect lesser, more pragmatic gains such as equal treatment under law, safer working conditions, protection by society of women and child laborers, and control of wages and hours—none of which had previously been considered a "right."

If man were poor and miserable, this was no longer the cast of the dice, but an absolute ill with a deliberate cause. Where to place the blame? The most visible target was industrial capitalism. This became the focal point of attack; then and since, the Industrial Revolution has been depicted as the source of the workman's plight, and the creator of urban squalor.

This was irony turned full circle. Without industry and its accompanying technology, society could not have entertained the idea of broad economic progress. Moreover, industry inself was not the proximate cause of urban poverty. An urban proletariat existed long before the Industrial Revolution, and in the eighteenth and nineteenth centuries it was often the nonindustrial workers whose life was most grim. As grisly a view of urban European life as one can imagine appears in Hogarth's etchings and Dickens' novels. Yet Hogarth dates from before the Industrial Revolution, and the unfortunates Charles Dickens described were for the most part not factory workers. If one had to single out, in macabre fashion, the most pathetic example of humanity in all of Europe, one would probably not look to the factory, but would fasten upon the farm hand. He was the lowest paid and most helpless of men. Edwin Markham was hardly exaggerating when he saw "the emptiness of ages in his face, and on his back the burden of the world."

Industrial capitalism, on the other hand, had a particularly ugly countenance and a high degree of public visibility. It involved not just a few craft or field workers, but hundreds of mill hands, accelerating the crush of urban poor in communities totally unable to cope with the attendant problems. Abominations of industrial architecture blighted dozens of cities, and to this day blacken the face of much of Europe (and for that matter, of America). The regimentation of work schedules and the brutality of some factory overseers were widely advertised, leaving a pall which has never fully lifted.

It is now clear that many of the horror stories circulating from this period are distortions. Tales of vicious factory owners exploiting defenseless workers, and especially women and children, were partly founded in fact, but were embellished as social protest. Conveniently ignored was the example of such capitalists as Robert Owen, who built homes and streets around his mills at New Lanark, Scotland, raised wages and reduced working hours, provided for the education of workers' children, and lobbied for child labor laws. Owen was an extraordinary man, but he was far from alone in his desire to better the workman's lot. Many of his contemporaries shared that objective even though they rejected Owen's ultimate dream of building a communal society.

What is clear now was not so easily seen then. Had the early industrial society been given a loftier vantage, to glimpse future possibilities and correctives, civilization might have come through this period with minimum disruption. But the problems of the time had immediate urgency, and no momentary solution was at hand.

The factories of the eighteenth and nineteenth centuries were low in productivity and high in the need for unskilled manpower. Neither is a quality associated with rapid increases in living standards. An obvious answer was to increase industrial efficiency through the introduction of new technology. From the point of view of the factory owners this was the only logical course to follow, for commercial competition was on the rise. From the point of view of their employees new tools meant lost jobs and, among a labor force of little skill and no education, lost jobs meant disaster.

At the heart of the problem lay the fact that there was at this time a surplus of labor in Europe. Finding another job was a difficult task and, for some, all but impossible. It was all very well to say, and it was true, that in the long run technology was creating more jobs than it destroyed. It was also said, and again was true, that those future jobs would be better paid and otherwise superior. But this was small comfort to workers caught in the jaws of change. They were not taking the long view; they were looking at lost jobs and starving families. Who would support them? They had no savings. Who stood ready to retrain them? No one. Where were the new jobs? Miles (and maybe years) away, in factories they had never heard of, often not yet built. What "workmen's compensation" was offered to cushion the shock? At most, some inadequate Poor Laws enacted too late.

Let inventors and mill owners celebrate the virtues of the flying shuttle and the power loom. To the workers, an ounce of prevention was worth a pound of grief. They took to the streets.

When textile machinery was introduced in France during the mid-eighteenth century, the importer was met by such fury that he had to flee in disguise. Other victims of mob fear were John Kay, whose flying shuttle forced him into hiding, and Thimonnier, inventor of the sewing machine. After angry tailors and seamstresses smashed Thimonnier's early models, he was afraid to pursue the invention. The sewing machine had to be reinvented later by an American.

The most violent outbursts were the Luddite riots in England between 1811 and 1815. Bands of bitter textile workers roamed the countryside destroying stocking frames, power looms, shearing frames, and sometimes whole factories. A favored weapon was the "Great Enoch," a heavy hammer made by Enoch and James Taylor. The symbol of leadership was the banner of "King Ludd," who was never captured and who is assumed to have been mythical.

The Luddite uprising left deep wounds. Several people were killed by the mobs, and the government moved swiftly to repress what its more conservative members regarded as an open insurrection. In the panic to preserve "law and order," some Luddites went to the gallows, including a sixteen-year-old boy whose crime was to act as sentinel while his brothers put a mill to the torch.

Incidents such as these were fuel for the fires of revolutionaries, and were taken as a final indictment of capitalism by Saint-Simon, Fourier, Marx, Engels, Lassalle, and Lenin. The principal prophets of despair were Marx and the economist, David Ricardo. Ricardo's gloomy analysis, which lent to economics the name "the dismal science," envisioned an Iron Law controlling wages: no matter how profitable an enterprise may become, its employees can never rise above the level of bare subsistence.

To Marx, this signaled revolt, not only against the capitalists who held title to the tools of production, but also against established governments which guaranteed that title. This was the only answer to what he saw as an inevitable class struggle, with workers and employer striving for opposite goals, forever irreconcilable.

The dignity of labor was not a basic issue to Marx. He began and ended with a materialistic interpretation in which economic forces overwhelm other human drives. He cared little for the subjective or moral questions surrounding man's work.

Nor was technology at issue. To the contrary, Marx had a childlike faith in science and mechanization, and expected them to bring an industrial society without poverty or peasantry. It was preposterous, he believed, to "protect" small peasant landholdings, for this would keep too much of the population on the farm, and slow industrial progress. It was equally wrong to oppose technical change.

Marx's objective was not to limit industry but to transfer its ownership to the proletariat. With this in mind, Marx saw the likely success of communism in England, then the most industrialized country of Europe, and in Germany, which was moving rapidly toward an industrial economy. Russia, with its vast distances and agrarian economy, was rejected as an unlikely home for communism.[2]

The Marxist prophecy proved wrong in almost every respect. Capturing the land to the east, Marxism turned into a dictatorship not of the proletariat, but over them. The government did not "wither away" as forecast, but became a behemoth with a grip on one-third of the world's population. Western Europe, instead of abolishing capitalism, reformed and extended it, and prospered. What Marx had assumed to be the death rattle of capitalism proved instead to be the outbursts of an adolescent, needing restraint but capable of mature behavior. What Marx had assumed to be the hopeless plight of the proletariat proved to be a step toward a wholly new standard of living, a tragic, sacrificial step for some, to be sure, but a forward step nonetheless, Ricardo's Iron Law has rusted into oblivion.

The consequences remain. The nineteenth-century spirit of enterprise survived, and brought gains to millions, but many others were left disenchanted and embittered, if not enslaved. The unbridled enthusiasm for technology was tempered by a new awareness of the human costs of change, and by a growing concern about man's ability to cope with his own creations. The legacy of fear still exists and has delayed technical change on more than one occasion.

At a time when differences among social classes showed signs of waning, a new split appeared. As Sir Norman Angell has remarked, the net effect of the leftist movement was to convince many workers that "there is no such thing as a community of interest between employer and employee," and that "for a man to produce his maximum is to do some mate out of a job." That doctrine has proved as infectious as it is destructive. It has been persuasive to employers as well as employees, and continues to pervade their relationship. The hyphenated term, labor-management relations, in itself implies a rift.

Could the worst of those problems have been avoided?

That is a moot question. Had there been some mechanism for easing the impact of change, had the work force been more mobile, had warning voices been heeded, and had leaders of government and industry been more concerned with people and less with things, this part of history might make happier reading today. But hindsight is not much help. The forces for conflict were powerful and all too real. Industrialists turned of necessity to technology, and gave society a broader base for future economic progress. Workers responded out of desperation, and desperate men are not satisfied with promises. A community of interest was proposed but rejected; perhaps under the circumstances none was possible, except in the unfulfilled dreams of utopia, and the tortured dreams of Marx.

Society learned painful lessons, at a cost it can ill afford to pay more than once. As for the question of what might have happened under different and more favorable conditions, we do have an answer—the American economy, fashioned by commerce and technology, the beneficiary of Europe's experience yet not the victim of her problems. We turn to this chapter in history next.

AN AMERICAN SYNTHESIS

To build a great country, Robert Frost once advised, start with a fine piece of geography. America did. The nation was blessed with extraordinary natural resources and with a favorable turn of fortune's wheel. The timing was perfect. The colonists could hardly have picked a better time to leave Europe. They left behind a continent torn by war and picked to pieces by diplomats. In the whole of the seventeenth century in Europe, there were not five years together which were free from armed conflict.

Louis XIV spent much of the century trying to force the authority of France on the rest of Europe, and nearly succeeded. Spain fought to preserve her position, and failed. Sweden ran full cycle in less than a century, building an empire and losing it. England was split by civil war and religious quarrels. The Low Countries were divided, a center of international controversy, and would remain so for many years. What is now Germany was not a nation at all, but an unruly collection of more than 350 provinces. Already a political shambles, it was reduced to an economic one by the succession of wars.

Hired armies swept back and forth across Europe like the tides, inundating cropland and leaving destitution in their wake. Hundreds of thousands of Europeans, having committed no crime beyond living in the wrong place at the wrong time, were literally harassed or starved to death. Thinking of the hardships the colonists faced in the New

World, one must also acknowledge the miseries they left behind.

Yet the good fortune of being somewhere else, in a new land of natural bounty, cannot of itself explain America's success. How could a collection of agrarian colonies lacking commercial organizations and industry, desperately short of capital and grossly underpopulated, be transformed in nine generations into the most prosperous nation in the world? What accounts for this remarkable rise?

The "secret" of America's success was a matter of both economic policy and political and social outlook. Although physically removed from the problems of Europe, Americans were not cut off from ideas. They were able to borrow the good ones and avoid most of the bad. The more fortuitous features of life in the seventeenth and eighteenth centuries—including the skills Europe had developed in technology and economic organization—were transported intact to the New World and put into service. With some notable exceptions, the worst of the difficulties that marked industrialization in Europe were left there.

America chose to build its economy on the basis of competitive capitalism, through an approach that strongly favored consolidation and encouraged the application of technology. The approach was further distinguished by a boundless enthusiasm for work, with results that proved phenomenal.

Of the factors implicit in national growth, the one that deserves first attention is the American attitude. The country was born pro-work; and here, more than in any other major civilization, man's faith in his own perfectability became an instrument of economic improvement. Enterprise was reinforced by public sanction, on the implicit premise that it would work to the public good. Far from condemning the man of commerce or relegating him to an inferior status, society accepted and encouraged him. Technology, far from generating fear, was welcomed in America as a beneficent force, and made an ally in social and economic progress.

Above all, to use the term of historian Arthur Meier

Schlesinger, the "habit of work" pervaded the American experiment. There was enthusiasm for accomplishment, a yearning to build, a sense of mobility, a restless urge to get on with it, a penchant for the new and novel coupled with a stubborn sense of duty and a concern for the well-being of the common man. Taken together, these generated the momentum to carry the United States to economic pre-eminence by the end of the nineteenth century.

In the first years, the land and not the people imposed the conditions of life. In place of the neatly partitioned farms and centuries-old towns of Europe, the early colonists found only the silent forest, touching the ocean's edge. Wealth was there but it was hidden from view. Despite rumors circulated in Europe, there was no Aztec gold in North America. There was something far more valuable, but it had to be earned. Before the soil would yield its riches, it had to be cleared of trees, stones, and, sometimes, Indians. Mineral resources lay undiscovered, to be mined only at expense of toil.

The climate was not greatly different from that of Europe, but the colonists were poorly prepared for it and found it far from hospitable. Recalling the first year at Plymouth Plantation, William Bradford wrote, ". . . they that know the winters of that country know them to be sharp and violent, and subject to cruel and fierce storms . . . that which was most sad and lamentable was that in two or three months' time half of [the Plymouth] company died, especially in January and February, being the depth of winter, and wanting houses and other comforts."[1]

Yet even in such years of trial, the colonists had great ambitions. They would not settle for mere survival. The first Virginians came with commerce in mind. The first Puritan immigrants came to build "A Citty upon a hill," to show the world what a community of Christians could accomplish. In later years America's vision turned to the frontier, to the settlement of the vast plains beyond the Appalachians, to the creation of a unified nation "from sea to shining sea." This was seen as a mission ordained by Providence, America's Manifest Destiny.

There were other objectives: to conquer what Mark Twain called "the ancient dominion of pain," to build factories and whaling fleets, to explore, to found schools and colleges, to take a "democracy in rags" and turn her into a gracious symbol of justice and prosperity. Not all these hopes were realized. America's grasp fell short of her vision. But the unlimited nature of these dreams, the very audacity with which they were fashioned, lent energy and purpose to the effort.

America took literally the admonition of Ecclesiastes: "Whatsoever thy hand findeth to do, do it with thy might." Slackers were condemned. The village loafer, who might have been regarded with amused tolerance in a less demanding land, became an enemy of society in colonial America, and a fit subject for forced labor or the stocks.

From pulpit and penny press came repeated urgings to diligence. Through the pages of *Poor Richard's Almanac,* Benjamin Franklin called his fellows to their duty:

Laziness travels so slowly that poverty soon overtakes him.

Leisure is a time for doing something useful.

He that hath a calling hath an office of profit and honor.

Ralph Waldo Emerson, essayist and lecturer of the transcendentalist stamp, brought his usual grace of expression to the topic:

I look upon that man as happy who, when there is a question of success, looks into his work for a reply.
Success in your work, the finding of a better method, the better understanding that insures the better performing is hat and coat, is food and wine, is fire and horse and health and holiday.

James Russell Lowell found "ample recompense in work done squarely and unwasted days." Longfellow wrote of the "joy that springs from labor." Theodore Roosevelt, advocate of the strenuous life and heir to two and one-half centuries of its tradition, said, "Far and away the best prize that life offers is the chance to work hard at work worth doing."

Respect for work shone through all levels of education and income. William Manning, a colonial farmer who "never had the advantage of six months' schooling," reflected the conventional wisdom in a homespun offering called *The Key of Libberty*:

It is undoubtedly the duty of every person that is blessed with the facultyes of a sound body & mind, to apply himselfe industeriously to some honest cauling for the benefit of himselfe & Society.

Lucy Larcom, a mill girl in Massachusetts during the young years of the textile industry, wrote a poetic "Idyl of Work," prefaced by unashamed pride:

It is the laborer's privilege to ennoble his work by the aim with which he undertakes it, and by the enthusiasm and faithfulness he puts into it.[2]

As a reflection of the American outlook, however, there is no rival to the celebrated McGuffey *Reader*. William Holmes McGuffey, who compiled this series of anthologies beginning in the 1830s, was an unvarnished moralist. He held all virtues as very, very good, and all vices, horrid. Toil was equated with piety; laziness, with Lucifer.

For nearly seventy years schoolchildren cinched McGuffey in their bookstraps and grudgingly committed his selections to memory. By 1900, it is estimated that the circulation of the *Readers* totaled 100 million, a sum that gains meaning from the fact that the population of the United States, during these years, averaged something less than 40 million.

McGuffey was a tedious doctrinaire and a stuffed shirt, but his books matched the political and social spirit. Was this not the land of the self-made man, where every individual was instructed by God to be "architect of his own destiny," and where all things were possible? It was indeed, said McGuffey and many more.

Of Heroes and Heredity

America had no hereditary aristocracy and wanted none. John Adams helped stamp this into the American character: "Nobles we never had. Nothing hereditary ever existed in the Country: Nor will the Country require or admit of any such thing."

Adams had company on his point, even among men who, in another nation, would have comprised the titled aristocracy. The framers of the Constitution, for example, were as cultured and distinguished a company as America knew, yet they saw fit to include in their document a specific prohibition of all titles of nobility.

If a man wanted honors, let him work for them. If he wanted his children to fare as well, let him imbue them with a firm sense of service and a proper horror of parasitism. The successful English entrepreneur, rubbing elbows with the nobility, would have been proud that his sons did not work for a living; his American counterpart would have been ashamed to admit it. Even today, a touch of guilt attaches to inherited wealth in America, finding expression in such folk-forecasts as "shirtsleeves to shirtsleeves in three generations," and in inheritance tax codes that go a long way toward fulfilling that prophecy.

In a nation inclined to hero worship, high accolades were offered leaders from humble beginnings—Franklin, Jackson, Lincoln. If they were log-cabin stock, so much the better. Where necessary, the facts could be adjusted to fit the legend. Fourth of July orators happily claimed Andrew Jackson as a plain-dirt farmer, conveniently ignoring the fact that "The Hermitage" is something more than a sodbuster's shanty. "The American Cincinnatus," they dubbed him, reviving the legend of the Roman called from the plow to defend his country in battle and lead it in peace; Jackson's adult acquaintance with plows was remote at best, but what the nation wanted was not accurate biography but a restatement of a dream.

Popular music, often a clue to public attitudes, offered a willing audience an endless stream of songs about people at work. Some were laments to the loneliness of the cowhand and the dangers of the deep, but more were light, bright ditties bearing such titles as "Down on the Farm," "The Boatman's Dance," "The Fireman's Song," "Down in a Coal Mine," "The Faithful Engineer," "The Newsboy," "The Gay Young Clerk in the Dry Goods Store," and "The Diligent Hose Company Quick Step."[3]

Artists idealized toil and lent a heroic cast to their subjects. When John Neagle was commissioned to paint a portrait of Pat Lyon, a successful businessman of the early nineteenth century, his client insisted on being posed as a blacksmith, sleeves rolled up, hammer in hand. This had been Lyon's first trade. A famous portrait of President Jackson gave him the matted hair style and forehead curl of Napoleon Bonaparte. As it happens, Jackson had a wavy, high shock of hair, but Napoleon was a hero, a man who made his way to greatness on the strength of his own will. Down with the loose locks; paint in the flat curl.

In the prints of Currier and Ives, hunters and trappers are well dressed, farmhouses are in good repair, and the harvests are invariably bountiful. The purveyors of genre art were far too shrewd to show the harsh realities. They knew what the customers wanted, and it was not the "ashcan school."

The legends of America made giants of men. There was Mike Fink, dauntless keelboatman who could outwork and outfight any man of the canals. There was John Henry, a steel-driving man swinging a twenty-pound hammer in each hand. There were oilmen like Gig Morgan, who built a drilling rig so high they had to hinge the top to let the moon go by; steelmen like Joe Magaras, hefting 2000-pound bars; lumbermen like Whiskey Jack, a seven-footer who could lift a log raft; and firemen like Mighty Mose

Humphreys, hauling the pumper down Main Street faster than horses could run. There were the Nantucket whalers and the Forty-Niners, Casey Jones and Paul Bunyan, Daniel Boone and Davy Crockett, some real and some imagined, all magnified larger than life but engravings of the deepest truth, reflecting the way people looked at themselves.

Help Wanted: Apply U.S.A.

In its approach to technology, America was the most fortunate of nations. It had everything to gain from innovation, and nothing to lose. While there were occasional protests against the introduction of new tools and techniques—John Henry's classic battle against the steam hammer is a case in point—there was no concerted uprising comparable to the Luddite riots in England. The forces pressed the other way.

Technology, instead of threatening to dispossess workers, offered a solution to a serious problem the young nation faced, the shortage of labor. Beginning with the founding of the first colony and extending well into the nineteenth century, there was a persistent scarcity of workers, especially skilled ones. The Virginia Colony had hardly been started when an urgent message was dispatched to the London sponsors to send more "honest, sufficient artificers, as carpenters, smiths, coopers, fishermen, brickmen, and such like."

Several decades later, when John Winthrop and a company of others established an ironworks at Saugus, Massachusetts, the principal problem was in finding men to operate the equipment. Other infant industries met the same difficulty, and some foundered because of it. Almost anywhere in early America, a man professing even moderate skills was treated with deference and hospitality. Jobs awaited wherever he went.

The labor shortage slowed expansion at first, but it had a compensating virtue. It stimulated innovation. As an example, Eli Whitney and Simeon North, gunmakers who helped develop the art of manufacture using interchangeable parts, were spurred to their efforts by the common dilemma. America needed guns, and there were simply not enough available workers trained in the handcraft. Whitney and North set out to make it more a machine craft.

Early textile producers quickly seized upon machine methods, dividing the work in the mills into a series of simple steps so that it could be done by women and children with minimal training. Latter-day moralists look askance at this development, but at the time it made sense to all parties. Women and children were the only available labor pool—the men were still needed on the farm—and the factory workers took it much more for granted than their grandchildren would have. A job in a mill, even at small wages, helped sustain the family, and offered an alternative to a life of farm toil. Many a young lady spent a few years at the loom, carefully saved her money, and then left the factory for another career or for marriage. Lucy Larcom, for instance, went into the mills at Lowell, Massachusetts, at the age of eleven, left in her early twenties to go West, and became a schoolteacher.

The labor shortage ended in the middle decades of the nineteenth century, when a sharp increase in immigration brought an abundance of low-skill labor, desperate for work, to America's farms and factory gates. Much of the strife and tragedy associated with the industrialization of America date from the time of this change.

By this date, however, America had acquired two hundred years of experience with the advance of commerce and technology. A highly organized economy with a growing industrial arm already had demonstrated its ability to create higher living standards, and to charm the public with an array of new products and services. In America, in contrast to Europe, the benefits of change were well established before the problems became apparent. The nation was spared much of the violence that might have marked the transition to an industrial economy, and escaped the class warfare Europe suffered.

A Technical Focus

Nations, like people, can get the right reputation for the wrong reasons. This is the case with America's vaunted reputation as an innovator. We still have with us the legend of the Yankee inventor, an inspired, versatile, and self-taught tinkerer who concocted inventions to order. But he is a myth.

Technology became a major force in the nation's advance, not because Americans brought unique gifts to it but because they knew how to apply it. If the colonist displayed certain ingenuity, it was in devising makeshift substitutes for products and tools familiar to him in Europe but unavailable in the New World. The pilgrim had little time for the tedious and frustrating pursuit of technology. He was too busy scratching a livelihood out of the soil. Scientists of note emerged in America—Franklin, David Rittenhouse, John Clayton and Benjamin Silliman, to mention but four on a list of dozens—but they were a small corps of elite, and not distinctly American in intellectual pursuits. They saw themselves as members of an informal, international company of scientists and amateur experimentalists headquartered in Europe, where men had leisure and money for such lofty activities. Science, with other refinements of life, was a luxury few Americans could afford.

With no important exceptions, the mechanical inventions introduced in America before 1776 were European in origin. Many later advances, including the railroad, steamboat, and the use of interchangeable parts in manufacture, stemmed from European antecedents. The U. S. Patent Office had almost nothing to do when it opened its doors in 1790. Thomas Jefferson ran it as a part-time job, processing only three applications the first year.

The two most significant American inventions before

1800 were the cotton gin, which Eli Whitney patented in 1794, and Oliver Evans' automatic flour mill, an authentic work of genius, years ahead of its time, in which grain was carried to the grinding stones, milled, spread, raked, and barreled by machinery controlled by a single workman. These, though, were exceptional offerings, products of two extraordinary minds dwelling in that special province of creativity that defies dates and national boundaries.

The nineteenth century is the period best remembered for the prowess of the American inventor, and it was indeed productive. By the time the nation paused to mark its centennial with a fair at Philadelphia, the domestic list of accomplishments included the sewing machine (developed independently here after being sidetracked in Europe), the telegraph, farm tools by the dozens, the elevator, vulcanized rubber, notable advances in road and bridge construction, and a new device, introduced at the Philadelphia Exposition and almost overlooked in the shuffle, called the telephone.

What was most remarkable about the century, however, was not the daring originality of American ideas, but America's hospitality to inventions of all descriptions. Once it was clear that their handiwork was wanted, inventors tumbled over each other to offer improvements. Mr. Jefferson's successors had their work cut out for them. By 1850, the Patent Office was processing applications at a rate of more than 2000 a year. Within a few more years the volume of U.S. patents passed that of Great Britain, then the most heavily industrialized nation in the world. In 1870, 13,518 patents were issued in the United States; in 1890, 28,304.

Cyrus McCormick developed his reaper in the 1830s; by 1850 annual sales were 3000 units; by 1860, 20,000. The first telegraph line was strung in 1844, connecting Washington and Baltimore. Less than five years later, service reached from New York to Albany and as far west as Milwaukee.

The first locomotive appeared here in 1830, when Peter

Cooper's "Tom Thumb" made a hesitant journey along a single line of track at Baltimore. By 1840 there were 3000 miles of track in the United States. At the beginning of the Civil War, "Tom Thumb's" 13-mile ribbon of iron had stretched to 31,000 miles. The conduct of the war itself was greatly influenced by the railroad. As the primary means of moving troops and supplies, rail lines were a constant bone of contention. No less than 125 skirmishes, raids, and battles were fought along the lines of the Baltimore and Ohio Railroad. Advancing troops secured railroad facilities as a priority mission. Retreating armies ripped track sections from the ties, heated the rails over fires, and bent them into "bow ties." Cities such as Chattanooga were strategically vital because they were rail centers, and therefore marshaling areas and supply points. Sherman's campaign in Georgia was possible only because his engineers and infantry were able to keep open a rail line from Tennessee. The major strike against him was an attempt to cut that lifeline.

With the war's end, railroads expanded more rapidly than ever. In 1869 construction crews from East and West met at Promontory, Utah, and the commemorative golden spike was driven; the railroad, still less than forty years of age, spanned the North American continent. During the next thirty years, enough additional track mileage was added each year, on the average, to cross the nation again. In 1900, 38,000 locomotives were hauling passengers and freight along 200,000 miles of main-line track.

The yen for progress was so great, and the opportunities for larceny so enticing, that many inventors spent less time in the workshop than in the courtroom. Even before Whitney's cotton gin had cleared the Patent Office, imitations appeared. The gin was mechanically simple (at least to the people who broke into his shop to look at it) and easy to build. It was bootlegged all over the South and revitalized the cotton business, but only occasionally put royalty payments in Mr. Whitney's pockets. McCormick and Goodyear, to mention but two other perpetual plaintiffs, also spent years trying to curb infringements of their patents.

Their difficulties were compounded by the fact that it was much easier to win a patent in the nineteenth century than it is now. Small modifications often were accorded status as separate inventions, and the courts had monumental problems unraveling conflicting claims. As a sample of what they had to deal with, more than 12,000 patents were issued on harvesting apparatus before the year 1905, and an equal number on different kinds of plowing equipment. It would take more than mortal judges to decide the questions of priority that resulted. Many of the accused patent pirates must be held guiltless, for in truth there was often no sure way to know who owned what. Confronted by a booming market, entrepreneurs frequently decided to sell whatever they knew how to make, and let the dust settle by itself.

For all the courtroom squabbles, which often descended to the level of a saloon fight, the patent system was a useful device. Even a clouded claim was better than no claim at all, and to the inventor, usually a man of little wealth, patents offered a protective cloak under which he could seek financing, develop his wonder child, and make his bid for riches. Equally important, by requiring public disclosure of the details of each patented invention, the patent system accelerated the spread of technical ideas and spawned subsequent innovation.

Without this sheltering canopy of law, the nation's more ingenious citizens might well have kept their ideas to themselves, to be developed in secrecy. The authors of the Constitution were alert to this problem; when they provided for a patent system, their goal was not so much to protect the individual inventor as to encourage public declaration of technology, and thus advance society's interests. In fundamental purpose, the law that founded the modern patent system was not a defense of special privilege, but an important act of social legislation.

Consolidate and Integrate

The urge to consolidate commerce, to undertake projects of increasing dimensions, and to diversify the economic base was as marked as the passion for technology. Although farming was the first business of America, trade was pursued on an impressive scale even during the colonial period. In 1631, with the English colony at Massachusetts barely a decade old, a ship was built expressly for coastal trade and communication with the Dutch settlement at New Amsterdam. The *Blessings of the Bay* was a modest thirty-tonner, but the fact that she was built at all is a testimonial to the enterprise of the colonists. By 1680 about 1000 vessels were in the colonial trade, and by 1760 America was producing 300 to 400 craft a year, including merchantmen as large as any built elsewhere. At this date, one-third of the merchant tonnage sailing under the British flag had been built in American yards.

In the year the Revolution began, colonial products with a value of two million pounds sterling were exported. A domestic whaling industry with 300 ships was in existence. Paper mills were commonplace. Sawmills numbered 100 or more, some with a capacity of more than 5000 board feet per day. There were more furnaces and forges in the Colonies than in England and Wales combined, and the Americans were entertaining subversive thoughts about Europe's monopoly on the manufacture of consumer products.

This was a monopoly in perpetuity (as contrasted to the limited term of a patent monopoly), and it had the effect of keeping the Colonies in a dependent economic status. In the seventeenth century, it would have meant little, but by the late eighteenth century, with a solid base of commerce to build on, America was as ready to bid for economic independence as for political freedom.

Textile production, the first of America's major manufacturing industries, began in the last years of the century (closely pressed in some areas by the manufacture of "spiritous liquors"). By 1811, eighty-seven cotton mills were in operation, and in the next four years that number doubled. As of 1815, 76,000 people were earning a living in textile manufacture, and 135,000 spindles were in service.

Initially, production was directly patterned on European models. Very directly, in fact. American entrepreneurs, angered by England's continuing efforts to keep them servile, did a bit of unauthorized "borrowing" of technology. The first beneficiary of this art was Moses Brown, a Rhode Island merchant who employed Samuel Slater to operate textile machinery for him. Slater was an Englishman who had superintended a hosiery mill and constructed a factory for Richard Arkwright, the developer of water-frame spinning. Slater was lured from home by a newspaper story that an American had paid a bounty of £100 for the design of textile machinery. The law prohibited his leaving England with plans or notes, but Slater had something just as good, an excellent memory on which he imprinted a full set of drawings.

Brown jubilantly set Slater to work building a new factory at Pawtucket and, after problems had been resolved, it ran admirably well. Completed in 1793, it was the first full-scale industrial plant in the United States. Slater became a wealthy man, and a grateful nation made him a hero. President Jackson gave him the title "Father of American Manufactures." He should have split the credit with Moses Brown, who had the daring to undertake a wholly new venture on the strength of one man's memory.

Once begun, American industry quickly expanded and went off on its own tack. The European answer to an expanding market was simply to build more machines and hire more people. There were plenty available. This was no answer in the United States, where additional workers were hard to find. What the American mill owner needed was a way to obtain more output from each worker. The result was the integrated factory, where tools and workers were combined in such a way that the efficiency of the system, as well as its capacity, was multiplied.

The English carried out the weaving operation as a separate step, remote from the other stages of textile production. They continued to use hand looms long after power machines were available. The Americans combined all stages into a single, smooth-flowing process, and turned to power immediately. Francis Cabot Lowell, the man for whom the Massachusetts city and its textile works were named, designed a power loom in 1813 and built his first mill in 1815 (at Waltham; the Lowell mills came a few years later). Within a little more than a decade a highly mechanized, tightly integrated factory was in operation, with all parts of the process under a single roof. The "Lowell System," with its superior efficiency, became an identifying mark of manufacture in America, although all the separate pieces of its technology had been available in Europe fully a half-century earlier.

Half the time, American entrepreneurs were operating more on nerve than on solid engineering or sound financing. When the Erie Canal was planned, for example, neither the tools nor the talent for its accomplishment were at hand. It was far and away the most ambitious engineering project attempted to that time in America, and the only thing that held this delirious dream together was the bravado of DeWitt Clinton, governor of New York. "Clinton's Gutter," as his opponents uncharitably called it, opened in 1825 and did everything its optimistic sponsor had promised. The canal stimulated settlement of the western territories, greatly encouraged commerce, and showed everyone what fine engineers America had. It might be added, though, that when the 363-mile ditch was started, trained engineers were as scarce as millionaires on the frontier. To celebrate the Erie Canal properly, we ought to put it down as America's grandest example of an on-the-job-training program.

On paper, the decision to challenge England's supremacy at sea was equally intemperate. No one had presented a real threat to England's sea power since the Spaniards sent their armada on its futile journey into the Channel in 1588. The struggling American republic was hardly in a position to undertake a shipbuilding race.

Undeterred, the Americans built their whalers, coastal traders, transatlantic freight carriers, and light-heeled clipper ships. The United States flag began to appear in ports all over the world. By 1875 the American merchant service numbered more than 32,000 vessels. It was returning generous profits to its builders, and was on the way to becoming the largest merchant marine in the world.

Another limit to enterprise, this one more effective, was the scarcity of funds for investment. Alexander Hamilton's 1791 "Report on Manufactures" cited this as the most serious brake on economic progress, and many ambitious Americans, nursing dreams of building a business, knew at first hand what Hamilton meant. Most people had almost no cash income. Raising five hundred or a thousand dollars to start a small sawmill was a major project. Building an ironworks or a textile mill, which might require $250,000, called for resources only a handful of people in the nation could command.

One answer was to turn to Europe. E. I. du Pont's powder mill was a case in point. The original unit of the present chemical company, this mill was established in 1802 along Brandywine Creek in Delaware. The project had the personal blessing of President Jefferson, for America needed explosives for hunting, for road building and land clearing, and for defense. Du Pont had been trained in explosives manufacture in France, and Jefferson was eager to see the project succeed.

It cost $36,000, most of which came from Europe, this being the only source he could find for such princely sums. The mill prospered, but du Pont within his lifetime was unable to retire all of the initial debt; $36,000 was more than even a successful firm could pay back in a few decades.

Many larger projects could be pursued only with public aid. No private combine could muster the funds to finance the Erie Canal, to build the transcontinental railroad, or to lay the Atlantic cable. A private syndicate could build a wooden ship, but could not meet the costs of converting the merchant fleet from sail to steam and wood to iron. Government involvement in business thus has a long history in America, dating from the nation's first confrontation with large-scale economic needs.

DeWitt Clinton, having campaigned for governor on the promise of building the canal, obtained New York State funds to pay for it. Robert Fulton was given a monopoly to encourage his steamboat service on the Hudson River, and it was renewed several times despite Fulton's early failures to meet commitments. Mail subsidies helped keep transatlantic steamships on schedule. Withdrawal of such a subsidy, following a series of disasters, brought final ruin to one of the largest shipping companies of the times, the Collins Line. Railroads received substantial financial aid plus grants of as much land as there is in all of Pennsylvania, New York, and New England. Congress helped Cyrus Field pay for the Atlantic cable project, again in the face of failure—the first cable broke and the second went silent after a brief period of service—and far beyond the initial cost estimates.

Government, though, could not and would not pay for everything, and was far from consistent in dispensing largess. Some projects were supported by Congress and state legislatures, while other ventures of equal or greater merit (but lacking equally persuasive advocates) were rejected. Moreover, legislators were under considerable pressure to turn down all such requests, for the continued appeals for subsidy ran counter to the popular credo: "The best government is the least government."

Public opinion was hardly more consistent. People clamored for economic expansion, but retained a blind spot toward the role of capital in its development. No one expected Providence to supply the raw materials and energy for production, but somehow it was supposed, with reference to investment funds, that God would provide. A stable monetary system was needed for the orderly growth of commerce and industry, but pleas for it were mostly lip service, and serious efforts to fill the need were at times opposed even by the people who would have benefited most. The independent treasury system, forerunner of the present Federal Reserve System, did not gain a solid foothold until 1846. Banking, and especially credit, was viewed with an almost medieval suspicion, even though a passing thought (or a look at medieval history) would have shown the hopelessness of trying to build a major economic structure with cash-on-the-barrelhead.

Partly, this was politics. Backwoods citizens felt deep in their bones that eastern financiers were up to no good, and stump orators won votes by saying so. Partly, the problem was caused simply by inexperience. Eminent and otherwise farsighted economists, business leaders, and public spokesmen saw that industry could multiply everyone's income—and thus escaped the pitfalls that trapped Ricardo, Malthus, and Marx—but they failed to attach any great importance to industry's problem of raising capital. Horace Greeley capsuled their opinions in his Cooper Union speech in 1867, when he said it was just "vulgar error" to suppose America needed any large amount of capital. The frontiersman would have applauded; the one thousand New Yorkers in his audience did.

Greeley and company were behind the times. They were applying the standards of their youth to the problems of a changed nation. America already ranked fourth among nations in industrial power, and would reach first position within thirty years. The population was 37 million and was moving toward urban centers. When Greeley was born, only one person in twenty lived in a community of eight thousand or more. When he made his speech, the figure was one in five. His city of New York had long since become a community of more than one million people.

Agriculture had only one more decade in which to hold its claim to a majority of the labor force. Farms as well as factories had gained in efficiency, thus releasing an increasing share of the population to trade and manufacturing. Already, 400,000 business firms were in operation, and nonfarm production accounted for far more than one-half of the value of the nation's output.

In the closing years of the nineteenth century and the early years of this one, the drive for profit and the expansion of the economy brought a swift increase in the number of business firms. Most of them, as today, were small organizations providing a livelihood for a proprietor and one or two employees. However, a rising portion of commercial activity, especially in manufacturing, came from large-scale enterprise. Work increasingly became an institutional function with employees grouped in units of hundreds or thousands.

Manufacturing output quintupled between 1865 and 1900, doubled again by 1920, and has quadrupled since. Wholesale and retail trade added something less than $1 billion per year to national income during the 1860s and 1870s, grew to more than $5 billion by 1910, and soared past $50 billion a year during the 1950s.

Chain stores were unknown a century ago. By the turn of the century, nearly one hundred firms had multiple outlets; by 1920 the number had passed one thousand. The communications industry of the 1870s had a few thousand employees. By 1920 employment reached one-quarter million, a number that has since quadrupled.

Why such consolidation? The rise in population and in economic ambitions were two factors. A third, less obvious, was technology. As tools became more powerful and sophisticated, the "critical mass" of factories rose. The small waterwheel mills could be run by a handful of workers, but in later and more productive factories the minimum size for efficiency was measured in hundreds of "hands." The key was the steam-driven prime mover that supplied the plant's power. Below a certain limit, it was not worth installing. Above that level, it pointed the way to profits.

At the Philadelphia Centennial Exposition, the prize of the show was the Machinery Hall, in which all of the tools were powered by a 1600-horsepower Corliss engine. Towering over the rest of the exhibits, it symbolized the theme of the fair, "Power," and suggested the coming trend of events. By modern standards it was a monument to inefficiency, but in 1876 it was the most powerful engine ever built, and one of the wonders of the world. George Pullman bought it after the show to put in his railway equipment factory.

During the 1870s, prime movers generating a total of about 20 million horsepower were in service in transportation and manufacturing. By 1920 the figure was eight times as large, not counting the most fashionable kind of power plant, introduced at the turn of the century, the auto engine.

Having contributed to the consolidating process, technology itself became inextricably involved with business. This development only occasionally draws comment, but it was a significant event in the history of science and engineering, and deserves to be marked as a vital step in economic development.

Until late in the nineteenth century, science, engineering, and industry had been allied in the United States only in informal ways. Most men of technical talent worked only part-time at science or invention, and no industry maintained a formal research program. Such support for technology as there was came mostly from personal resources, and usually entailed personal sacrifice. Although he was the outstanding scientist in America in his day, Benjamin Franklin did not support himself from his research. His printing business paid the way. Samuel Morse was not an inventor by trade but a portrait painter, and a good if impecunious one. John Fitch, the visionary steamboat builder, was an itinerant map salesman, and not a good one; he nearly starved. Eli Whitney began as a schoolmaster. The two Cyruses, McCormick and Field, both had private fortunes to sustain their dreams. Elias Howe had only a job in a machine shop, though the sewing machine later made him wealthy.

Technologists were first drawn to industry as consultants, and soon after as staff members. When it was suggested that petroleum might be mined in quantity, George H.

Bissell called upon Benjamin Silliman, a Yale chemistry professor, to evaluate the possible applications. It was largely Silliman's optimistic report, forecasting many profitable uses, that started the oil industry on its giddy rise. A little later John D. Rockefeller, as skillful at picking associates as in undoing competitors, added Samuel Andrews and Herman Frasch to his staff. They improved refining techniques and product quality, and gave Rockefeller a technical advantage that was an important element in the success of Standard Oil.

Immediately after the turn of the century, General Electric and Du Pont established research laboratories of their own, the first in American industry. Within four years, Du Pont was spending $300,000 per year on research and development, a sum that only a large and prosperous industrial organization could spare for such a then-debatable purpose. From this time on, through the expansion of industrial laboratories and the growth of universities and private foundations (which, industrialists correctly point out, were largely financed by the benefactions of industrialists), technology became a full-time occupation for a growing army of scientists and engineers, adding new leverage to economic growth through development of new products, and creating millions of new job opportunities.

The Modern Corporate Form

Consolidation was marked by a change in the structure as well as the size of institutions. The corporate form of organization, hardly known before the Civil War, steadily gained in favor thereafter, to become the principal employer and major source of production in America.

The corporation had much in its favor. It was adaptable and permanent, it could undertake large-scale projects, and it offered some insulation against the shocks to which enterprise was exposed. It attracted support on all three counts. Unlike a partnership, whose participants are personally responsible in the event of claims against the organization, a corporation offered limited liability. The most its owners could lose was the price they paid for its stock. Such other personal assets as they had were immune to loss or legal claim. One would doubt that this made much difference to the knights of commerce—the Carnegies, Rockefellers, Vanderbilts, and others of immense personal fortunes. They had learned to play for high stakes, and they could afford to. Business to them was life's best adventure, and risk a part of the game. However, to investors whose means were more modest, and who were less inclined to risk house and carriage on a business proposition, the legal limitation of corporate liability was undeniably appealing.

What these investors lacked in affluence, they made up in personal numbers. Corporations, drawing dozens and then hundreds of such people together, raised the money to tackle projects beyond the reach of any giant of finance. The most impressive deal of the rugged individualists was Andrew Carnegie's sale of his steel mills to J. P. Morgan in 1901. Morgan paid him $492 million. But the corporation Morgan was putting together, United States Steel, began with assets three times that great, and in less than twenty years the iron and steel industry had grown in book value beyond $7 billion. There neither were nor are any private fortunes of that size.

Other industries followed similar patterns of capital growth, attaining dimensions that could be reached only through multiple ownership. By 1920, the chemical industry represented an investment of nearly $3 billion; textiles, nearly $7 billion; transportation equipment, nearly $2.5 billion; other machinery, $5.6 billion. Overall, American manufacturing in 1920 showed a book value of more than $40 billion. The sum is now five times greater.

Employees as well as dollars flowed toward this form of organization. In 1904 more than 70 per cent of the production workers in manufacturing were employed by corporations; in 1920, more than 85 per cent.

From the point of view of the public, the corporation brought a needed sense of order to the economy. A proprietorship or partnership is a transient arrangement. No matter how well it is run, it expires with its owners if not sooner, and must be brought back to life by the next generation.

To the colonial population this made little difference. The demise of a craft shop or small mill was at worst a local inconvenience. However, a busy, interdependent economy, interlacing the lives of millions of people, could hardly function on such precarious terms. A well-ordered flow of manufactured goods was now a necessity, and the corporation was one instrument of its attainment.

The incorporated business survives independent of its founders. As the French put it, it is a *société anonyme*, an organization anonymous not in any surreptitious sense of the word (for it is obliged by law to name its incorporators), but in the sense that it has a separate, impersonal identity. It is more cumbersome than a personal proprietorship, but it has greater stability and continuity, and these were appealing virtues to nineteenth-century America.

In the past one hundred years, the corporate form of organization has drawn enormous numbers of adherents. Some of them have failed; many have survived and profited; a few have grown and prospered far more rapidly than the nation as a whole. By way of completing the equation, it must be added that these same organizations, especially the last ones mentioned, have been principal contributors to America's economic expansion. They are certainly its beneficiaries, but they are in equal measure its benefactors.

The Pains of Progress

This sounds tidy and painless, as though it were all accomplished without grief or error. In truth, there was an abundant measure of both, and we are still living with the consequences. The drive toward economic expansion was accompanied by some gross obtuseness and startling examples of the human capacity for avarice. Success did not always come to the people who worked the hardest for it. Wrongs were not always set right. Credit did not always reach the deserving.

What many in America regarded as the rightful course of empire was taken in a different light by some Americans. The Indian, for example, doubtless did not see it as his Manifest Destiny to be shot or herded into the confines of a reservation. The fact that his skin was red and his adversary's pink hardly abrogates the Indian's claim, as Indians still point out.

What some apologists term our national "growing pains," and dismiss as reflections of the ethical standards of the times, appeared to a lot of people on the scene, as well as to many of our own generation, to be cases of simple bestiality. The slave trade, for example, survived for decades after it was morally denounced and officially outlawed in America. Southern congressmen encouraged the Navy to look the other way when the slave ships went by; Yankee captains lined their holds with black cargo; and shipowners north and south banked the proceeds. Some of America's most genteel fortunes began in this fashion.

While America made heroes of many men who deserved immortality, and some who did not, the nation ignored or abused a number of its most useful citizens. Oliver Evans, honored now as one of the giants of American technology, was in his own time just another unsung inventor. His automatic mill found use in all the wheat growing sections of the nation, but others made the profits on it. He invented a steam engine, a better one than Watt's, put it in a dredging barge, made the rig amphibious, and still drew few admirers.

For John Fitch, life was a pathetic and unsuccessful struggle for recognition. His steamboat worked. It was running on the Schuylkill River at Philadelphia while the Constitution was being drafted. Yet Fitch could get almost no one, including the men working on that document, to take him seriously. Some of them came to the riverbank and went away unimpressed. The effort to commercialize the steamboat did not succeed until it was taken over by a poorer engineer but better salesman, Robert Fulton. Evans and Fitch were but two of many prophets without honor in their time.

In the swing toward industrialization and consolidation, the pendulum went too far. In the hands of some entrepreneurs, pleas for efficiency masked deliberate exploitation, and consolidation became a convenient euphemism for monopoly. Watered stock was foisted on the credulous. Worthless patent medicines were sold to the gullible. Rising aggregations of capital did not always finance new industries, but sometimes found circuitous routes to the pockets of legislators and judges—a commentary on the ethics of sellers as well as buyers of special favors. There was more than one occasion when the old adage came true, and people got the best government money could buy.

Labor was not only subdivided but in many instances was overspecialized and stripped of skill and dignity. This trend toward alienation was noted and protested even before industrialization had gained full momentum, but the warnings went unheeded. Tocqueville commented in detail on the problem, but it was a full century later, in the 1930s, when the full cost of this misstep received general acknowledgment, and corrective steps began in a number of industries. Workers were regarded as a commodity, as interchangeable as machines, with the key difference that workers could be kept in debt to the company store, thereby permitting employers to recover a substantial part of their "investment" in labor.

Arriving in the land of the free and the brave, many nineteenth-century immigrants were met at the pier by some special representatives of American enterprise, small business division: Dockside gyps persuaded the newcomers to part with their foreign-looking properties—a fine and valuable beaver hat, for example—and to accept in trade a genuine American replacement—a cheap cotton cap. Having been so favored by these haberdashers, the new arrivals were then shepherded to suitable housing—a tenement owned by a rapacious landlord—and found jobs—very often in the employ of another paragon of American

enterprise, the owner of a grimy, dimlit sweatshop. Entrepreneurs who today find it difficult to accept the behavior
of many labor leaders need only refer back, for the sake of
perspective, to the ground rules staked out by some of our
commercial ancestors.

In a less tragic vein, but one that also has wide significance today, the pendulum may have swung too far with
respect to the entry of government into commerce. It has
since become apparent that it is a great deal easier to get
government into business than to get it out. But it was
businessmen who pleaded with government to provide subsidies and privileges, thus making government a partner
in enterprise. It was businessmen, for the most part, who
asked for legislative protection as a curb on entrepreneurs
who had succeeded in building monopolies. It was the actions of businessmen, if not their personal request, that
prompted the enaction of food and drug laws, the establishment of codes setting minimum wages and working
conditions, and the control of interstate commerce.

This line of comment must not be carried too far. The
abuses of enterprise in America, lengthy as the catalog may
be, have been specific rather than general. Most people
did not work in sweatshops. Observers who saw and compared working and living conditions in the United States
and Europe (such as Dickens and James Bryce) were
quick to praise American standards. Recent research in
social and economic history suggests that these on-the-
scene appraisals were more realistic, and more indicative
of general conditions, than later muckraking exposés.
Here, even more than in Europe, the literature of protest is distinguished more as an angry cry of outrage than
as a report of general applicability.

Most businessmen, with judges and legislators, must on
the strength of the record be credited with a respectable
code of honor. Compared to the experience of a number
of other nations, the relationship between business and
government in the United States has been remarkably free
from corruption. Law and social pressure did bring flagrant
offenders to heel, if belatedly. The process of reform,

while it did not prevent all future malefactions, did move soon enough and far enough to constrain unbridled capitalism, and to protect the public's confidence in a competitive, open economy. The American problem was not to make the idea of capitalism acceptable—it was accepted from the start—but to provide checks and balances as operable in the economic arena as in the political one.

The American economic synthesis, with its penchant for technical improvement and consolidation, has survived by public consensus. It developed to its present level because its virtues have been impressive and its faults capable of correction. For most Americans (the major exception is those who have been out of the economic mainstream, by virtue of race, geographic immobility, or other circumstances), the evolution of this economic structure meant improved working conditions and rising living standards. This approach to work and this method of organizing it have been retained and encouraged because people have seen this as a logical way to fill economic needs, and a way that is consistent with the idea of freedom.[4]

CORPORATE BAEDEKER

It is time now to return to the questions raised at the beginning, and examine work in the institutional frame today. The focus already has been narrowed to the United States and the commercial organization. Now it narrows still further, to a consideration of the large industrial firms that have come to symbolize the "corporation." They employ a larger segment of the work force than any other single type of organization, and, in terms of this inquiry, provide ideal access to the points most worth considering. To a greater extent than at any earlier time in history, man at work is today man incorporate. How he fares within the corporate interior, and what he stands to gain or lose by working there, are matters of considerable consequence.

Let it be noted before going further that the corporations in question here are numerically no more than a fraction of 1 per cent of all U.S. corporations. The privilege of incorporation extends to all manner of organizations, and by the tens of thousands noncommercial as well as commercial groups avail themselves of its advantages. MIT is a corporation. So is the Sloan Foundation. So are civic associations, libraries, and yacht clubs by the gross. More than one million corporations make profit or try to, but most of them are small firms, and many represent no more than the prescribed minimum (usually three persons) required for corporate franchise.

The concern here is not with these smaller companies, but with the profit-centered corporations that fall under the title "big business." There are about 3500 of them, counting on the basis of 1000 or more employees, and they are at the hub of American economic life. Including only companies in manufacturing, they generate sales of more than $200 billion a year, and employ about 10 million people. (This is about one-seventh of the civilian labor force, a little less than twice the employment in farming, and about the same as the civilian employment in government.) They have become centers of scientific research and major instruments for the application of new technology. This, plus their much vaunted capacity for mass production, makes them as much an arm of national security as the defense forces themselves.

Partly by virtue of their individual size, and partly because of their collective importance as employers and producers, these big corporations are a constant subject of discussion. People are interested not only in corporate size, but also in corporate power and corporate behavior, and the implications of both to the individual. Knowing that the evolution of big corporations solved some problems (and created some) during the nineteenth century, people quite naturally ask whether such economic organizations solve twentieth-century problems (or create them). Acknowledging that business morality has ranged in the past from very high to abominable, the next question is where the level falls today. How adequate are the controls of corporate conduct, and to what degree is the modern corporation—especially the big one—truly accountable to society?

There are plenty of answers around. A considerable body of literature surrounds the large corporation, and the corpus expands at a rate of about one new book per day. Many of these probe the corporate ethic and psyche, as do countless articles in academic and lay periodicals. Relationships with competitors and the public are examined in legislative hearings and scrutinized in court. Corporate *modus operandi* are dissected in case studies at some six hundred colleges and universities offering degrees in business administration. The "social responsibility" of big business is debated endlessly, although there is some question as to just what the term signifies, and what the standard for the corporation should be.

There is a maxim in commerce that, when a man handles money, it is wise to have someone looking over his shoulder. The large corporation has a whole nation of monitors. Its annual report is spot news to the public press, and a document of compelling interest to security analysts, financial writers, and occasionally a dissident band of stockholders.

All this is as it should be. Society has good reason to examine its subordinate parts, especially when they grow to such dimensions. The process of diagnosis and prescription may not always be agreeable to the patient, but it is healthy. Like cod liver oil, it is not so bad once you get used to it, and it may do some good. For one thing, it has provoked a certain amount of introspection in industry. As but one sign of this, trade and technical magazines, along with the popular press, now look upon the community responsibilities of corporations as regular editorial fare. Discussions of the role of business in the urban crisis are commonplace in *Fortune* and *Harvard Business Review*. As specialized a publication as *Chemical and Engineering News* sports a two-page headline, "Social Criticism and the Chemical Industry." Such a headline is in itself something of a social revolution.

Granting the value of all this probing and testing, it nonetheless has a built-in limitation. With rare exceptions, critiques of the corporation are academic. Whether the commentary is benign or destructive, dispassionate or heated, it is usually unaccompanied by extensive personal experience within the corporate interior. To set up an analogy, it is as though the assessment of our political or social institutions were left entirely to foreign visitors, with no reports from U.S. residents. This could be risky. We might be fortunate enough to draw another Tocqueville to our shores, but suppose we got another Mrs. Trollope instead?[1]

The vantage point here is from the inside looking out,

with the remainder of this book comprising a series of essays on the life of man incorporate as seen by a participant. To be discussed are the people who populate the plants and offices of big business, the management of such companies, the relationship of the individual to the "anonymous society," and last, the role and control of these organizations in society. These are essays from personal experience, drawn from two decades of employment in a quartet of corporations—an electrical manufacturer, a chain-owned newspaper, a New York publishing house, and a chemical manufacturer, all big—supplemented by exposure to the personnel and facilities of numerous other large companies.

Four corporations do not an economy make, and one man's reaction is inevitably tinted by what he happens to see or miss. However, an intramural view perhaps has some general application. Separate companies are not wholly unique. They operate under common legal conditions and social forces. They recruit in a common marketplace of talent. They differ in product lines but not so markedly in commercial objectives or in basic structure. They have not all achieved the same degree of rapport with employees, nor are they equally sensitive to what might loosely be called the public will, but big companies are increasingly aware, as a group, that their relationships with the individual and the public are inevitably factors in business success or failure. In view of these similarities, close exposure to this limited but diverse assortment of companies may be as good as any other guide to the corporate interior.

The Corporate Waxworks

It surely is not necessary to begin a guided tour with a restatement of the obvious. Research men do research, plants produce products, salesmen sell them, and the treasurer's office counts the money, as everybody knows. Well and good. Questions at the next level are more interesting. What kind of people sell? What kinds of challenges remain, if any, within the production divisions of companies gone to automation? What sorts of personal tensions and cross-currents does corporate life produce? Here, the answers may not be obvious, especially in view of the quaint notions circulating in some of our literature. These are so bizarre that, for fun if not illumination, it is worth pausing at the door of the corporate waxworks for a look at some life-sized, stereotyped figures. They would fit nicely in a zoo, or in a diorama at the natural history museum, for, as the fiction has it, the corporation is a jungle and lives by the code of same.

In the corporate veld, as kings of beasts, dwell the lions of finance and industry. Insular, ruthless, and arrogant, they devour smaller rivals, and plot raids on each other's hunting grounds.

At the next stage down in the jungle peck order are the aspirants to power. These are lean and energetic felines, identical in appearance, who have already marked out for themselves a place at the top. Some of them will get there eventually, the ones who know how to use their claws in the clinches.

At the edge of the game preserve we find a chattering band of scoundrels and noisemakers. There are silver-tongued pitchmen, exuding confidence and false friendship, as corpulent as elephants and as gregarious as jackals. There are ad men and "PR" types, obsequious scavengers who spend most of their time drinking at the better watering holes.

Up in the trees, out of the reach of the carnivores, are the owls and other eggheads. They chatter in a language no one else understands. For unknown reasons, they seem to have bad digestion, for they are all small and wan. There are no fat eggheads.

The only sympathetic creature in this peaceable kingdom is the poor beast that does the work. He is a decent but pathetic specimen, the only animal in the corporate jungle that can be made to carry a pack.

So much for nature study. Few passers-by would confuse wax figures with the live article. Along with the absent-minded professor and the string-tie congressman, these caricatures belong in comic books. Some people in the corporate world sputter indignantly at their cartoon image (and some here and there fit it) but there is small danger that the world at large is being deceived. We pause here only to make note of the stereotypes, and to suggest that the corporate population, if not fitted to the costumes of central casting, may yet be an interesting and colorful cast of characters.

While there is much talk about the uniformity of corporate employees, their distinguishing feature is diversity. People join the large corporation just as they affiliate with other kinds of organizations—social, military, academic, or spiritual—for all sorts of reasons ranging from dedication to happenstance. They bring with them all ranges of ambition, talent, and independence of spirit. They are "family types," "suburban types," "business types," "engineer types," and a few dozen other types. If somehow this adds up to "corporate types," so be it.

Some are iconoclasts, some are joiners, and some are security seekers. Some are extremely bright and some barely adequate. Most undoubtedly fall somewhere in between. If this signifies "corporate mediocrity," so be it. Literally, "mediocrity" means "man in the middle," and corporations, together with other institutions embracing thousands of people, must candidly admit a considerable population of middling men in their ranks, along with minorities at the respective ends of the pole.

Corporate employees are, of course, "conformists" in that, with most of their compatriots in society, they behave in more or less predictable ways. With occasional exceptions the corporate animal can be expected to eat three meals a day, drive on the right-hand side of the road, and wear shoes instead of sandals. So can most oboe players, poetry critics, and other nonconformists. Conformity is what you are used to, and it should excite no wonder that corporate employees, spread more or less uniformly across the national population, are used to the same conventions and

standards of behavior as tens of millions of others. Critics
of the organized life may read dire meaning into this, but
the conformity of man incorporate is quite literally unex-
ceptionable. By what logic would one expect him to walk
out of step with everybody else?

Generalizations may be less revealing than specific examples. What does man incorporate look like in action?
Take as a case study the corporation with the auspicious
name of E. I. du Pont de Nemours and Company, Inc.
If people in any company ought to be subject to type-
casting, one would expect to find evidence here. Du Pont
is a very old company and a big one. It has more than
100,000 people on the payroll, plants in more than two
dozen states, and operations in nearly that many other
countries. It is very partial to technology, efficiency, and
profits.[2]

Its outward countenance is austere. Like *The New York
Times* and Lloyd's of London, Du Pont has acquired a certain gray eminence which, for better or worse, sets it apart.
Perhaps because Du Pont is so closely associated with its
founding family (though they are no longer sole owners),
and as a reflection of conservative traditions, the company
presents a stern, unruffled, anachronistic exterior. The
headquarters buildings, massive and granitic, sit like a
Buddha near the banks of Brandywine Creek at Wilmington, Delaware. The architecture is drab, joyless, and unen-
livened. The corridors are lined with marble (high initial
cost; low maintenance—a choice made years ago by a
management which expected the company to be around
a long time), but Du Pont has no fancy reception room
and no chorus line of charming girl guides. Visitors, it is
assumed, can read the name-boards at the entrances, and
follow the arrows. There are no executive elevators, no
executive dining rooms, and no fleet of chauffeured limou-
sines. Executive offices are not spartan, but neither are they
opulent. Many a journeyman lawyer has an office that
puts Du Pont's presidential quarters to shame.

The directors' meeting room is the only place of palatial
elegance in Du Pont headquarters. Lighted by chandeliers

and hung with ancestral portraits, it looks more like a ball-room than a conference room. But it is not sacrosanct territory. When the directors are not in session, the room is used by other groups needing a large space. Hallowed is tradition, but reigning is sober practicality.

Here, then, are the outward signs, and they are deceiving. They suggest that the corporate arteries have hardened, but financial statements suggest otherwise. The company remains uncommonly successful, with sales of about $3 billion a year, and a return on investment that is the envy of Du Pont's rivals. It is hard to think of any other business firm (Rothschilds? the Medici banks?) that has done as well over as long a period of time as Du Pont. But what of its people?

The Executive Type

In the executive offices, one would half expect to find celluloid collars and high-button shoes. Instead, a personal tour reveals a variegated assortment of disparate personalities and backgrounds. The only universal characteristics are long experience in Du Pont and a stomach for long working hours. (Both are distinguishing features of the company. Promote-from-within is a nearly inviolable policy, and office hours begin at eight o'clock for vice presidents as well as stenographers.)

As one "executive type" in Du Pont, there is a distinguished, gray-haired gentleman who once played saxophone in a dance band and who now collects antique woodwinds as a hobby. This unlikely background, which certainly would be disapproved by any Committee on Stereotypes, did not disqualify him from high corporate office. After twenty-eight years of company service, he was elected a vice president.

Another corporate type, more in keeping with the conventional model, is an ebullient, club-joining, golf-playing extrovert, a musical-comedy buff and a staunch supporter of the Republican party, Hamiltonian division. He recently retired, having headed in succession three manufacturing departments, each the size of a major corporation.

Set in contrast to him, tempering generalizations, is a man who has drawn equal promotions, but who lives miles out in the country, attends the theater only under duress, avoids country clubs like the plague, and keeps his political leanings, if any, to himself.

The man who, at this date of writing, is president of Du Pont, Charles B. McCoy, is a studious, plain-spoken man who keeps his working hours long and his sentences short. Ostentation is not in his makeup. While some executives advertise their promotions by building a bigger house, McCoy has taken the opposite tack. When he bought his present home, he tore off one wing and lowered another, claiming that the place was too big for a family with grown children. The head of the Finance Committee, and a former company president, Crawford H. Greenewalt, is an urbane conversationalist with an interest in literature and a soft spot for whodunits. His recent avocation has been hummingbirds. To this last topic he devoted more than fifteen years of spare-time labor, producing a book of text and photographs that ornithologists have acclaimed an outstanding work. The project is a late entry on his list of interests. Though he was trained in science and began his industrial career in a laboratory, his field was chemistry, not zoology; and in his early years in the company, when there were slow moments on the night shift, he killed time not by reading bird guides but by practicing the clarinet.

Among their associates on the board, and for many years in active management, are a former professor of chemical engineering from MIT, and a Du Pont family member who was a pioneer aviator in the days of leather helmets and celluloid windscreens. As a concession to passing years, he has turned in his joystick, but continues to challenge the elements from the cockpit of a yawl in bluewater races. He spends most of his time now working on urban affairs, as a director and prime mover in a community development council.

Some of the men in this executive group hold Ph.D.s in

science, some had little if any formal technical training, and a few did not complete college. (This last group is small and getting smaller but claims in Du Pont the most elite of leaders, Walter S. Carpenter, Jr., former company president and chairman, now honorary board chairman. He left college before completing his senior year.) Some work in pin-neat offices with scarcely a notepad to mar the expanse of walnut desk and credenza. Others thrive in clutter, with books, magazines, and reports stacked on side tables and spilling onto adjacent chairs.

As would be expected, the executive ranks hold men skilled in the arts of public address. But there also are men with little experience in this realm and no inclination to practice. Some years ago when one such man was offered a senior position at Du Pont, he demanded exemption from such chores and got it, in writing. He never broke his self-imposed rule, though on one occasion, when he was being presented a high national award in science, some remarks were read for him.

What is true of executives is true throughout the organization. Some employees are narrow in interest and perspective, leaving a track in life that is a mile deep but only an inch wide. Others reverse those dimensions, and approach their work with the broadest of views. There are individuals who shoot from the hip and others who meticulously measure range and wind velocity before firing a round. There are pragmatists and theorists, mild individuals and fractious ones, men infused with "team spirit" and men who recoil in horror from it, tough-guy supervisors and Dutch-uncle types, men who suffer fools gladly and men whose patience is exhausted by the first hint of incompetence. They are working for a corporate employer not because they fall in the same color band of the psychological spectrum, but because someone, somewhere, saw useful talent and potential in them, and made them a job offer.

They might have drawn attention for any number of reasons, for in terms of talents as well as personalities, the corporate labor force is one of the most mobile and variegated of all human groupings. Change is its normal condition. This of itself scarcely deserves mention, for change is the nearly universal condition, but its magnitude in the business organization is worth noting. Particularly in large industrial corporations, the prerequisite for prosperity (personal or corporate) is an ability to adapt to persistent, often drastic, frequently unforeseeable change. As corporate jesters put it, if you don't like the way things are done around here, wait a minute. That applies to job skills, the variety of job assignment, and, for many people, job location.

A few of the manifestations are seen on the surface, and apply throughout the U.S. labor force. Women workers, for instance, are increasingly a factor in corporate operations, just as they are in other sectors of the work force. Today, the ratio is one to three: one woman in three holds a job for pay outside her home; one job in three in the labor force is held by a woman.

The educational level of the work force is rising, and an increasing percentage carries professional credentials, notably in science and engineering. In but one decade, 1955–64, the number of professional and technical workers in the United States rose nearly 50 per cent. One corporation that checked recently reported that nearly one-sixth of its employees were college graduates, and that more than half of these held technical degrees. Among the younger employees, those with less than fifteen years of service, few had less than a high-school education. The office work force is growing swiftly, both in real numbers and as a percentage of the labor force. For the past half century, the number of office workers has been increasing twice as fast as the average for the work force as a whole.

Subcurrents run beneath the surface. What is notable about women in industry, for example, is not their presence but their shifting occupations. They came into industry as factory operatives—the shirtwaist was familiar to New England textile mills before the denim collar. Next they were given jobs in the office, and stenography and bookkeeping swiftly became "woman's work." For some decades, that was the status quo. Now, reflecting changes that began no more than twenty years ago, women are also employed in industry as (to quote but one corporation's list) engineers, lawyers, physicists, chemists, physicians (and, of course, nurses), draftsmen, sales service representatives, translators, writers, editors, data programmers, biologists, patent specialists, and mathematicians. They have even begun to enter, one by one, into that bastion of masculine privilege, management. The number of women in professional and managerial jobs is not earth-shaking, but neither are these examples singular. A nation that has more than 80,000 women working as accountants and auditors and roughly 16,000 physicians and surgeons is overdue for a redefinition of "woman's work."

A second undercurrent, and one which has drawn less notice, is a return toward personalization of work, even in some occupations noted for specialization. It has been said countless times that technology makes jobs anonymous. Once true, the assertion is now false for many employees in certain industries and debatable for workers in others. The contribution of the individual has become more distinct and identifiable, and calls for more responsibility.

It should be noted that these internal trends are not reflected in organization charts. Such cryptic documents, which are all that many people ever see of the corporate innards, go coldly about the business of putting people in boxes and attaching familiar labels. One might easily infer—the chart does not imply otherwise—that employees assigned to a common box are more or less interchangeable. Were that the case, personnel directors could spend the rest of their lives with their feet on the desk. They are not to be let off so lightly.

The Hole and the Peg

Organization charts ignore details because they have to, but in this case the details are all-important. It is by no means remarkable for a large corporation to include more than three hundred different entries in its lexicon of occupations. Each job is subject to shadings and variations, made necessary by differences in individual temperament and talent. Technical work, which occupies an increasing fraction of employees in manufacturing, provides the outstanding example, and the pattern that prevails there is beginning to emerge, slowly but significantly, in other sectors of the work force. While there may be a dozen engineers in a development laboratory, all classified with a single job title, no two of them automatically could exchange projects. In research, some assignments are so personal that when shifts are called for, it often happens that the project must be changed. It is easier to rebore the hole than to alter the peg.

In practice, it rarely happens that people and jobs can be matched at a rudimentary level. The process is far more complicated. A technical director organizing a staff would never be so crude as to think only of "scientists" or "engineers." He would make his first cut at the level of electrical engineers, mechanical engineers, and chemical engineers, and subdivide from there. To find a man for a particular mission, he would scour the staff for an electrical engineer with background in nuclear reactors and a predilection for statistics. If he had more than one such man, as he might in a large company, and one could be spared from other projects, and that one was personally enthusiastic about turning to a new problem at that moment, the director would then begin to count himself blessed.

The example is still oversimplified. It is all but unheard of for a single specialist to have the manifold talents required for a major project. Commonly, an activity of any long-range substance calls for a combination of skills beyond any one individual's cerebral span. A typical product development, from the time research begins to the day of commercial introduction, will involve five to fifteen years of work by people representing fifteen subdivisions of science and at least a half dozen branches of engineering. With this in mind, a corporation with diverse interests tries to recruit as varied a group of scientists and engineers as would do credit to a university. No one corporation represents a norm, but simply to cite a figure, the Du Pont Company reports that it has nearly 2500 Ph.D.s on the payroll, a number few universities could match.

One would expect such an organization to become narrowly specialized in its technical work, but in the corporation as in the university, the opposite is true. The current demand is for scientists and engineers who can operate beyond the borders of one specialty. It is a little like the historical divisions of Continental Europe: The more that the map was carved into small pieces, the more flimsy the borders became. The same pattern prevails in science, with the walls dividing disciplines being breached on all sides.

The Knights of the Road

In other divisions of the corporate effort, the organization chart is equally uninformative. To confine itself to a single page, it dumps the sales function into one box, but this makes for strange bedfellows. The familiar drummer is still to be found—some things in life do not change—but when the salesmen meet in convention, the back-slapping pitchman must search to find a kindred soul.

Once, the worst that could be said of a salesman was, "He doesn't know the territory." Today, the "territory" extends beyond geography, to encompass the textbooks of science and engineering. Instead of meeting Professor Harold Hill, of *Music Man* fame, the salesman now finds himself surrounded by fellows who talk about catalyst recovery, high-temperature dissipation of the strength of materials, arcing through insulating films, court decisions governing sea transit of bulk chemicals, and foreign tariffs affecting U.S. exports of aircraft parts—salesmen all.

The gentle art of persuasion remains useful, but in many corporate markets, pitch and personality no longer suffice unless backed with technical training. I once traveled in the Midwest with a man who sells pigments for plastics, paints, and inks. He spends more time in his customers' laboratories than in the purchasing agents' offices, for this is a type of industry with technical problems, and he is the type of salesman who can help solve them. He has a Ph.D. in chemistry, and spent fifteen years in research and development before transferring to sales. The Ph.D. is a little unusual, but otherwise the example is not. Among the 1500 salesmen in the company that employs this man, 900 are college graduates.

Selling has become a process rather than a single event, a many-man activity involving backup forces in advertising, market analysis, technical service, and troubleshooting. The span of these activities varies with the industry and product in question. For old-line products whose uses have been tested by time and which are subject to little variation, the problems are basically those of marketing strategy, and supporting services are concentrated there. At the opposite end of the scale are products subject to modification and new applications, going to (or coming from) technically advanced industries. Here, the requisite services range all over the map. As an example, one salesman who handles petroleum chemicals used in East Coast refineries ran a count of the different specialists who stand behind him, and came up with thirty-nine. They ranged from a man who studies jet-fuel combustion to a mechanic specializing in test-car instrumentation.

How far industry has gone in this diversification of the sales process is suggested by a 170-acre complex of sales service facilities maintained by Du Pont a few miles from its home office buildings. There are eight laboratories there, staffed by about two thousand people who concern themselves with such matters as electroplating, tire making, weaving, paper making, and injection molding. Du Pont is not engaged in these lines of manufacture but its customers are, and in the chemical industry, which is extremely competitive, a seller will go a long way to keep a customer happy. In this case, Du Pont spent millions of dollars to duplicate in microcosm the production and test facilities of customer industries, hoping to find new or better ways for them to use Du Pont products. It is all part of the sales effort, justified on the grounds that long range, Du Pont cannot make a profit unless its customers do. It is interesting to note that the number of people employed at this set of laboratories is greater than the number in Du Pont's direct sales force.

This type of activity is more common than most people realize. Just as General Motors maintains test tracks and U. S. Plywood builds test houses, corporations producing industrial materials operate sales service laboratories. The only difference is in their customers. One sells readily identifiable products; the other, reaching for industrial markets, is farther removed from public view. In either case, there is a constantly increasing assortment of jobs contained in the label "sales."

The Production Corps

"Production" too is a catch-all term which fails by a wide margin to describe its people. Taken in a narrow sense, the word would identify something less than one-half of the employees in many modern plants. Employees who operate production machinery are outnumbered by a corps of people worrying about quality control, raw materials supply, freight rates, machine maintenance, pollution control, power generation, payroll deductions, and shift schedules. Strictly speaking, they are "nonproduction," although they do not appreciate the description, and one would have trouble running a plant without them.

There have been so many shifts, of such profound sweep, in the patterns of production within the past twenty-five years that the classical portrait of the factory worker has been turned into a charade. "Mass production" is not the same as it was in the 1920s or 1930s. The endless, unvarying replication of products which once characterized most industrial output now is identified only with selected industries and product lines. Elsewhere, while goods are produced in increasing quantity, few items march off production lines like tin soldiers. It follows that the people participating in this production process are less like tin soldiers themselves.[3]

For some years, it has been technically possible to build industrial plants that can be adapted, more or less instantaneously, to turn out a number of product variations. There is no one date when this originated, for it has occurred in different industries at different times and usually has been acknowledged belatedly; but it ought to be remarked as an important development in the history of man and his work. Industry has been moving back to the "custom order" business.

Once it became possible for manufacturers to offer something more than a large volume of goods at low cost, it became necessary. Customers issued the dictum. This complicated the manufacturer's problem. From Ford's point of view, it would still be easiest to make every car the same and paint it black, the way grandfather Henry did. Du Pont would be delighted to manufacture one variety of nylon and sell it to all customers for all uses. But industry can no longer operate this way. Henry Ford II, trying to hold a husky share of the current auto market (and no doubt remembering the near disaster that occurred at Ford because Henry Sr. resisted model changes and variation), gears his assembly lines to tens of thousands of combinations of engines, bodies, colors, and "optional extras." The only time a visitor sees a batch of identical vehicles at an auto assembly plant is when a fleet order comes off the line, and even there the customer wants features not found on other models, such as special lights for police cars. Du Pont, to sell nylon in competition with other producers and in rivalry with other textile fibers, finds itself concocting somewhat more than one thousand variations of nylon, modifying denier, surface coating, and other qualities to suit customers' needs.

Little fixity of outlook is possible anywhere in the production organization. Engineers are pressed to design process equipment that is more versatile as well as more productive. Quality control specifications are written to closer tolerances. Scheduling and inventory control are asked to work to tighter margins. Too much raw material in the storage bins pushes capital requirements beyond reason; too little, or too much of the wrong items means delay and unfilled orders. These are problems of no great dimension when there are only three or four variables in the production process, but the alternatives now number in the thousands, which is one reason computers have become standard equipment in manufacturing. They can handle many-variable problems and not lose track of what they are doing.

The production worker is as much affected by these new patterns as anyone else, and the prerequisites of his work show the change. The question is no longer how to simplify rudimentary and redundant tasks for a work force of functional illiterates, but how to keep a diversified plant crew attuned to constantly changing requirements. To that end, the personal qualification of highest merit is the ability to learn, backed by a willingness to do so.

Several years ago a General Electric spokesman predicted the arrival of a time when a young man would no longer be able to select a trade that would sustain him unchanged through his working life. That time is here. While old-line crafts survive, tools and materials change, old products are supplanted by new, and job descriptions are altered. Apprenticeship to a new job is now a familiar role for many industrial employees who have picked up the twenty-five-year service pin and blown out the candles on the fiftieth birthday cake.

For some workers training is continuous. An example is the instrument mechanic who maintains delicate control and metering devices in the chemicals and petro-chemicals industries. This is no spot for the boy who used to stare out the window in math class, wondering how soon he could quit school and get a good honest job. The instrument mechanic works with constantly changing apparatus, and he stays in school to learn how to repair it. He has his own classroom in the middle of the plant, attendance is compulsory, and high-school mathematics is a minimum prerequisite. This is an exceptional case, but it reflects a broader trend that shows no sign of reversing.

On-the-job training programs are fast becoming a universal facet of corporate life. One estimate holds that they already represent an effort one-third as large as the nation's formal education program. The figure could be wrong—numbers like this are mostly guesswork—but there is no question that the training and retraining effort is big and getting bigger. The major reason is the change in the attitude toward process obsolescence. Technology rather than old age now is the deciding factor. A century ago industrial plants were built on the assumption that machines would run until they wore out. Today, few installations are expected to function without change even for a decade.

By the time a new plant has its opening celebration, and the corporate hosts are showing off the "very latest" in twentieth-century technology, the design division is at work on process improvements and the research staff is thinking about other products or processes altogether. As engineers say only half jokingly, they are now so good at their jobs that they can build nothing but obsolete plants. If they waited until all possible advances were in hand, and tried to draw an ideal set of blueprints, they would never build a plant at all.

The evolution of industrial work has all but destroyed the meaning of the terms traditionally applied to the work force. "Blue collar" and "white collar," for instance, have lost all but marginal value in many large corporations. People still are divided into those who work in offices and those who do not, but the distinction is misleading and the labels only confuse the issue. Some production men work in air-conditioned control rooms, in greater comfort and with far more privacy than is found in the bookkeeping bullpen. On an index measuring training, income, or cleanliness of fingernails, operators score higher than many office workers. "White collar" still has a status that carries weight around the water cooler, but this is more a matter of prejudice than logic. There is little correlation between the color of clothing and the magnitude of the individual contribution.

In the literal sense, the blue-white distinction loses even marginal meaning. In the South and Southwest, where many newer industrial plants are located, clerks, machinists, and shift supervisors all arrive at the plant gate in sports shirts. Plant managers do too, though as a concession to tradition (and as protection against unexpected visits by the brass), a tie and coat are hiding in the office closet.

The division between "skilled" and "unskilled" is similarly uninformative. In plants associated with segmented, assembly-line operations, it is hard today to know where the dividing lines fall. The woman who assembles radio components is by no means the illiterate who used to clean vegetables at the cannery, but neither has she spent years learning her present trade, as has an electronics repairman or a tool and die maker. The usual dodge is to call assembly tasks semi-skilled, a term of such vagueness that it can be made to cover almost anything.

In more highly mechanized industries, where the repetitive hand work is minimal, the skilled-unskilled categorization has become a logical absurdity; almost everybody has moved to the left side of the hyphen. Apart from yard work and a few pick-and-shovel jobs, there are no jobs for unskilled laborers. In companies with technical leadership, it is probably safe to say that not more than six to eight workers in one hundred are unskilled; some companies set their own figure at three or four per hundred, and admit that there are borderline cases among that small handful.

The difficulty is that we continue to use one word, "skill," to signify both the things that a man can do with his hands and the things that he knows in his head. They are not comparable, and merely to say that a worker is "skilled" is to say nothing of the changes continually reshaping his job. To offer but one of many examples, those instrument mechanics have always carried a top-skill label, but their work changes year by year. Simple thermometers and pressure recorders have given way to a battery of new measuring and monitoring devices, each with internal mysteries, each to be supplanted as time goes on by still more elaborate apparatus. About a decade ago, an instrument mechanic spent 20 per cent of his time figuring out what needed doing, and 80 per cent doing it. Today, those percentages are the other way around. This required a complete overhaul of the training and selection program, with increased emphasis on learning potential, but there were no changes in labels. Throughout the production process, physical demands are declining. The chemical operator attending a modern plant unit needs less dexterity than he required as a boy making model airplanes, and he burns fewer calories at work than at the bowling alley. His job looks deceptively simple, and plays hob with "fair day's work" formulas. The operator seems to spend most of his time wandering around the control room and process area. He looks at dials and adjusts valves, and does very little that would excite a dynamometer.

What he is being paid for, at a rate schoolteachers envy, is experience, judgment, a sense of responsibility, and a certain knowledge of what to do in a crisis. The operator controls an assortment of machinery valued in the millions of dollars. It is integrated with other process units, all of which function profitably only when dozens of process variables are kept within close tolerances. In some processes, equipment must operate continuously or not at all; if the flow stops, liquids in the system "freeze" and the unit has to be dismantled with sledge hammers.

A blunder by an operator—or more likely, his inattentiveness—can disrupt a schedule that reaches all the way through the plant, into the freight yard, and on to the customer's receiving dock. Mistakes are expensive and can be dangerous. For all the technical acumen of the engineers, it is still not possible to build an error-proof plant. Hence, operators draw high pay, and earn it best when they appear to work the least.

Is this type of work more or less skilled than that of a machinist or mechanic? Who can say? The physical obligations are smaller and the psychic tensions greater. The main point is not to get bogged down in semantics. Each form of effort is essential to the production process, and each is skilled in a way hardly known in industry a century ago.

Making Waves

One element is still missing, and no corporate Baedeker would be complete without it. Discussions of work in industry—and so far this one would have to be included—usually leave the feeling that everything is done in marvelously good order. In a well-run organization, everyone is supposed to know where his function fits. Lines of jurisdiction are supposed to be clear. Overlaps and conflicts are supposed to be resolved.

That is all very neat: in fact, too neat. Such an organization is a practical impossibility and would be an operational disaster. Overlap and conflict are inevitable, and the attempt to eliminate them would rob the corporation of most of its bright people and all of its vigor. A certain amount of tension is necessary to keep up the circulation and to guard against what John W. Gardner calls "organizational dry rot."[4]

The natural play of personalities will automatically create some pulling and tugging. Sparks are bound to fly when a methodical temperament meets with impatience, or when the ambitious and energetic mind is met and balked by the conservatism and rule worship that appear in a bureaucracy. One has cause for concern only when the squabbling dies out, for a total absence of conflict means that nobody cares enough to fight.

Instead of trying to stamp out the conflict, some corporations load the dice to provoke it. Du Pont, to return to that company, has promoted into its management ranks a number of fairly testy men, including a few who have earned the reputation of being outright provocators. One in particular is personally amiable, but pushes for projects that leave some of his colleagues apoplectic (while others, of course, are cheering him on). He is enough of a realist to admit that only a fraction of his proposals will be adopted, but he persists anyway, for he assumes that he was put where he is to do precisely what he is doing.

As he once said to me, "Five years ago, they would never have put a fellow like me in this job. But right now, they seem to want a guy to rock the boat a bit. Who knows, maybe five years from now they'll toss me overboard."

One doubts it, for his ideas, good or bad, are undeniably stimulating, and this corporation regards stagnation as a greater danger than heresy. It has even acknowledged this in a formal way, through a special bonus program that provides impressive sums to employees who make very extraordinary contributions. The bonus is made all the sweeter if the employee accomplishment is made in the face of opposition.

Personalities aside, there is an innate reason for conflict. Business problems do not come in neat packages. Alternate routes are offered, with risks that are only partly capable of rational, quantitative assessment. There is not always a right answer or "ideal course," but only a set of options, each with its own uncertainties. Assuming maximum objectivity and good will on the part of all concerned, the possibilities for disagreement are still almost endless.

Let us take some not so hypothetical examples. A research group is exploring new compositions of matter, looking for a molecular chain that will produce a textile fiber. This alone is no great trick; modern chemistry can produce thousands of new formulations and, to a degree, tailor molecules to order. The problems emerge when management adds the rest of the requirements. The fiber must offer physical properties superior to those of existing materials. It must take and hold dyes and finishes. It has to be capable of being manufactured at some reasonable cost. There must be a market for it, latent if not already established; and an investment in the new product must be as attractive, in terms of profit per dollar of risk, as other prospective uses for the company's funds. Different people assess the potential product at different points along the way, measuring with different yardsticks and rendering judgment, as often as not, on the basis of less than complete data. It would be extraordinary if they all came to the same conclusion.

Commonly, after several years and several million dollars' worth of laboratory exploration, there would be more than one candidate product to investigate. This further multiplies the alternatives. One candidate may offer the best final properties but require the expensive raw materials, implying a fairly high selling price. Another may be easier and cheaper to manufacture but have less predictable market potential. Which candidate do you choose?

The research division in all likelihood would like more time to examine additional formulations, while sale management may be anxious to establish a position in a new market at the earliest possible moment. Design engineers, in turn, will point out that it is imperative to scale up to the pilot plant level immediately, if there is to be any hope of putting the product into full commercial production within three or four years. It is relatively inexpensive to stay in the laboratory, but no one can be sure that another year "on the bench" will make any difference. Full-scale development, on the other hand, costs plenty; $50-to-$80 million may be committed before anyone will be sure the venture is going to succeed. Do you bid low and stay in the laboratory, or push ahead with the cards in hand? Is this the type of venture to which the company should commit several hundred technical and merchandising employees for a period that may run five years or more? Is this the time to launch a new textile material— or should you put the money into making farm chemicals or a new paint plant?

At some point the mental gymnastics comes to an end with either a "go" or a "no go" decision, but that decision, so simple on the surface, will be well larded with what psychologists call interpersonal conflicts. As suggested earlier, the case cited here is not imaginary. This is precisely the process that led to "Dacron" polyester fiber and several other widely used man-made textile materials. The figures as given are of the correct order of magnitude.

Consider a second case, again based on actual product lines but this time dealing with materials already on the market. The product is a plastic, and Sales believes that volume would almost double if this product could be engineered for automotive structural use. Engineering says it can do the job but the cost, including plant modifications, will run to five million dollars. This means the price has to go up ten cents a pound. "Too much," answers Sales; at that price plastic cannot compete with machined metal. Try a three-cent increase. Okay all around, but this means that it will take the company five years longer to recover its cash outlay. Treasurer's looks pained.

"Don't worry," interjects Research. "They'll never get this one off the ground. In five years we'll have an inexpensive sintered metal out of the laboratory, and knock all those cost figures into a cocked hat."

Two more chaps are yet to be heard from. Enter stage left a statistician trailing a train of computer print-out sheets. Development, he announces, has put the whole problem into Monte Carlo language, and for $2.42 worth of electricity the computer has delivered the answer. The chances of making 10 per cent net return on the plastics project are 64 to 36, favorable (if all the input assumptions are correct).

Let her rip? Not quite yet. Legal's courier has just arrived with the news that new patents awarded a competitor in West Germany are technically close to Engineering's ideas, so close that it may be impossible to use the production process without royalty payments.

Go—no go? A neat package for decision-makers, well calculated to make for some more of those invigorating interpersonal conflicts.

Tension has its price. It is easy for conflict to become destructive. Given poor leadership or an unfortunate mixture of personalities, diversity may degenerate into factionalism and internecine war.[5] The next chapter discusses this in terms of management responsibilities. In closing this chapter, suffice it to say that conflict and diversity are inseparable parts of the corporate scene, and can be a vital stimulus.

How useful this can be was suggested to me by a corporate friend who received a tempting offer to leave industry, and turned it down. He is a highly employable fellow, holding a handful of degrees including a Ph.D. in statistics, a field in which jobs outnumber applicants and the bidding for manpower is spirited. His credentials are such that a Big Ten university offered him a professorship and a chance to be second-in-command of a department. The job was glamorous; the budget was big; the salary offer was higher, I am all but certain, than this man's Du Pont salary.

Those who know him well were surprised at his decision. He has been battered more than most by the corporate crosswinds. His ideas have lost out more often than they have prevailed, and he has had the personal disappointment of watching other men catch and pass him, even though few people anywhere in the corporation work as hard as he. The university offer must have been tempting. But he chose to stay where he is. Why? His own explanation is that he wants to finish the projects he has begun, a job that will take three years at the minimum. My opinion is that a deeper and more persuasive reason is contained in one of his offhand comments:

"This is a funny life for a man like me, and sometimes I think the company is going to drive me nuts. But it's fascinating."

THE MANDATE OF MANAGEMENT

Given the diversity and variety of its population, the corporation would appear to be in no danger of becoming mired in sameness, or too ponderous to move. The greater danger is that, like the famous horseman, it will leap into action and ride off in all directions at once. The force that keeps this from happening, and gives the organization a sense of direction, is management.

As a minimal responsibility, management must balance a multitude of individual efforts and keep peace in the corridors. Should it fail in this the organization can only destroy itself. To put it in engineering parlance, a large corporation is a system in dynamic equilibrium; its parts are moving fast, and if they run in gross imbalance, centrifugal force will tear them apart.

The supervisory role is primary, then, but taken alone it is insufficient. Management is supposed to be something more than a balance wheel or a referee at the intramural corporate games. As the cliché pompously puts it, the manager is expected to be "creative." This is a vague if august charter. In what way creative? The word covers all manner of crimes against the language. Presumably what it means—this is what it signifies here at any rate— is that management must generate energy as well as channel it. It should not only lend cohesion to an otherwise fragmented activity, but also should add a motive power of its own.

Most important, the administration must infuse a sense

of common purpose into the organization, to draw forth such talent as is available and to point that talent toward objectives that are considered worthwhile. It is not enough to recruit and train individuals so that they can make a contribution. For the organization to prosper, managers must convince other employees (or at least offer them the hope) that the institution is useful to society, and that the individual's contribution is distinguishable and significant. This kind of corporate climate cannot be concocted by formula, but its creation is management's basic business.

Most people in management are not given to such high-minded generalizations. They are more comfortable dealing with concrete problems, and leave the philosophizing to their speech writers.[1] In justice to the manager's cause, it must be said that he uses some wonderfully ingenious tools and systems in the day-to-day business of control and administration. The technique of his job is important, and will be given further attention in a moment. What must be recognized, though, is that all administrative systems and devices are secondary and supportive. They are the tools of the manager's trade, not the bonding force that holds the organization together, nor the energizing agent that supplies momentum and direction. More than is commonly realized, corporate success or failure is measured not according to supervisory structure or financial control, but in proportion to management's ability to draw the best talents out of people.

On paper, the large corporation is arranged vertically and directed autocratically. There is a chain of command through which orders can flow from top to bottom, military style. Companies used to operate this way. Perhaps some still do, though no examples come to mind. The traditional hierarchy remains (it must, for a reason which will be pointed out), but in practice the flow of communication is as much up as down. Giving orders has become the least of the manager's job. It might even be said, without stretching the point, that a corporation's management can fairly be judged by the degree to which it succeeds in making that flow of communication move upward.[2]

Good-by to Little Caesar

We are apparently witnessing in this generation the last and final passing of militant management. There are still tyrants and tin gods flying corporate colors and making life miserable for subordinates, but as a working philosophy, autocratic management is on its way out. Little Caesar is an anachronism. However noisily he struts around the board room, whatever his personal degree of ownership control, he is failing in the one mission that counts the most in his own ledger: bringing in the profit. As a passing speculation, the possibility occurs that the "great man" theory of business management has been oversold historically. From the Medici to the house of Morgan, and including such pillars of independence as Ford, Hearst, and Rockefeller, one distinguishing feature of success was the ability of the leader to surround himself with exceptionally able lieutenants who did more than merely carry out orders, and who somehow found ways to get along with the boss without becoming yes men.

The present confronts the manager with two facts he has no power to change. First, participation in the corporate work force is voluntary. Management can entice and cajole. It can to an extent "lock in" employees through pension plans, deferred bonuses, and other financial programs that pay off only for people who stay with the company. But management cannot compel loyalty, and its effective economic grip has been greatly weakened with the passing years.

We no longer have the kind of economy, as we had in the depression of the thirties or in the nineteenth century, when wholesale numbers of people lived in terror of losing their jobs. Corporate employees are free to "disaffiliate" and, to a greater extent than ever before, they have the financial means to do so. Quitting work would be a genuine hardship for some corporate employees (as an example, for textile workers in the smaller southern cities, where one corporation may be the predominant if not the only major source of work), but for many others loss of a job would be but an inconvenience and temporary sacrifice. This pertains especially to well educated employees with relatively high income. They comprise, by rough measure, about one-half of the civilian labor force, and they of all people have portable talents. They also are hard to replace, and they know it. To hold their support, management must look to incentives rather than coercion, and autocrats have never been as good with the carrot as with the stick.

Second, what might be called the incremental differences among companies are becoming decisive. As competition increases, rival firms move closer together in measurable capabilities. As noted earlier, they look to the same schools for their scientists and engineers, and hire people with similar backgrounds. Administrators in different companies have access to a common set of techniques; there are few secrets in this business to be patented or jealously hidden from outside view. Differences in personal talent, while they doubtless exist, ordinarily are more significant in small companies than in large. In big corporations, by the sheer weight of numbers, such differences tend to cancel out. Variations in financial strength, which govern a company's ability to undertake competitive risks, have become less singular and limiting. Except in a few specialized fields of defense technology, where government rides herd over the corporate effort (and the profits), there are no longer important sectors of the competitive marketplace where a single producer has a clear field simply by virtue of his size. Companies of all sizes have well-heeled competitors to contend with. Boeing may look formidable to a small company supplying fuel hoses, but North American is not awed, and it is with North American that Boeing must compete.

Searching for ways to hold a competitive position, the corporate manager must look to another element, the human factor. Increasingly, what distinguishes one company from another is the ability to bring forth an incremental extra effort from employees, a small but crucial contribution that goes beyond formulas for "a fair day's pay for a fair day's work." It is not the sort of thing that is found in contracts. In terms of daily output or number of new products invented, the margin may be miniscule; but its effect is cumulative and eventually impressive.

Here, too, the autocrat is at a disadvantage. Nothing in his training or temperament prepares him for this kind of problem. He cannot use fear for incentive, and he lacks the power of compulsion that would be his in a military organization. His inability to cope with the human element sooner or later, and probably sooner, will be reflected in the stern logic of the earnings statement. Meanwhile, he lives on borrowed time.

The Many-Man Approach

Most corporations long ago saw the perils of one-man management and turned to the many-man approach, distributing authority through the organization according to a set of house rules limiting the jurisdiction of men at different levels. How widely this dissemination of authority has been carried is indicated by the experience of Du Pont, one of the earliest and staunchest advocates of managerial diversification. That company was no stranger to nineteenth-century iron-man rule. For three decades after the Civil War, its decisions were made by one man, Henry du Pont (significantly, he had been a general). His imperious ways would not do for the twentieth century, however. Following his death, and without benefit of formal theory or precedent, the company diversified both its product lines and the decision-making function, establishing a committee system of management that has been widely imitated. Today, senior operating responsibility in Du Pont is vested by the directors in an Executive Committee of the president and eight vice presidents. Below them are fourteen levels of management, ranging down to the plant foreman. More than seven thousand employees, or one out of fifteen on the payroll, fill some supervisory function.

Much the same arrangement is to be found in other large corporations. The "Generals" (Electric, Motors, Dynamics, Foods), the "Standards" (Oil, Brands), and the acronyms (FMC, SCM, TRW, and RAC) all operate through decentralized management.

Centuries ago military and church organizations discovered the value of staff services as a supplement to line organization. The corporation has taken a leaf from their book, and established auxiliary departments to assist management. There are staff divisions assigned to forecasting and planning; staff employees who count the money, calculate the taxes due on it, and suggest where the residue can most profitably be invested; staff men who deal with health and safety programs; with advertising, publicity, and public and employee relations; with purchasing, traffic, and legal affairs; with long-range research; and with engineering and construction.

These people by definition carry no responsibility for making and selling product lines. They are the corporate adjutants and outriders, the specialists in communications and logistics. As such, they are not management per se, but aides and auxiliaries of management, and a further example of the wide dissemination of authority with the corporate structure. They are labeled "overhead," and their contribution, being indirect and expensive, is sometimes regarded as superfluous; but in appropriate measure staff services more than pay for themselves.

How much is enough? Both for staff services and for dissemination of line authority, the question is legitimate but unanswerable except in a general way. Parkinson's Law can take hold, and there can be an almost endless lamination of management levels, to no avail or profit. Services can be overdone. At best, their value is difficult to compute except in a few areas (e.g., finance, engineering) where monetary yardsticks apply.

As a general observation, it appears that we have not as yet reached a point of diminishing returns. Looking to the broad evidence, companies that have used staff services most abundantly, and integrated these into a decentralized management system, have been consistent leaders in profits. General Motors and Du Pont (which has 15 per cent of its employees in staff departments) are notable examples. On a narrower base, drawing upon examples that do submit to measurement, the conclusion still holds. As but one of many instances, a staff mathematician in an engineering research laboratory, 2000 miles removed from a Texas chemical plant, wrote a set of equations to simulate what was happening in the plant's production apparatus, programmed a computer to try thousands of combinations of variables, and arrived at an optimum set of production conditions. The result was a 25 per cent increase in the output of one production unit, with no change in equipment. Triumphs of this magnitude are exceptional, but it would not take many such examples to convince a skeptic of the value of staff services.

In any case, the many-man approach to management and the overlay of staff services carry an air of inevitability today. Top management turns to them in self-defense, for it is not possible for one man, or a small group, to keep track of the myriad details that affect corporate performance. Even if time permitted a single officer to make all key decisions, he could not judge intelligently among the multitude of proposals crossing his desk, some couched in the language of science, others demanding an expert knowledge of law, still others calling for extensive background in banking and finance. The dissemination of authority, if it does nothing more, supplies senior management with translation services, and gives these men a little time to think.

They have paid for it. For many-man management, apart from its built-in complexities, carries with it a fundamental dilemma. Authority to make decisions can be delegated, but responsibility for the results cannot. As stewards of the stockholders' property, top management is answerable both in law and in conscience for the corporate performance. There is no way short of abdication to dilute this accountability. If the ship runs on a reef, it is the captain who is called before the Court of Inquiry. To protest that he was in the wardroom eating dinner while a junior officer handled the ship only makes the captain's position the more embarrassing. This is the reason organization charts, like military chains of command, are drawn as pyramids; they picture a hierarchy of responsibility.

They do not illustrate the flow of decisions and ideas through corporate channels. That is a far more complicated matter, whose diagram looks like a cat's cradle. A few years ago, at a conference which brought together a group of college professors and Du Pont's top management, this point was raised in specific terms. One of the professors, a sociologist as I recall, patiently listened to an introductory talk, then took the floor to say this:

"In any human institution from a tribe to a nation, we find an overt and external frame of organization, plus an underlying set of relationships controlling the actual, everyday decision-making process. [I am being as faithful to the professor's style as memory permits.]

"In your company, certainly there must be such a substructure. Quite apart from the organization chart, you must listen more to some people than to others. Seminal ideas must emerge in unexpected places. How do they cross over the lines you have drawn? There must be times when you play hunches. Are there not advisers you especially respect, men whose judgment you trust even though the chart does not assign them authority?

"I see your organization chart," he said in conclusion, "but what I want to know is how the underlying chart would look. Just how does Du Pont actually operate?"

The answer came from Walter S. Carpenter, Jr., then chairman of the board, a man who at that date had fifty years of experience in management:

"If you can find out," he said, "I wish you would let me know."

A candid executive in any other large corporation would have given the same answer. When I worked at General Electric, there was a standing offer of a vice presidency for any man who could describe in five hundred words or less the inner workings of that company. As far as I know, that prize is still unclaimed. No one is likely to earn it, for the "substructure" that so intrigued the professor is not a structure at all. Corporations are not that systematic or rigid. They are constantly in flux, and refuse to stand still long enough for microscopic examination.

The error lies in thinking of the corporation as though it were a puppet controlled from one place where all the strings come together. In practice, only the lines of responsibility remain stable—otherwise there could be no organization chart of any kind. Decisions and day-to-day relationships among employees are strongly influenced by personal factors, and by differences in the kinds of work people do. Certain types of projects may be managed strictly according to Hoyle, with approvals granted consecutively as proposals are reviewed by successively higher levels of management. The decision to build a new plant would be an illustration. For other types of decisions, the chart is followed mostly for protocol. When a problem calls for a single area of expert knowledge, the man in charge is likely to turn directly to the employee who knows the most about it. From common courtesy (corporations pay much more attention to the niceties of life than is often supposed) the request may be run through channels, but it skips along without interruption; the manager knows just whose opinion he wants.

The lines of corporate contact cross and interlock in changing patterns. Job assignments and people change, and the links among them are broken and reconnected. Groups are reshuffled as often as market conditions and other factors require. People move from department to department, and from specialty to specialty. In Du Pont, there is a promotion of someone, somewhere, on the average of once every ten minutes. Some "experts" are more expert than others. One manager may be content with an opinion from a single subordinate; another group head, less certain of his own ground or of the individual wisdom of his people (or perhaps just less opinionated) may prefer to work from a consensus.

In such organizations there can be no finished piece of

paper architecture to position and tie together thousands of people. There can be only general scaffolding, shaped in rough accordance with the pyramid of responsibility, but subject to change.

This sounds slightly chaotic, but when two qualifications are met, such organizations operate with remarkable dispatch. Decentralization must exist in fact as well as name. It is all too easy, in any large organization, for decisions to be made in pre-meeting political sessions attended by a select few. In that event, the many-man approach does little more than pour holy water on essentially autocratic decisions. Some of this is inevitable, especially among executives who have strong opinions about the rightness of their own ideas. But as academicians have pointed out, this approach is more prevalent in corporations—and in universities, government offices, and churches—than devotees of decentralized management care to admit, and where it prevails, it makes a mockery of their claims.

As a second qualification, the people involved in a decentralized system must respect and trust each other, and have a common goal. At this point we are dealing with a truism bordering on banality, but there really is no other way to put it. This form of organization does in fact work, and every attempt to explain why ultimately can be reduced to this simple point.

If a corporation is to thrive, there must be a singularity of purpose, together with an enormous amount of personal give and take, for these are needed to offset the tensions among people and absorb the impact of collisions. This elasticity cannot be legislated. It exists only to the degree that individuals agree upon general objectives, and management succeeds in convincing them that, as individuals, they count for something in attaining those objectives.

It is for these reasons that an effective corporate manager strives to maximize the sense of individuality of his subordinates, and to provide recognition for accomplishment. His own interests are served if he succeeds. This is hardly a new idea, and the only thing remarkable about it is that it is so often ignored.

It is for these reasons, too, that promote-from-within is such a laudable policy in corporate management. As is often noted, the grow-your-own approach to management has the advantage of providing a maximum number of target jobs for ambitious juniors. This helps, but an equally important virtue is that it builds a feeling of community in management, and strips men down to their basic character. The value of this should not be underestimated. Men who have worked together for decades develop an intuitive sense of each other's strengths and sensitivities. They can agree to disagree without malice. They know who is sincere and who is synthetic. Having shared sandwiches and coffee on the graveyard shift in their cub years, and sweated out together the problem years as junior managers, they have developed a rapport that is difficult to match on short acquaintance. Most important, when the time comes for a promotion, the candidates are not ciphers or dossiers, but individuals whose qualifications and sense of values are well known to the men making the selection. If this does not guarantee optimum wisdom, it greatly enhances the chances of a reasonable selection.

The Rational Manager

There have been many attempts to systematize management, both to reduce the risks of enterprise and to bring a greater sense of order to the corporation's internal activities. The effort has been so successful, in the areas where it can succeed at all, that one classic problem of management is disappearing, and another has cropped up to take its place. Traditionally, management was hampered by a shortage of data. The statistics needed to assess the health of the business were slow to arrive and often prohibitively expensive to collect. That problem is no more. Management is surfeited with data, and the question is not how to obtain more figures but what to do with the ones at hand. The danger is that management will drown itself in paper or, worse still, that it will try to apply quantitative measures to problems that are not fully quantifiable.

Modern recording and communications equipment, coupled to data-processing tools, makes it possible to analyze output and efficiency almost instantaneously, plant by plant and even hour by hour. Computers, darting through thousands of computations per minute, can be programmed to slice and tabulate sales or production statistics to any desired degree of refinement, sending the manager anything from a summary figure to a tidal wave of detail. Manufacturing activities can be monitored as they run. Traffic men can keep track of box cars and tank trailers scattered across the country. Inventory can be counted mechanically, with signals automatically relayed to purchasing and production offices when stocks run low.

All this helps. In organizations that in every month churn hundreds of thousands of inventory entries, sales invoices, production reports, paychecks, and accounts payable entries, there is obviously much to be said for accurate, high-velocity adding machines. If management uses these tools to excess, and wastes money and time tabulating the insignificant, it has no one to blame but itself.

The major virtue of these tools, though, lies beyond the realm of bookkeeping. After all, in the years before the "computer revolution," when electronics was still in the gee-whiz stage, corporations somehow managed to meet the payroll and keep track of inventory. The fundamental contribution of the new tools is that they permit a systematic approach to many business problems that previously defied rational solution. Management can measure more and guess less.

The case histories mentioned in the previous chapter hint at the possibilities of the new rationalism, and it is easy to find additional examples. In Du Pont's product portfolio, for instance, there is one chemical material that can be manufactured at any of four locations. It is sold to industrial customers in various parts of the country. Where should each order be made? To save on shipping charges it would seem best to fill orders from the plant closest to the customer. But distance is only one of several dozen factors. The product can be shipped by water as well as land; it may cost less to move it a thousand miles by sea than to send it three hundred miles overland. Raw material prices and other costs vary from plant to plant and month to month. The backlog of other orders has to be kept in mind, as well as the speed with which each customer needs delivery.

The problem is already beyond the level of a manual calculator, but it is subject to further complexities. Some variables are functions of others. The efficiency of a plant, for instance, depends in part on how closely it operates to its designed capacity; that in turn depends on whether or not the plant is assigned the order in question.

Problems of these dimensions can be manipulated mentally, but no corporation could afford the price or the delay. Thousands of clerks and dozens of mathematicians would be required, and it would be ludicrous to await their answers. A decision is needed this week, not next year. Moreover, this brings to mind a preposterous picture of a clutch of mathematicians, tucked away in the corporate basement, cranking out figures with monastic patience. Mathematicians are too scarce, and their talent too much in demand, for management to bore them with such assignments.

The routine approach, and for years the only one possible, was to look at a few variables and ignore the rest. Give the order to the nearest plant with available capacity. Today, the answer is to translate the problem into symbolic language, put it on magnetic tape, and feed it to a computer. Within the hour, the computer will compare hundreds of alternatives and determine how much each of them means in dollars. Theoretically, such problems always have been rational; they are now subject to more rational and thorough analysis.

Similar problems are encountered throughout a corporation, and are now approached statistically. In research, through strategic programming of computers, it is possible to plot in advance the sequence of laboratory tests that will give a maximum amount of useful information with a minimum number of experimental runs. In engineering, using already conventional office tools, it is possible to assemble and organize information about the thousands of individual tasks that must be performed in constructing an industrial plant. These may then be laid out on a visual flow chart to show the sequence in which jobs must be completed, the dates on which each must be begun and finished if construction is to stay on schedule, and the amount of money involved if any job has to be rushed through on overtime.

Marketing is a tougher nut to crack. The variables are more variable. But if statistics of past performance can be projected into general expectations for the future, it is possible for management to map tactics in advertising and distribution. There will be no certainty of success, but the sales force at least will know, given the conditions at hand, that money and energy are being spent in the way that offers a decent probability of profit.

These systems have brought a welcome increase in the precision of the corporate effort, but they have not yet reduced management to a deterministic, fully systematic game. They never will, for fascinating as these techniques may be, they have structural limitations which cannot be wafted away with electronic wizardry.

In the first place, the tools are not that good. The real world gives us too many variables. There is no computer in existence or conceived that can deal with problems of business strategy in their full richness and complexity, evaluating all alternatives to produce decisions that are unassailably correct. Computers provide a means of manipulating thousands of factors, but for even a comparatively simple business problem, a full and rigorous statement would reveal hundreds of thousands or millions of options and germane factors—not all of them known or even in existence at the time the machine is programmed.

As a useful digression, consider the game of checkers. The opening move poses what is intellectually quite a limited problem. There are only sixty-four spaces on the board, twenty-four of them already occupied, and moves are permitted only in certain ways. However, what one player does alters the options open to the other, and the strategy must be calculated not only for all possible first moves, but also for every move and countermove that can follow, out to the end of the game. The number of those options is calculable. Using the fastest computing equipment at hand, that problem can be solved in a fully systematic way in 10^{21} centuries, after which it can be guaranteed that the opening player will defeat his opponent.

Computers can be taught to play checkers or chess, but they will not play perfectly. Like people, all they need to "learn" is to play well enough to win. The real world, it must be admitted with some joy, is considerably more complex than a sixty-four-square game with fixed ground rules. Even the best of tools provides management only a strategy and a set of probabilities, not certainties.

Mathematicized management is restricted by the limits of its inputs. Either the data going into the computer are based on assumptions (which may prove wrong), or these figures lead to answers which deal only with part of the managers' questions—the easy part.

Research managers can decide logically how to approach a given set of experiments, but no amount of mathematical maneuvering is likely to show whether these experiments are the best route to new knowledge, or whether that new knowledge will in any way be useful. The production manager can tell where to manufacture the next tank car of hydrogen peroxide, but possibly his operation would be more profitable if it were converted to other product lines entirely. On this question office machines are mute.

There are parallel cases in sales, planning, and other areas of administration. As long as knowledge is expanding, as we are always being told it is, and as long as the market remains open to new ideas and alternatives, the future cannot be regarded statistically. However refined the tools and techniques of management, the key questions must of necessity remain subjective. Going back to that classic case, there was no way to prove that Gutenberg was right to develop the printing process, until he did it.

As I mentioned earlier, those who yearn for wholly dependable, objective approaches to human affairs have on occasion tried to find rules and "laws" governing the management function. It has been a frustrating search. The ground rules that work effectively in one situation have to be modified to fit another. The "ten easy steps" approach is naive in the extreme; it attributes simplicity to a subject that is inherently not simple, and confuses techniques of management with objectives. The only "law" that seems to pertain generally to management is a negative one. To grace it with a title, it is the Law of Inverse Certainty: The more important the management decision, the less precise the tools to deal with it.

This is not the sort of law that appeals to scientists, and it certainly will not draw much applause from the devotees of mathematical management. But it states the case. When a manager wants to know the cost of converting to a higher grade of iron ore, he can have the answer to the penny. When he asks a broader question—All things told, is it profitable for us to add another product line?—the response is touched with conjecture. The widest and most general question—Where are we going and how do we get there?—is clouded with uncertainties, immeasurables, and unforeseeable turns of events. Yet this is the most vital question of all. The answers or the refusal of management to give answers will set the corporate course for years ahead, and will give this disparate, variegated institution whatever sense of commercial unity it is to have. In keeping with the pyramidal structure of the corporation, it becomes the certain duty of top management to make decisions in the areas of maximum uncertainty.

There is a First Consequence of the Law of Inverse Certainty: The more important the decision, the longer it will be before anyone knows whether it was right. When a company embarks on a new product variation, the market soon lets it be known, in precise if cold-blooded terms, whether that move was well taken. To shift the company in an entirely different direction, perhaps moving into another industry, increases the ante and lengthens the time for doubting. By the time an appraisal is possible, millions of dollars are over the dam, and it may be too late to turn back. It is in this area that management earns its keep and gets its ulcers.

This also means that an incompetent or self-serving decision-maker, if he once succeeds in gaining a high position, can hold office for years before a case can be built for impeachment. Given a job in research management, for example, such a man can focus his division on projects that are in a "hot" field of science (science, too, has its fads). If he is glib enough in his sales pitch, he can pry loose major appropriations (no one wants to be behind the times in research, do they?), build a substantial technical empire, and use this as a steppingstone to a higher post. (He did a great job of building the team, didn't he?)

This may take several years. But time is on his side, for it may take even longer to obtain an audit of results, and see that the project, as far as his company is concerned, was technically barren from the start. A man can feather himself quite a nest this way, all the while claiming, of course, that he is only thinking of "the good of the company."

The Team Builder plays one of the most destructive of corporate games. Not only does his approach lose money and reward dishonesty; it also is likely to frustrate subordinates who have sound technical judgment, and cause them to seek employment elsewhere. These are the men a company can least afford to lose. When the reasons for their departure hit the grapevine, the company will find they are not easily replaced.

Another example of the breed is the Cost Cutter, the man who builds a reputation by slashing projects and people left and right. It is no trick to save money if that is all a manager wants to do, and in periods of declining earnings such single-minded men find ready-made opportunities. The true cost may not become apparent throughout the company until the axe man is long gone from the scene, and snugly ensconced in a vice presidential chair.

A particularly lurid case history along this line was related to me by an ex-employee (his group was abolished, without warning or explanation, one Christmas week several years ago) of one of the twenty largest U.S. corporations. The Cost Cutter slashed divisional overhead more than $1 million in jig time. He also destroyed the morale of a design staff, shredded the accounting and control group, and according to this report nearly wrecked the competitive capability of the division. Was it worth the price? It may be years before top management can answer that question. The Cost Cutter is now a full-fledged member of headquarters elite, in a choice position to defend his actions. The "malcontents" who might make a case against him have left the company. The division may have enough momentum to keep rolling for a while. When and if it finally slows to stalling speed, who will know why?

There is no reason to suppose the percentage of Empire Builders and ambitious men is any lower in corporations than in other types of institutions. Nor is there any sure way to prevent some of them from "making it." The promote-from-within policy helps (as Mr. Lincoln suggested, the more people you have to fool, and the longer, the harder it gets); but it is no panacea. The best prevention is to have men in top management who are knowledgeable about the business under their jurisdiction, and sensitive to the personality traits of their subordinates. The first is a matter of objective control, of charts and data and professional experience; the second is a matter of subjective judgment, ephemeral and imprecise, but in this case, an indispensable quality.

With this for background, it is clear that there can be no ideal "manager type" or management system. It takes all sorts, both in personality and methodology. Assuming minimal personal civility, which is a lubricant if not an absolute necessity in human affairs, the manager's approach cannot be correlated to neat rules and fixed standards. What counts is his ability to deal with problems that fall into his bailiwick, whatever type they may be, and to draw from his subordinates an enthusiasm and feeling of common purpose. This cannot be put into a manual on The Ten Rules of Successful Management, or learned in charm school.

The teachable aspects of management are not to be scorned, but they should be carefully identified. The results of management training programs suggest that many procedural and technical skills can be taught to potential managers. The ability to identify and evaluate relevant data can be enhanced. It is possible to change attitudes, to a degree, and improve a manager's awareness of the importance of personal factors (the feeling of respect, credibility, etc.) in the manager-subordinate relationship. It is very doubtful that it is possible (or perhaps even desirable) to change significantly the actual behavior of managers in their approach to the human problems they face. From all indications, these behavior patterns are well set by the time a man leaves college, or before. Such patterns are likely to stay with him through life. If as a young man he acts with slight sensitivity to the feelings of others, he probably will remain that way with or without a management portfolio, and with or without special training. If the humanistic touch is there at the start, he and his employer can build on it.

It follows that, in choosing candidates for supervisory roles, senior managers first have to ask themselves a basic question: Does the job require only a hard-headed, operational ability; does it require the somewhat different talents associated with the nurture and guidance of other individuals; or does it call for both?

If only technical competence were required, there would be less of a shortage of men with management potential; but as men advance into higher echelons, an increasing portion of their responsibility lies in those nebulous areas of human relations and personnel development. The "technical manager" is perhaps adequate to the solution of the short-term, limited-range problems, but the "humanistic manager" is needed further up the line. Unfortunately, unless the emerging manager already has the requisite humanistic outlook, experience in technical decision-making will not equip him to deal with senior management's problems.

This is one of the serious problems of the large organization, for humanistic managers are hard to identify at an early age, especially in corporations where most college-trained employees come with degrees in science or engineering. The natural temptation is to fill lower-level supervisory posts with men whose talents are most immediately useful (i.e., with "technical managers"). Only in later years, when the organization encounters deep-seated labor problems or deficiencies in personnel, does it become clear that the short-term management needs were filled at the expense of long-term organizational health.

Of Science and Nonsense

Essays about management often revolve around a now-tired debate: Resolved—management is a science; Opposed —it is an art. I turn to this point last, tangentially, in the conviction that as far as the large corporation is concerned, the terminology is ambiguous, the debate is irrelevant, and the arguments on both sides are a bore. Management is an art, a science, or neither, depending on how you look at it. For more than semantic reasons, the debate ought to be laid to rest once and for all. To continue it is but to perpetuate an attitude toward the management function that has caused incalculable mischief and misery. There was a time, within the memory of many men still living, when "scientific management" had a particularly ominous, destructive connotation. Instead of identifying a rational approach to the supervision of work, it signaled a wholly impersonal, mechanistic outlook that ignored or subordinated the most important variable of all—man. It therefore was no science at all, but only a misadventure for which managers and employees and the whole nation are still paying.

It derived innocently enough, from a passion for efficiency that swept industry during the late years of the nineteenth century and the early years of this one. Where it went askew was in a single premise: In the drive to "engineer" the production process, it was mistakenly assumed that humans as well as tools would submit to the process without complaint, and that, indeed, the same approach would raise the output of both. The highest manifestation of this, although not the only one, came in the form of a cult that acquired the specific label "scientific management." Efficiency was its god and Frederick Winslow Taylor was its prophet. Its icon was the stopwatch.

Taylor and his disciples atomized industrial production into its tiniest particles. They relocated tools and reordered the flow of work, analyzed each motion of hand and eye, rearranged every manipulation to gain the ultimate in productivity from the expenditure of energy.

In many ways this approach made sense, and its appeal to managers was obvious. It fulfilled the yearning for precision and it had measurable results. Waste was reduced. Output and profits climbed. On the surface it should also have appealed to production workers, for it implied higher wages with no more, and usually less, exertion.

The premise, though, had its fatal flaw. Efficiency is not entirely an engineering matter. It is now clear, courtesy of that marvelous instrument called hindsight, that atomized work is far from the engineer's dream it was once thought to be. In recent decades, it has been shown again and again that higher efficiency lies in production systems built around the versatile and ingenious qualities of man. Values once scorned as "subjective" and "imprecise" pay off in profits.

"Scientific management" not only by-passed the workman's personal feeling of involvement in his job; it denied him status entirely. No one asked or cared what he thought. In fact, the less he thought the better, for that meant one less variable to play with in the time and motion studies. The result was that for tens of thousands of people life in industry was reduced to the ineffable logic of the slide rule.

Man's horizon narrowed to the dimensions of a single machine, to be fed and tended not according to the workman's individual skills, and certainly not according to any personal notions he might have, but in compliance with the dictates of a flow chart, hour after hour, until an evening whistle broke the trance.

Taylor himself saw what this meant. Speaking of one pick-and-shovel job he had quadrupled in efficiency, he observed that "One of the very first requirements for a man who is fit [for this work] is that he shall be so stupid and so phlegmatic that he more nearly resembles an ox than any other type."[3]

The sentiment was not lost on workers. Some, to protect their sanity, learned to block off a compartment in the mind, and function unthinkingly and mechanically. If they were to be regarded as children, they would act as such. The analogy is a fair one. Mentally retarded adults have been found to be well suited emotionally to such jobs.

Those were the malleable ones. Tougher-minded people fought back. One could well conclude, looking back at this period (or, for that matter, looking at the current scene in some corporations), that the men a psychiatrist would regard as the most mature were the ones labeled "troublemakers." They were adult and too intelligent to accept a return to childhood, so they lashed out in protest. The stopwatch was assailed as a symbol of oppression. Time and motion studies, innocent enough in themselves and very useful as a means of reducing needless drudgery, became the mark of the "speed-up."

It is too much to say that this spirit of protest built the militant labor movement—other forces were hard at work—but this was precisely the type of issue needed to organize factory workers. As George Meany has observed, one important aspect of the union movement was its promise of a sense of dignity for the laborer, by involving him in decisions about his work.[4] "Scientific management" gave the early organizers a unifying cause, a target to substitute for the class consciousness that had never fully developed in America. Unions clamored for a voice in the establishment of output quotas and the size of working crews. Frequently, they got it. The "fair day's work" is still a negotiable item in many labor contracts, refined in some cases to a point where it can be stated in ergs of energy and caloric consumption.

Coupled with this were demands for higher wages and improved working conditions. Part of this was the workman's natural yen for a share of the nation's rising economic wealth. But in part it was the voice of frustration. Discontent, employers discovered, has a high price.

Fortunately for business organizations, "scientific management" was never universally adopted. Although it had a wide following (interestingly, one zealot was Nikolai Lenin, who sought to apply it in Russia), many industrial leaders shied away completely or borrowed from it selectively, enhancing efficiency but sidestepping the worst problems. Nonetheless, the movement had tremendous impact on people's thinking, leaving a cloud that to this day overshadows the management process and, most seriously, poisons the relationship between managers and employees in hundreds of corporations. This is tragic for all concerned for, to paraphrase a familiar saying, management is not as "scientific" as it used to be, and it never was.

In the corporation today, management borrows techniques from science; if this alone is the criterion, then it is all right to call management scientific. (It is also all right to call music, advertising, or yacht design scientific, for these too, along with innumerable other activities, call upon the tools of science.) Corporate management strives for precision, and has had more success in the improvement of measurement and control than anyone thought possible a few decades ago, even the advocates of "scientific management."

Yet limitations remain. The instruments of science can respond only to questions that can be put scientifically. With respect to those management questions that are speculative, conjectural, and nonrational, there is no way for managers to think "scientifically," and no reason why they should try.

There is art in management. Some executives, like some painters and composers, have a truly aesthetic talent, an unexplained but undeniable ability to generate elegant or exciting ideas. They look at the obvious and see the new. But whatever the alchemy or genetics that produces such minds, artists and managers remain distant cousins. No one has confused Ben Fairless with Ben Shahn.

The difference does not necessarily lie in how "socially useful" or "creative" each may be. The artist and businessman march to different drummers. Practitioners of the fine arts (ideally) set their own standards of performance, personally and without reference to absolutes. The manager's work (eventually) is measured with tangible yardsticks, graduated in established units. Until there is a conversion scale by which we can compare aesthetics and the coin of profit, managers and artists will pass through the forest on different trails.

Art or science? It makes no difference. All that matters is that management is a useful and necessary function, capable of increasing the individual's contact and satisfaction in his work. Management admits to subjective judgments but it can claim no mystique. It deliberately subdivides and disperses its authority, yet it cannot divest or dilute its responsibility. Its performance is assessed in arithmetical terms, but behind its success or failure is a nonlinear quality, the human factor. The underlying relationship among individuals, as the central element in corporate success, remains the main business of management. How pointedly this applies is seen in the comments of two men working in a manufacturing division of Du Pont where technical progress has been notably swift. Asked about the impact this is having on them and their fellow workers, one said that his prime job was "to get people ready for change, so they won't be hurt." The other said, "The people side of it is none of my business; I'm in engineering."

The first is a manager. The second, one fondly hopes, will never be.

THE INDIVIDUAL IN THE ORGANIZATION

A professor of history at the University of Delaware, Dr. Walther Kirchner, approaches his courses with a provocative reverse twist. Instead of confirming commonplace ideas about history, he urges students to examine the textbook generalizations to see where they do not apply. He does not do this to be contrary, or to show everyone how clever he is. What he is trying to show is that history, being made up of people, lends itself reluctantly to simplification.

To offer one of the professor's examples, the seventeenth century marks the introduction of the Age of Reason and epitomizes the Age of Absolute Monarchy. Yet on close examination it is hard to find an important country in Europe in which a monarch had absolute power at that time, France and Louis XIV included. Further, one can make an excellent case for the seventeenth century as an Age of Faith, contrarationalism.

Clio the Muse, as the professor notes, has a perverse streak: "When you have history all straight in your mind and everything falls into place, you may be fairly certain that you have got it wrong."

This backhand approach is stimulating, for it shows students that history has limitless variety, and therefore is a subject worth bothering with. The same technique has utility here in an assessment of the curious relationship between individuals and corporations. It is a relationship—or, more accurately, a host of relationships—that does not submit gracefully to simplification. It too is bounded by conventional generalizations. It too is a subject worth attention, for it is the modern example of man confronting institution, and trying to maintain his identity. How well he fares is a matter of deep consequence in any society that honestly claims to embrace freedom.

This chapter discusses the relationship of the organization to the people inside; the next chapter examines the relationship of the corporate organization to the society outside. Both begin and end with the premise that a large corporation retains its legitimacy and deserves to survive only if its actions are in keeping with the tenets of a free society. That premise is not examined—it seems so basic to me as to need no defense. What is to be explored is the substance and basis of the individual's relationship with the large corporation, and that exploration, as the professor would say, brings us out in a somewhat different place from where we went in.

What are the commonplace notions about the personal side of corporate life, and how vulnerable are they to a contrary line of argument? As seen from this vantage, the conventional generalizations submit very nicely to reversal. They look better turned upside down.

It is often said, for example, that large corporations are cold and pro forma in their relationships with employees. Consumed by a passion for technical gadgetry, given over to the hands of men who think in terms of numbers, these companies have lost altogether any personal touch they may have had. Men and women today are ciphers on an IBM card, magnetic bits on a computer tape. Hired according to scores on entrance tests, they are ranked, paid, and promoted according to sums on rating sheets, and even fired by machine-printed notices. So the allegation has it, and so it is believed by many. One of the marchers in the Berkeley student protests carried a sign in the shape of a punch card. "I am a human being: do not fold, spindle, or mutilate."

Looking to the opposite side of the coin, it may also be argued—and is by others as well as by me[1]—that the difficulty lies in quite another direction. Many supervisors, aware of the danger of managing by the numbers, try so hard to protect the personal relationship that they end up managing by sentiment. Determined to take full account of subjective factors, and fearing they will judge subordinates too harshly, they procrastinate and duck unpleasant decisions. Were they a little more cold-blooded, countless ineffectual employees would be lectured sternly and demoted, transferred, or bounced.

Good Old Joe

For all concerned, this should be done at the earliest possible date, sparing no feelings. Once an employee has twenty years of service he becomes Good Old Joe; to fire him sends a shudder through the whole organization, and raises a moral question. A man at forty-five is not as employable as he was at twenty-five. If he is so inept now, why was this not admitted earlier, when Joe had a better chance for a second start?

Sentiment is often misplaced anyway. In 1958 a Du Pont engineering group went through what is euphemistically called a reduction in force, with the result that a large number of engineers, most of them young, found themselves out in the street. Few suffered more than a minor shock. On their own or through a placement bureau set up by Du Pont, they all located other openings. Follow-up contacts showed that many of them felt they were better off for the change, and were glad it had happened when it did. One of the group told me that the jolt forced him to review his own ambitions, and led him to look for a spot where he could work in the field he had pursued as a graduate student. He is now with Esso Research, doing just that and blessing his good fortune.

From firsthand experience I know what he went through. In a moment of youthful indiscretion and hunger, I once talked myself into a job as *Argosy* magazine's feature editor. It was a trial marriage based only on hope, and it became clear overnight that the alliance could never last. I was ill suited to the job, and to *Argosy* the liaison must have seemed a disaster, for the then editor, Jerry Mason, threw me out after six weeks. He did us both a favor, for which I here thank him publicly (I neglected to do so at the time).

How many other bosses in similar circumstances would have had the objectivity to admit the error, and the kindness to set it right so promptly?

To be sure, it is easy for engineers to find work, and staffers of national magazines develop extraordinary survival instincts; they manage in one way or another. But what about the many people trained to less mobile trades? Perhaps they have been bumped from their jobs by automated machines, or by a declining market for their product. Are they too to be summarily shoved through the gate?

That would be callous, but it would be just as reprehensible for management to lean to the other extreme, and give artificial shelter to dying trades and dying products. This only delays the inevitable and makes the personal problems worse. The answer is not to put Good Old Joe in the feather bed, but to make him more mobile by helping him prepare for other work, either with the same employer or with another.

To the credit of many corporations and unions, people are now looking around the corner to anticipate problems of this kind, to prevent later hardships and prepare for new opportunities. Douglas Aircraft, as one instance, has a program that gives maintenance and production workers 8000 hours of on-the-job training plus 700 hours or more of evening studies at any of eight colleges in California. One objective is to give employees a broad enough technical background so that they themselves will be able to master new skills and adapt to change. A single project like that is worth a thousand make-work jobs, and costs less.

It is now clear that the forces reshaping American industry are of such magnitude as to require much more than a lateral transfer among craft talents. The direction has to be upward. Merely to retrain a displaced worker for another craft may prove to be but a temporary expedient. It may only continue the problem of overspecialization, which already has been pushed too far in industry. For the time being, it may be the only answer but in another five years, the man's new craft may also pass and he will be in the same predicament all over again.

What is needed is a way to break the cycle, and this can only be done through programs that permit employees to gain education as well as training. There is a world of difference between those two words. Training implies a specific set of activities. Education, as used here, fits the aphorism: learning how to learn. It is with this distinction in mind that programs such as the one at Douglas deserve special mention, for they are adding another dimension to the industrial worker's mobility.

On Mobility

It would be helpful if there was similar mobility geographically. However broad the training efforts, there is no way for an employer to guarantee job opportunities indefinitely at a fixed location. In the most prosperous times and far-sighted companies, there are plant closings and personnel cutbacks. Realistically, more of the same must be expected in the future.

The prospect of transfer harbors all sorts of problems, and they are especially acute among production and maintenance workers. Companies are not enthusiastic about moving large numbers of workers into a new area, where they may be competing with local residents. Employees themselves often resist moving, as do many union representatives, who point to the fantastic seniority snarls that can result. Nevertheless, if the work cannot be brought to the man, the man must go to the work. Full mobility is the price of an economy that aspires to full employment.

The difficulties of transfer are a bit exaggerated. America is no longer the rooted society it was a century ago, with the typical citizen living, working, and dying within fifty miles of his birthplace. Among salaried employees the transfer has become more or less routine, an accepted part of the process of getting ahead. Among others in the corporate employ, there is visibly less of the provincialism that makes a trauma of a transfer. Vacation travel, plus a stint in the armed forces, has had a broadening effect on millions of people.

Some people remain greatly upset by the idea of mobility. They still lean to the serenity and sense of permanence of small-town America (which, as Sinclair Lewis pointed out in *Main Street,* was not quite what it was cracked up to be, but that is another matter). Their argument would be understandable in Europe, where for centuries many a family has remained in the same town or city. In America, it is indeed a curious track to follow. We are encouraged as youngsters to admire the colonists who clipped home ties and set forth to a strange new life, and the pioneers who rode Conestogas to the frontier, often to face conditions a good deal worse than they had bargained for. These, the schoolbooks tell us, are the kinds of people who built this country. How is it, then, that it has become a problem of magnitude to transfer a man from Cleveland to St. Louis?

Perhaps it is the frequency and involuntary nature of transfer, more than the general idea, that is bothersome. Corporations often shift sales and supervisory personnel three, four, or a half dozen times in the course of a career. It is said that this produces anxiety and an inability to develop anything deeper than superficial social relationships with other individuals. There is even a term for it, "mobility insecurity." Some, carrying the argument to the extreme, accuse corporations of deliberately using transfers as a means of destroying the individual's attachment to all institutions except his employer, thus keeping people totally dependent on the company. I cannot respond to this charge, except to say that it is clearly paranoiac, hinting as it does at dark plots and evil schemes.

It boils down to differences of outlook. Some organisms

do not adjust readily to repeated changes of environment. Some people are centered on home, possessions, and community status. The suggestion that they leave familiar surroundings and set up shop in a new town represents a direct threat to all they hold dear. To others, home is where you hang your hat. The excitement of change or the prospect of advancement outweighs the inconvenience of moving, and the thought of beginning anew with strangers holds no terrors. If it is a disservice to transfer the first type of man, it would be equally a disservice not to transfer the second.

Are transfers obligatory? Unless a plant or sales office is being shut down, few companies will flatly demand that an employee move. Instead, he is offered a new job. "Offer" is a euphemism—or, to be more specific, it is a word subject to two interpretations, both correct. It means than an opening exists and that the man in question is considered qualified to fill it. In that sense, it stands as a compliment and, if accepted, as an opportunity. Suppose the man does not want to move. What does it mean then? Not Siberia, but limitations—limitations the employee may be quite prepared to accept.

Transfers are not capricious. They are part of the effort to broaden an employee's experience and utility, and with few exceptions they are accompanied by higher pay and responsibility. Only in special cases, as for example in construction work where men move from project to project, is this generally not the case. Where a corporate transfer is rejected, it signifies that the man in question probably will not be able to offer, in years ahead, as varied a background as some of his more mobile compatriots. His chances of attaining a top position are therefore reduced. Transfer, then, has a mandatory ring only for individuals who aspire to the highest slot they can reach on the organization chart. For those who read personal success in other terms, and prefer to let others compete for the top, there is rarely any compulsion about moving.

In any event, the corporate employee who takes to the road has plenty of company. His index of transience is no higher, and may well be lower, than that of several other major groups in society. The armed forces and the academic community are examples. Academicians take it for granted that a young man will do his undergraduate work in one university, take graduate training in another, move to a third to begin teaching and finish his doctoral thesis, gain tenure in a fourth, and spend his sabbaticals in still other locations, often foreign. Wives and "faculty brats" trail along in his wake, not always uncomplainingly but aware that the professorial life is semi-nomadic. A faculty brat myself, I lived in seven different towns at three corners of the country—South, West, and North—before going to college. I am unaware of any irreparable damage done to my psyche, nor was I aware before the age of eight or ten that other people lived differently. On the block where I now live, we have the pleasure of the company of corporate employees ranging from a Midwesterner who runs a General Motors assembly plant to an expatriate Icelander out of western New York. Of eleven houses on the block only one, to my knowledge, houses natives of this city. None of us is under treatment for mobility insecurity.

Alien Men

Moving to another of the imputed problems, it is reported that large segments of the corporate work force have been deprived of all sense of personal involvement in their work. Anomie, a lack of fulfillment, isolation from a finished or complete product, the desiccating rhythm of routine and monotonous jobs, the absence of participation in decision—all these are cited as symptomatic of a broad spiritual malaise within the production work force. "Alienation" is the trade term for it and, as one sociologist, Robert Blauner, points out, the word has become the "intellectual's shorthand" to describe the fate of the manual worker.

The idea of alienation is not hard to trace. It had its origin in the Marxian analysis of industrial life. It was reinforced by the experience of mass production industries in the period of roughly 1900 to 1940. Working conditions associated with it are still to be found and, on this basis, "alienation" remains a catchword in the literature of sociology, freely used by industrial sociologists and psychologists who are non-Marxian and anti-Marxian, but who cling to this fragment of the faith.

However, the issue of alienation grows weaker with each passing year. The recent trends of industry have been away from the conditions that produced this catchy but questionable word. As sociologists themselves have recently pointed out, there are vast differences in the atmosphere of work in various industries. For some reason, scholarly attention has focused heavily on the auto industry, and the ways of work there simply cannot be generalized to cover all industry. Blauner is particularly sensitive to this point. He has held factory jobs himself, and in a recent book discusses studies of four industries—autos, textiles, printing, and chemicals—demolishing any notion that what is true for one may safely be assumed to apply to all others.[2] Moreover, what was true of the auto industry in the 1930s and 1940s, when the bibliography of alienation began to grow fat, no longer applies to all of the production force in that industry alone, or to many other industries. As Blauner notes, assembly-line workers—the group most vulnerable to alienation—probably do not represent more than 5 per cent of the U.S. labor force today. Atomized work has all but vanished in such industries as chemical manufacture and petroleum refining (where it had only marginal application anyway), and has diminished in other heavy industries such as steel making. It is declining in industries such as appliance manufacture and textiles, which in the past were citadels of redundant and impersonal jobs.

The large corporation has not yet found its way out of this forest. Millions of workers still spend their hours at dull tasks utilizing only a fraction of their talents—and making, it may be added, only a fraction of the contribution they might make to the corporation. But it is no longer reasonable to speak of the work force in sweeping generalizations. For millions of other workers have from their own experience gained a sense of participation and responsibility from their jobs. They would be greatly amused, if not offended, to be told that learned papers are being written about their alienation.

The Pursuit of Equity

Sometimes justly, corporations are charged with inequity in their treatment of employees and in selecting candidates for advancement. In a big company it is nearly impossible to assure that the same ground rules apply to everyone. Then too, there is the sting of truth in George Orwell's observation that some men are created more equal than others. Again, though, the argument looks better upside down. Management can become so preoccupied with the need for equity that it loses flexibility and all vestiges of horse sense. The company becomes entombed in its own rules.

General Electric once locked horns on such a matter with its illustrious Charles Steinmetz. At issue was his love of cigars, and a rule against on-the-job smoking.

The inventor announced his decision: "No smoking, no Steinmetz." He stayed, the rule went, and GE is still around to tell the story.

The "togetherness" syndrome is a related malady. Much is made of "morale" and "teamwork," but the words are overused and it might be best to drop them from the vocabulary altogether. To many people they signify a one-big-happy-family approach, a route of maximum folly for any large corporation. Any business organization of more than a dozen men, striving to deal with individuals as in a private family, would be an incredibly dull place to work in and a perilous investment. Extraordinary and disquieting personalities, which often mark the most creative minds, can be readily accommodated in a business or professional relationship. People go their separate ways at the end of the day, and there is a veneer of custom and courtesy that smoothes the more abrasive moments. But in the confines of the family, masks are harder to keep in place. Tempers flare. Politesse is swept aside. If there are true mavericks in the family, peace is preserved only at the cost of disciplinary action. Harmony, Inc., the company with the happiness chaps in charge, is a business with predictably small growth potential.

That approach has been tried, with disastrous results. Walter Buckingham, a Georgia Tech professor, points to the case of the United States Electric Light Company, which found the inventive mind of Hiram Maxim intolerably disruptive—he produced ideas so fast as to make the company's apparatus always obsolete. Maxim was banished to England on a lifetime pension. While the English were knighting him for his continued creativity, United States Electric Light was going out of business.[3]

The moral of that story, and of the Steinmetz case, has been supplied by James Thurber, one of the wise men of the twentieth century. You might as well fall flat on your face, he said, as lean over too far backward.

Who gets ahead, and why? The mythology of promotion is familiar, but here too the problem, assuming there is one, is due less to inequity than to an overzealous insistence on absolute (and unattainable) objectivity. By now it should be evident that few corporations can afford to select men for advancement on a favored-son basis. Few try, for in that dice game the statistics are all against you. The preordained promotion line, with a handful of "whiz kids" pushed through a prescribed sequence of jobs—and everybody else pushed aside—remains a golden dream of some corporate planners, but no one has yet found a way to pick the right batch of candidates. In commerce as in horse races, some run with "early foot" while others scamper faster in the stretch. Administrative talent comes in many forms, and people begin to demonstrate it, if at all, in various ways and at different times in their lives.

Rather than freeze the promotion system, which would guarantee the loss of some late-blooming candidates, corporations would do better to keep the structure as flexible as possible, reviewing performance and potential periodically (some companies already have this down to an annual or semi-annual basis), for every employee at every level. Ability should be judged not on the basis of a single project but on the cumulative record; and, to avoid either of Mr. Thurber's extremes, it would be wise for each employee's work to be reviewed by two or more supervisors, to guard against judgments too gentle as well as too harsh.

The Corporate Comedy

Similar problems arise with the tribal rites, ceremonials, and status symbols commonly attributed to corporated life. The company picnic, office Christmas party, and twenty-five-year service ceremony are cited in amused tolerance as evidence of corporate immaturity. Granted, funny things happen in corporations. It is reported, for example, that adult males at times gather in convention splendor and extol their company and boss in song. This is hearsay; I have never been privileged to witness such a spectacle. The only company song I know is a bawdy parody about Du Pont, unfit for mixed company or publication.

Before drawing conclusions about the corporate comedy, though, it pays to look further. Perhaps everyone's house is made of glass. The wags who are so amused by the "tribal rites" of business are often found in organizations much more given to ritual than any corporation. Consider for example the university, with its mortarboards and gowns—a ludicrous getup, when you think about it—its processionals and convocation ceremonies, and its faculty teas, not to mention the rah-rah and the bonfires, the pep rallies and the panty raids, and other juvenilia for which the faculty is not accountable. (Some observations along this line were once made by a corporation president in a speech at Princeton. He admits it was not his most popular speech.)

As for status symbols, there are corporations which indulge in rules about carpeting, corner offices, private elevators, and keys to the executive washroom. Telephone protocol is a standing joke, with secretaries sparring with each other to see who will put her boss on the line first. In the wonderful world of status symbols, though, the corporation is no match for the government, where a man's stature may be measured by the number of phones on his desk, the brand of car he is assigned, and whether his wastebasket is made of walnut or inferior stock.

It is well to tread lightly here, and not only to avoid broken glass. There is virtue in ceremony, and it may even be in order to say a kind word for status symbols. The parade of academicians flying their school colors, and the ritual of the church service, like the family gathering to decorate the Christmas tree, have a merit in tradition which all but the most cynical will concede. Using care to distinguish the silly from the useful, the demeaning from the distinguishing, one can make a good case for ritual and adornment.

Corporations might be better off if they had more of both. Their employees come from a society which, for the most part, makes public acknowledgment of private accomplishment. They have been to schools where the honor roll is posted and the parchment says, to those who have earned it, *magna cum laude*. They have been in military service, where rank or rating adorn shoulder and sleeve. They have heard the applause at class elections or on the basketball court. But in the corporation, they often find accomplishment is met by silence. One receives no merit badges to wear on a sash, and it is considered bad form to brag about pay raises. There are no honorary degrees, and the corporation offers no endowed chairs for distinguished performers and no tenure. Promotion brings a brief flurry of congratulatory notes and a squib in the local newspaper, but this is a paltry show compared to the ceremony of a naval change-of-command.

There is a man in our town who for a time had "Admiral" painted in front of his name on his mailbox. Who has ever seen a business executive put "Vice President" on his postbox? The notion sounds silly, but it is not far from a practice followed in some parts of Europe. An uncle of mine in Copenhagen has a sterling silver plaque on his front door. It is engraved "Jurgen Pedersen, Civil Engineer" (meaning not military) and it is polished daily, for in Denmark there is public honor in a title for the head of the house even if, as we would say in America, he is only a businessman. Perhaps the Danes have the right idea. American business may have gone too far in letting cash be its own anonymous reward.

Unwritten Commandments

There is a further and more serious issue to consider. It is often claimed that corporations intrude too much in the lives of employees, restricting their freedom of action and expression, and requiring a narrow conformity of them and their families.

In matters small and great, large companies are said to require obedience to unwritten commandments. The individual is not to indulge in controversial activities, especially political. "Public service" is permitted, even encouraged, but there is a problem of definition. One man's "public service" is another man's "partisan meddling." This is implicitly resolved by assuming that work on behalf of management's political party will be regarded as public service, while activities on behalf of the opposition will be scrutinized a bit more carefully.

The employee is expected to live among his peers and not aspire to a home in quarters of the town reserved for higher levels on the organization chart.

He is to drive a car suited to his rank, dress in a conservative manner, and of course do nothing so offensive or unusual as to grow a beard.

Reward and punishment, we are warned, will not be meted out openly. Corporate justice is more subtle. Compliance is marked by a gradual climb up the promotion ladder, with the final realization, after a suitable period of apprenticeship, that a man has made it; he is "in." Noncompliance is not discussed; that would be gauche. It is just that somewhere along the line, the edge of hope is blunted. Management loses confidence. People suspect that the unconformed employee does not "think right." The nonconformist is "out" and, by the usual magic of the grapevine, everyone else knows it before he does.

Despite the comic overtones, the allegation is dead serious. In a society whose cornerstone is the individuality of the individual, there would be grounds for swift action if organizations were to diminish the employee's right of privacy and freedom of choice. Not only prospective employees but the rest of society as well have a right to ask if corporations do intrude unfairly and in contravention of deep-rooted principles. Will the charge hold?

Let it be conceded immediately that in some instances it will. The least exposure to the corporate interior provides confirming case histories, involving invasions of personal rights too blatant to be explained away. There are employees who have lost their jobs because they opposed as private citizens an important customer's pet project, or because, again in a private role, they spoke out too fervently against industrial pollution. In some cities business leaders have constituted themselves into "The Establishment," and gone far to block dissent by employees or by other businessmen whose fortunes are tied to the leadership. But the broader and deeper the examination of this problem, the less simple and clear-cut the issue. The problems that are most general and serious only occasionally fit the familiar charge. If conflicts remain, it is often because there are no easy answers. Moreover, in the light of bitter past experience, most corporations have become uncommonly sensitive to problems of human relations. Efforts to treat the employee justly, on and off the job, are extensive and deliberate, and sincere if not always well executed. The point can be argued, but in some respects business leaders are better attuned to their responsibilities toward the individual than are some leaders of other types of organizations. As an example, one of my university friends, a scholar of the classics, discovered that the department she had headed for years was being abolished, and its functions assigned elsewhere. She gained the knowledge by reading a routine mimeographed faculty bulletin, and had neither been consulted nor privately notified. If a large corporation treated its wage-roll employees with such disregard for personal feelings, it would be inundated in grievances, and possibly face a charge of unfair labor practice. If this happened to salaried employees, it would stand as an open invitation to white-collar unionization.

With reference to the employee's life away from the job, the manager's first instinct is to follow a hands-off policy. Why should he care where an employee lives or what kind of car he drives? As far as the corporate purpose is concerned, such matters are irrelevant. To set up a rule requiring country club membership, or to consider in a promotion rating the "acceptability" of an employee's wife, only makes the manager's job more difficult. It is hard enough to find and train able people without injecting extraneous variables into the process. Why look for trouble?

Granted, employees themselves testify to corporate intrusions, and point out areas of corporate power subject to abuse. Pre-employment psychological tests can too easily be used as a screen against candidates who are opposed to church-going, or who fraternized too much on campus with unwashed folk singers. Get-out-the-vote campaigns can too easily be warped into management coercion to support candidates who "think right." Granting that such things happen, it is difficult to nail down specific cases, and my own attempts to document such intrusions suggest that the problem is exaggerated. As an example, one story recently contended that employees of an eastern railroad had received letters from their president telling them how to vote in a national election. Checking back, it appears that such a letter was mailed—during one of the Roosevelt campaigns in the Thirties.

Other "certified" cases have turned out to be episodes not of history but of the imagination. The rule about cars is a case in point. The hostess at one cocktail party informed me that she and her husband drove a Buick because that was the price range of transportation his position merited. She defended her point by pairing guests with the cars outside. The proof was there. Cars followed the organization chart from Corvair through Chrysler with a side excursion into foreign sports machinery (research man—beard also permissible).

Some days later I had a chance conversation with the man who directs this whole segment of the company (not invited to the party; rank too high). He did not know what kind of car this lady and her husband owned, and he thought it strange that anyone would ask. As for himself, at that time he drove a second-hand Plymouth nearing exhaustion. It would be unkind to point this out to the lady, for to conform to the system, she would have to send her husband off to work on a go-cart.

The crowning bit of data is supplied by a former president of the Du Pont Company. A member of the founding family and a man of great wealth and dignity, he left car and chauffeur at home and pedaled to work on a bicycle, his briefcase perched precariously on the handlebars. An eccentric? Hardly. An exception? Yes. But it is worth noting, considering the ground rules that are supposed to prevail, that the bicycle shops in the city of Wilmington gained nothing from his example. To this day they are singularly unaffluent shops. It is also worth noting, considering the prevalence of exceptions, that self-justifying prophecies are as possible to the corporate society as to any other. In this case, rules are being talked into existence at cocktail parties. This is a commentary on cocktail parties, not on corporations.

The lady in the Buick is not alone in inferring cause from coincidence. As in any large organization, people are prone to manufacture explanations to suit preconceptions. Thus the world hears of a battery of rules controlling housing, civic participation, and other decisions that belong to private domain—rules that would surprise the executives who supposedly concocted them. Rather than perpetuate the mythology of corporate life, it would be genuinely helpful—and vastly interesting—for sociologists and psychol-

ogists to explore the process by which these alleged rules
are born and nurtured.

The Private Domain

What of the rules that are not self-manufactured? Where
does the corporate jurisdiction end and the private domain
begin? To put it in the particular, what happens when an
employee indulges in political affairs that may affect the
company? Suppose he catches gambling fever and squan-
ders money his employer knows he cannot afford to lose?
What about the incipient alcoholic, or the employee who
turns up as the hypotenuse of a marital triangle? Can or
should the corporation intrude?

It is simple to say "No," even carrying the argument to
the point where the company should refuse to protect a
man against himself. As the cynical saying has it, "Every
man has the right to seek damnation in his own way."

But the glib answer will not do. Even in companies
which profess this as their policy, practice clouds the
denial. Alcoholism, to take that instance, is more than an
individual tragedy. Other people are involved, the wife
and children and fellow workers, and the "right" of an individual to be left to his private hell is debatable. By that
ethic, the insane should be left to batter their heads against
prison walls.

Loyalties and friendships built up over years of association at work cannot be tossed aside on the ground that
"it's company policy." Should the boss turn his back on
the ground that his corporate duty so requires, or does the
doctrine of brother's keeper inject itself? Anyone who thinks
this is a simple question is advised to spend a week with
the medical division of a large corporation. It is there that
the problem of the alcoholic worker comes to rest. There
too will be found the man's boss, soliciting counsel for his
own course of action, often almost as anguished and dis-
traught as the man whose job and perhaps life are at stake.

(As a personal by-note, one of my colleagues in the

newspaper world was an alcoholic. He kept his bottles in
the back of the water closet, and he missed enough dead-
lines to get a dozen men fired. The rest of us covered his
beat. To my knowledge, he was twice sent away for pro-
tracted periods of medical care, and I am told there were
other instances of this happening. His employer, the Gan-
nett newspaper chain, picked up the bill.)

Consider a less emotional example. Many corporate employees hold positions in government on a "released time"
basis. It would be a minor miracle if there were no conflicts
of interest. Suppose one arises. Can a man split his loyalties
like his office hours? Putting what he regards as public
duty first, he may have to recommend legislative action opposed by the corporation. This may satisfy his conscience,
but must the corporation suffer his action in silence?
Company management, after all, is obliged by law to act on
behalf of its stockholders. Who signs the waiver allowing
executives to ignore that duty? Yet corporate action invites
the charge that big brother has imposed a gag rule. This
is a classic case of a man trying to serve two masters.
With the best of good will and a maximum of objectivity,
all parties may stumble reaching for a compromise.

To depart for a moment from the case at hand, there is
an underlying dilemma here which, taken in broadest
terms, confronts any individual in any organization. To
what extent must the individual, as part of his compact
with the group, surrender personal volition? To what extent, approaching it from the other side, can he declare
himself free?

The question is usually put with reference to government, but it applies to the relationship between the individual and any sort of institution, be it spiritual or secular,
civic or economic. The search for a resolution has proved
difficult in the extreme. The pre-Socratics, Plato, and Aristotle were aware of the question, and counseled in varying degrees a dedication to higher—but not always well-
defined—ideals. Christ saw the nuances of the issue.
Theologians from Augustine through Aquinas, through the
Reformation and into our own times, have been acutely

sensitive to it, and have proposed all shades of balance among man, church, and temporal authority. Political theorists such as Locke, Mill, Montesquieu, and Jefferson groped for a solution that would make government possible, yet allow man to breathe free.

Looking at the world from one pole, one can argue that the group attains its fullest expression only if the individual gives totally of himself. This is but a step from absolutism. At the opposite extreme lies the refusal to surrender any shred of individuality to the group. Here is ultimate anarchy. In between is the great gray flannel of compromise, from which each generation strives to tailor its own ethic in the light of prevailing realities.

In reference to the corporation, the task of decision actually is less difficult than in other segments of life. A man cannot renege on his compact with society. He must abide by the law or exile himself from society altogether. With regard to economic institutions, he retains far broader personal option. No corporate majority can demand his obedience or continued participation. He can leave a company without resigning his citizenship or sacrificing his rights in the community.

This has a take-it-or-leave-it sound, but the bargain is not that one-sided. Equity demands that the interests of the group as well as the individual be considered. Rooting for the underdog, society expects the large corporation to behave with restraint and decency in its dealings with the individual. It is a reasonable demand, but no less should be required of the individual. He may do as he wishes, answering to society and his conscience, but he cannot always expect a corporation (or a university, government bureau, or church) to subsidize him while he does.

Decisions about one's personal life which clearly have no effect on the corporation—leisure activities, choice of friends, personal morality, and so forth—are none of the corporation's business.

Decisions which have an effect on the institution—as for example one's involvement in the governmental arena—

again rest with the individual but imply an obligation to the organization. If conscience and conviction place the individual in opposition to the group in which he works, he must make a choice of master. To deny this is to pursue an impossible tack in logic, for this would say, in effect, that men in groups have no rights versus men as individuals.

In day-to-day practice head-on collisions are uncommon. No doubt this sometimes means employees have been frightened into submission, but more often it signifies that large numbers of people acknowledge a moral contract with the organization, and find the terms are reasonable.

Corporate transgressions draw quick attack and wide notice; the bully is always the least popular boy in the block. A great deal less is heard about cases in which corporations scrupulously honor their side of the bargain, asking neither praise nor attention. To redress the balance slightly, and to suggest a further observation, several cases are in order.

Not long ago the administration of a university notified faculty and staff not to become embroiled in a particularly inflammatory local political squabble. To their credit, the faculty exploded. Meanwhile in the same community, while storms raged on campus, the town elected its new mayor. The campaign was partisan in the extreme, and one of the candidates was a Du Pont engineer. There was no hint of corporate displeasure, for there was no displeasure. As of this writing, this man is again running for political office.

Also living in that town is another Du Pont employee who had served two terms in the state legislature. He too suffered no reprimand for his partisan moonlighting, though on a number of occasions the legislature voted on bills that directly affected his employer. Du Pont has learned to take this in stride. At one plant in Kentucky three employees were serving in the state legislature at the same time; overall and by actual count, nearly one thousand employees hold elective or appointive posts in government. It would be interesting to know what the figure is in other big companies, but as far as I can determine no other large corporation has released a nose count of this sort.

In another instance, one that drew national attention, a company sought to build an oil refinery on Biscayne Bay in Florida, and met staunch opposition from civic groups, conservationists, and other local citizens. Among those most vocally opposed were an employee of Pan American World Airways, a man named Lloyd Miller, and some of the faculty of the University of Miami. An effort was made to censor the academicians; the university ordered that public utterances be cleared through its information offices. The airline received a number of calls protesting Miller's stand, but refused to fire him or to ask him to stop campaigning against the refinery. Pan Am asked only that he make it clear, in his pronouncements, that he spoke as a private citizen and not for the company. Pan Am's position was compounded by the fact that one of Miller's objectives was to win passage for an antipollution ordinance that might have affected refueling procedures for Pan Am and other carriers at the Miami airport. Yet the airline stuck to its decision.[4]

Corporations are not always so circumspect, and universities, all would pray, are not so busy preaching free speech that they have forgotten how to honor it. (In justice to the University of Miami, be it noted that a new president, taking office in the midst of this fight, promptly rescinded the censorship order.) The examples are meant only to show how difficult it is to generalize, and to suggest that the functions of an organization, whether they be commercial or otherwise, give it no corner on objectivity.

The Climate Inside

So far attention has focused on the individual's activities outside the organization. What happens to him inside? Are there adequate incentives for him? Is his contribution acknowledged? What sacrifices are demanded of him on his job?

Ironically, there is still an air of mystery and doubt shrouding the relationship of the corporation to the people in its plants and offices. It is ironic because the corporation has tried hard to explain its actions to various audiences. Perhaps it has tried too hard.

Sensitive to the criticism that business is inhumane, executives have made an extra effort to demonstrate their concern for the individual. Their programs have been more successful than their propaganda. The effort to humanize the corporation often appears to the public to be strained and synthetic. Trying to project a good image, as they say in the trade, corporations often manage to transmit only a note of insincerity. Platitudes have been bandied about at such length that all statements of good intention have a superficial sound, as though they were being recited by rote. "Morale," going back to that imprecise word, begins to look like a fetish. There is so much talk about "getting along with people" that one begins to wonder whether all that cordiality can be genuine. There is the suspicion, in sum, that it is all a façade, that once the public's back is turned, the mask will come off, the smile will vanish from management's face, and there will stand Mack the Knife.

Corporations need better propaganda. With the verbiage set aside, their objective is an uncomplicated one, and makes good sense. Neither the organization nor the individual cares very much whether the corporate climate abounds with good cheer or is merely marked by polite acquaintance. There is no need to build a relationship on a hyperthyroid basis. What does count—and this has been said before but it is worth repeating, for it is nearly the whole of the matter—is for the individual to feel that he makes a useful contribution in a worthwhile institution, that he is treated as a distinct person, with dignity and honor, and that his efforts and abilities are recognized. The corporation that can establish such a climate need make no apologies for its personnel relations. For those failing to create it, apologies are probably futile. They are in trouble, deeper trouble than they know, and such surface harmony as exists only obscures people's true feelings.

A delightful illustration of this comes in a story told by Chris Argyris, a Yale professor who has done extensive research and writing in the field of human relations in business. In a company he was studying—charitably, he refuses to name it—one senior manager spoke with particular pride of the healthy internal climate. Pay scales were liberal. Fringe benefits were generous. Personal relations were cordial; there were no "troublemakers" around. (That alone should have been a warning sign.)

At Dr. Argyris's urging, one group of plant workers was singled out as a model for study. The team was exemplary, hard-working, and loyal to supervision. Argyris spent several days with these men, talked at length with each one individually, and finally convinced them he was not a time-study man in disguise. He was then taken into their confidence, and shown something no eyes outside the group had ever seen. It was a large, silver loving cup, purchased by the men at great expense, kept behind lock and key in the washroom, and engraved with the names of several employees. This was the Goldbrick Trophy, given periodically to the man in the group who did the least work without getting caught.

What was wrong? The managers were not evil. They wanted to do the right thing. As Dr. Argyris analyzes it, their efforts related only to the material aspects of work. They thought solely in terms of pay and benefits. Beyond small talk, there was no communication and no rapport.[5]

Management was trying to run a "happy ship" but never thought to tell anyone where it was going. The men saw no purpose in their jobs, no reason why they or anyone else should do what they were being paid to do. Lacking any sense of personal involvement in the products or plant or company, the men played games to drive off boredom. Their genial manner toward management was not faked. The men liked their supervisors. Out of kindness as much as anything else, the employees had never expressed their true feelings about their work.

"The boss wouldn't understand," one said. "We would only hurt his feelings." Given the circumstances they were probably right.

In its negative way, this case has a world of meaning to those concerned with the relationship of the individual and the organization. This is an all too common instance of an all too human failing: managers were applying their own scale of values to other people. Employees were expected to respond to a fixed and rather formalized set of material incentives, when in fact there were deeper needs left unfilled.

Decent physical conditions and reasonable pay scales are obviously important to the individual, but these are not sufficient or always primary, and they offer a poor measure of what the working conditions are really like. Plants with the broadest lawns and best kept flower beds are not necessarily those with the proudest history of labor-management accord, as is indicated by some of the strikes that have hit modern plants in the aerospace and electrical equipment industries. Nor are antique facilities automatically seedbeds of dissension. An impressive record of long-term productivity and excellence in labor relations is held by an aged chemical works in one of the unloveliest sections of Newark, New Jersey. People get dirty working there. There are no acres of greensward, only old city buildings and sidewalks stained with the years' accumulation of grime. The product requires considerable manual attention, and is of such a nature that it cannot economically be made with pristine tools of the type companies display so proudly in their annual reports. The product is made a batch at a time, by men who work up a sweat. Yet here is a plant that is consistently productive, and one that has had no serious labor dispute in more than thirty years.

The explanation lies in the attitude of the people. Somehow, a sense of dignity and mutual respect has been infused into the relationship between boss and subordinate, not through a contrived system or "nice guy" approach, but through day-by-day consideration of employees as individuals. The managers have been open- and fair-minded men; subordinates have known that, whatever happened in the plant, whoever might come through the door tomorrow as a new plant manager, they would be judged and treated as individuals, not as numbers on a payroll check.

One of those plant managers is a man named Gary Cantwell. Now retired, he visited his company's home office recently to ask for information about an employee who had worked for him many years before.

He explained, "A long time ago an opportunity came up for this fellow, and I asked that he be left where he was. He was good, and I had nobody to replace him. Maybe I did the wrong thing, because when he did move on, his new assignment worked out badly. I was hoping that somebody else, coming after me, had given him a better deal." A manager that concerned about people, and that sensitive to his own fallibility, does not have to worry about green lawns and chrome-plated washrooms. The P.S. of this story is that someone else had stepped in—in fact, a half dozen supervisory people were familiar with the situation. The employee had long since been moved to another post at a higher rank.

How do corporations invest a manager with that sense of caring? The answer of course is that they don't. This is a mirror of the man himself, and of a personality trait imbued long before he joined the corporate ranks. Companies cannot expect to transform a thing-centered man into a people-centered one, no matter how much they spend on management development courses. They can only try to identify men like Gary Cantwell when they appear, to reinforce their strengths, and to utilize their talents in management.

If this facet of organizational life is poorly understood outside the corporation, it is just as badly understood inside. For unexplained reasons there is the feeling that relationships among individuals, when put into the atmosphere of work, no longer follow the principles that apply elsewhere. It is presumed that the usual guides to human conduct require special amendment for use in the corporation.

This remarkable hypothesis stands wholly unsupported,

yet it is taken for granted in many quarters. It rose to the surface, for example, in a survey conducted among industrial engineers. When asked where they felt their background was weak, and where their employer might offer formal aid, an astonishing number reported themselves untrained and deficient in human relations. They wanted to take a course to fill the gap.

Presumably, after years of "relating" to schoolteachers, grocery clerks, and golfing partners, they had worked out some sort of approach to other humans, but apparently they did not think this could be transposed into the corporate milieu. Instead, they wanted to brush up on human relations as they would on calculus.

No classroom syllabus would be likely to help. What new rules would the Professor of Interpersonal Relationships convey to them? What principles of conduct might he recommend for their use in the corporate office and laboratory, except those learned in childhood, and long since applied in everyday life? What is accomplished, in short, by injecting extra complications into the relationship between individuals and organizations?

The Matter of Incentives

There are problems enough in that relationship as it is. If people in large organizations are to feel that they make useful contributions, and that the gains to them outweigh the sacrifices, there must be visible opportunity and measurable reward. As François Mauriac has said, "One cannot preserve one's faith in himself all alone. We must have witness to our prowess: somebody who notes the hits, who counts the points, who crowns us on the day of rewards."[6]

In other words: incentives. This boils down to a question of yardsticks, and that, in turn, unleashes what may be the most tortuous and important question corporations have to deal with today: How do you get people to give of their best?

Once upon a time there was a simple answer: pay them.

Money equaled incentive, and corporate employers had more of it to dispense than anyone else. Financial reward never had the power to spur all men to action, but it spurred most of the ones industry wanted to attract, and industry cared little about the rest.

That has changed. Money has lost some of its magic as an incentive. Industry's manpower needs are diverse, and it must hold the interest of individuals to whom cash traditionally has not been the highest form of compensation. The search for alternative incentives is underway, but it started late and is proceeding slowly. However one may protest the crassness of materialism, money has one virtue that is hard to match. It is transferable. It can be used to suit the fancy of the recipient, and thus to cover manifold needs. Man's acquisitive urge may not be his noblest characteristic, but it obviously is one of his most general ones and, in the industrial and economic climate of the nineteenth and early twentieth centuries, it happened to be in very great demand.

No doubt it still is, but as they say of crime, it doesn't pay like it used to. There is not the same gnawing compulsion about getting and spending that there was when our whole economy bordered on subsistence. There are still people who are poor and thus desperate, but the vast majority of those who have made it into the middle class take it for granted that they will eat decently and find adequate shelter. Their financial ambitions center on discretionary income, the money they can spend any way they want. They will cheerfully accept a raise, but as an incentive in their lives money has lost some of its drawing power.

For those at higher income levels, there is a second fact of life to be faced. As wealthier Americans point out ruefully, money is the only form of compensation subject to reduction via taxation, and at progressive rates. To offer an invidious comparison, the Nobelist is not invited to tear his certificate along the dotted line and remit one-half the honor to the Internal Revenue Service. The four-striper is

not asked as he attains his captaincy to snip off one stripe
to decorate the uniform of an ensign.

Let this be no plea for the relief of men hard hit by the
graduated income tax. They have found other ways of
getting and keeping money, and less wealthy citizens
would be delighted to swap problems with them. The
comment here pertains only to the diminution of money
as an incentive. The bottom rung on the corporate salary
ladder is set by conditions in the recruiting market. There
are many steps from there up, and for a company to establish a sharp financial rise at each one, allowing for the
tax take along the way, the top salaries wind up in the
stratosphere. Even there, with compensation for many
corporate presidents quoted in hundreds of thousands of
dollars per year, men do not breathe as lustily as they once
did; the Sixteenth Amendment thins the air. (Let it be
noted, in passing, that middle- and top-level executives,
drawing most of their compensation from salary and tax-
able bonuses, pay tax at a far higher rate than still wealthier
citizens enjoying capital-gains privileges. As any tax accountant will counsel, the real route to riches in America
today is not through the executive ranks, but through
capital gains and investment in taxfree bonds. Though
there is no discernible shortage of men yearning for promotion, executives too are asking what else the corporation has to offer.)

Perhaps most important, the mood of the times has
changed and corporations are changing with it, though
they have been a bit slow in doing so. Peter Drucker, a
thoughtful observer of men in the business world, has
said that the classic weakness of the industrial corporation and market society was an inability to see that people
need individual status and function, measured in terms
beyond economic reward.[7] His comment is valid, and is
especially to be noted because he made it in a book published more than twenty years ago. Then and before, the
cumulative evidence indicated that corporations would
have to be more attentive to subjective, intangible incentives, and offer employees on all levels a sense of personal

participation in the direction of their work. Companies which took the message to heart, or were already intuitively operating on this basis, found it a profitable route to follow.

The literature of industrial sociology provides abundant corroboration. A notable example, related elsewhere by Drucker,[8] deals with a production crew being trained to make carbines. After becoming familiar with the production tools, they were encouraged to fire sample weapons, and to examine all the parts to see how they worked. They were shown weapons with off-quality parts, to see for themselves how small an error would make the carbine inoperable. Then each man, with an instructor at his side, worked out a production program for the parts he was to make, deciding on the sequence and rhythm of the work, and setting a goal for himself. Invariably, the workers set goals for themselves that were higher than the job-planners would have considered normal. Then, on a production basis, many of the workmen exceeded their own target standards. In a more recent example, Texas Instruments asked a group of girls to offer their ideas for simplifying their own assembly-line methods. Within a few weeks the girls had cut unit assembly time from 138 to 57 hours. Such would seem to be conclusive evidence, particularly in view of the fact that so many similar case histories exist.

The father-knows-best approach is going the way of the drugstore Indian, but it dies hard. It embarrasses some people to discover that subordinates may have better ideas than Daddy, especially when the ideas are simple and could have been seen long before. No doubt, too, there is an element of the protective society at work here, keeping graduate engineers on assignments that could be handled as well or better by technicians. Be this as it may, companies seem to be abandoning the condescending attitude, and, with an eye on the shortage of trained technical people, are beginning to look anew at the talents that have long lain latent in their work forces. As noted earlier, the intelligence of the industrial employee, from the bench worker up through the lower rungs of supervision, is one of the most underused resources in the United States, but this potential is at last drawing the attention it deserves. Industrial managers see this as one of the most promising areas for company improvement, and have come to appreciate its value as an incentive.

As a related and corollary move, some companies have put all employees on a salaried basis, eliminating the blue-collar, wage-roll classification. This can hardly be called a trend as yet; a survey a few years ago by the National Industrial Conference Board turned up only fifteen companies that had made this move. But it is an idea worth exploring, for it eliminates the feeling of second-class citizenship that still attaches to jobs that pay by the hour. It could open better routes for an upward flow of ideas, and give all employees the feeling that they are full-fledged participants in a single, unified effort.

A dozen arguments can be mustered against this course. In seasonal industries, where it is difficult to plan year-round work, the proposition may not be feasible without major changes in product lines and markets. Seniority and union problems abound. But these are largely procedural rather than substantive arguments, and the attendant fears (higher costs, absenteeism, abuse of sick pay provisions) simply are not creditable in many companies. Except in companies where the air has been poisoned by years of labor-management discord, there is no reason to expect wage-roll employees to behave any differently than salaried workers in meeting their responsibilities. The all-salary idea has drawn support from no less a company than IBM, which has put its whole work force on this basis. In the light of experience there and elsewhere, the idea deserves a wider trial. While it is too early to render judgment, I would expect the strongest advantage of this approach to lie in the least measurable quadrant. If it contributes to the employee's sense of dignity and utility, long range it could pay back its costs with dividends for all.

A New View Enters

One change within corporations, only touched upon thus far, deserves more attention in this evaluation of incentives. This is the entry into business organizations of large numbers of technical men and, most significantly, scientists. To the modern industrial organization, such people are no longer luxuries but necessities and, as everybody knows, they are in relatively short supply, or at least the bright ones are. The organization thus must offer incentives attractive to them. This has produced quite profound changes in management thinking, generating some trends and acclerating others.

Whatever anyone says to the contrary, scientists and engineers are not "just like everybody else." They very decidedly are not content with the portfolio of incentives that sufficed for so many executives for so many decades —good pay, a chance for promotion to top posts, and pleasant suburban quarters close to a golf course. If some scientists and engineers want these, many others (notably the most gifted ones) want much more—concerts and museums and libraries and, above all, the company of other good minds. A number of their corporate compatriots, looking to the example of the research group, have decided that they, too, want much more.

The technical men, in effect, have really started something. They have brought a multi-track system of advancement into being; encouraged a sense of self-criticism within organizations that could use more of it; helped lift standards of perfectionism and professionalism in work; and, in some communities and companies, revived the conviction that towns and corporations have obligations to each other. (I exaggerate for emphasis. Surely these trends have not appeared solely because AT&T and International Harvester have suddenly "got religion," and are trying to make jobs in plant communities attractive to MIT graduates. Still, this fact is very much in the middle of the issue. Moreover, returning to a point raised in Chapter 7, the rise of the technical forces makes it necessary to acknowledge problems that in some corporations would otherwise remain buried—for example, the continuing impersonality and facelessness of some lower-level jobs. If broader incentives are required for scientists and engineers, might not these incentives be necessary elsewhere, including on the production line? That question has been pressing itself even on unperceptive managers.)

Promotion to administrative duty is no longer taken as the universal or best symbol of recognition. Many corporate employees still owe their deepest gratitude, to use Kipling's words, to the one "who showed me the way to promotion and pay." But alternatives are now proffered in greater measure. There is increased respect, measured in pay and title as well as in professional honors, for scientists or engineers who hold no supervisory authority, but who have chosen instead to continue their careers in research or development. As a companion development if not a consequence, more of the same type of respect is now being shown to highly able craftsmen and staff specialists who are also out of the promotion line.

There is more of an air of exploration within the corporation. The man of research takes it for granted that inevitably, and probably frequently, experiments will turn out wrong. Were he right in all his decisions in the laboratory, right in all the answers he expected in his tests, he would not be doing research. In a gathering of research men and women, question and dissent are to be expected. No one takes this amiss, for this is part of what it means to be a professional, part of the process of testing ideas and closing off blind alleys. The corporation, now that it harbors large numbers of such people, is acclimating itself to an environment of open comment, and is finding it stimulating as well as productive. The corporation is learning to tolerate and encourage self-criticism, and to learn from mistakes. One of the first remarks made to me the day I reported for work as a corporate hand was, "You'll hear about a lot of rights and wrongs around here, but the one right we'll try hardest to protect for you is your right to be wrong." It is more than coincidence that the corporation in question has for decades been deeply committed to science and engineering.

Another ramification of professionalism is the premium placed on time. Time has become an incentive. As universities have long known, the professional tends to give first loyalty to his discipline, and only secondarily "belongs" to the institution paying his way. What he wants most is recognition by his colleagues and opportunities to associate with them. This he can only gain with time—time to pursue his own professional interests, to be with his fellow practitioners at professional meetings, to prepare papers for publications, or merely to stare out the window and recharge the battery. Three-weeks-with-pay and a pension at sixty-five are not quite what he has in mind. He thinks in terms of sabbaticals, and of trips to technical meetings at Edinburgh and Montreal.

Corporations now think in those terms, too. They know full well that the competitors for professional talent, chiefly the academic world and the federal government, have lifted their salary scales. The money gap no longer favors the corporation as it once did. In some cases, after allowance for other benefits, academe pays better. Moreover, apart from the body-snatching aspects of the situation, corporations have found it good business to think about the technical man's plea. It does not pay to lock a scientist in a cubicle, or tuck a bright engineer in a corner of the patent files indefinitely. It naturally occurs to employers and employees that the same may apply outside of the technical realm, with a bright lawyer or accountant or market analyst. It does not pay to separate any good mind from its sources of stimulation. Change and new challenges are the essence of intellectual growth, and if management can provide them, the corporate interest is well served.

Sabbaticals, leaves of absence, flexibility in choosing and guiding projects, a more relaxed approach toward working hours, tuition refund plans for those who want to continue academic studies—these and a number of other incentives are being offered by corporations to employees, sometimes all at once and in the same corporation. As I read the road signs, all of these changes are largely attributable to the corporation's new dependence on the professional.

One would expect these trends to persist, and produce still more changes in the corporate interior in the future. To stay alive in an increasingly competitive, technological society, commercial organizations will have to attract and hold larger numbers of people who are bright and broad-gauge. More will be expected of these employees, in formal education before they join the work force; in the informal, lifelong business of keeping up to date, which is part of what it means to be a professional; and in their enthusiasm for contributing their maximum talent.

Such people in turn will expect more of their managers: Quid pro quo. If the corporation demands excellence of them, it must set no lesser standards for those who supervise their efforts, and be more courageous about removing managers who become roadblocks. If a company expects its employees to develop judgment and perspective, management must be prepared to invest them, at an age young enough to make a difference, with responsibilities that will build and season their judgment.

If companies expect high-potential employees to be enthusiastic about corporate careers, managers will have to dispense with more of the Parkinsonian syndromes. SOP and NIH are useful examples. Standard Operating Procedure is often a necessary constraint, but it can also be a refuge for the ventureless mind. "There's no reason for it; it's just company policy" is a standing gag in big companies; but the washroom humor becomes unfunny when the employee quit-rate starts climbing. SOP is as good a way as any to drive imaginative men to other employers.

NIH—Not Invented Here—remains an unspoken criterion for the rejection of novel and disruptive ideas. NIH is a particularly debilitating malady not because it is widespread, but because it is so hard to diagnose. No one ever admits this is his real reason for turning down a suggestion.

Eventually, the truth worms its way to the surface—after one company unit goes to the trouble of reinventing what another company division has already done.

The cost is counted in more than time and money. NIH corrodes the souls of creative men and women. They long for a rational world in which ideas rise or fall on their merits rather than their source. Such men and women are the "high mobiles" in the employment market, and many of them have souls that oxidize rather easily. They respond to NIH by moving to less corrosive environments.

Above all, corporations still have to learn to communicate. This may seem a curious comment in view of the attention companies already give to internal communications. But what is needed for the future goes further and deeper than any but a few of the communications programs yet in evidence in American business.

Business seems to do reasonably well in the narrow aspects of communications. The boss really means it when he says, "My door is always open." (This could be challenged, but let the generalization stand for the moment, as a way to move to the next point.) The trouble is that, even when this is said sincerely, the comment has a ring of pathos. Open doors are not enough, and the supervisor knows it. Employees want more than someone to talk to; they also want to know where they stand, what their prospects are, how the promotion and salary systems work, where the division and department and company are trying to go, and where the company fits against the needs and problems of the times. Is it doing useful things, or working on trivia? Does it act responsibly in the marketplace and society more broadly, or is it part of the problem? Is management responsive to the ideas of employees, or are decisions made in spite of those ideas?

Too often, the man with the open-door policy is a line supervisor who cannot answer. He lacks information, or permission to pass it on. He responds with generalizations, or withdraws to that reference to "company policy." Employees can do better than that on the grapevine.

What is needed is strong, informed, two-way man-to-man communications, overlaid by the voice and muscle of top management. The senior men in management must come forth with frank and specific comment about the company's goals and policies, its prospects and problems. ". . . warts and all." There is no other way. Management must take employees into its confidence, not to the degree that they tell everybody everything, and tip the company's hand to the competition, but at least to acknowledge what everybody in the company already knows, that things are not perfect. If middle management fails here, it is because top management has lost its nerve. Executives may believe that confession is good for the soul, but few of them act as though they believe it is good for the corporation.

It can be. Candor is a disarming weapon. It can channel discontent into sympathy and, given a management that is trying to right the wrongs, that sympathy can be turned into support. The supervisor down the line can say all the same things, but that is not the same as having the president say them. The senior executive puts the company on record, and the very fact that he is aware of problems far below his level, and is willing to talk about them, creates a rapport between City Hall and the precincts.

It also has occurred to many people, in and out of corporations, that conditions in the community play an important role in the corporate success. Again, the lesson has been brought home by the professional staff. Having spent a minimum of four years and often as many as ten years on college and university campuses, places which by and large have cultural and aesthetic appeal, newcomers to the corporate employ are hardly impressed by a drab industrial environment. Their reaction to an organization wholly unconcerned with aesthetics may be unspoken, but it is predictable. Nor is it hard to guess the reaction when they are assigned to a plant in a remote town of the Midwest or the South, a hamlet that may be long on scenery but devoid of a decent library and short on stimulating intellectual companionship. As young men raising families, they ask first about the quality of the school system, and only secondly about prevalence of golf courses. Educational and other community facilities, along with on-the-job conditions, are now decided factors in the thinking of companies competing for brainpower.

These personal feelings, as noted, may not find overt expression, but their silent presence cannot safely be ignored. Consider architecture. To people accustomed to ivy and Campus Gothic, the unrelieved functionalism of Brick Industrial may seem less than magnetic. Businessmen sensibly ask how much it costs to add an aesthetic quotient to new plants and laboratories, and when they hear the figure they may blanch. Might they not also ask how much it costs them not to build with a sense of style? The cost may be higher still, measured not in out-of-pocket dollars, but in terms of the bright young metallurgist who resigned after a brief stay, leaving because he found the work atmosphere depressing, or because his wife found the community intolerable. On an exit interview, he will tell you he left to take a better job.

Here too it is easy to exaggerate. As noted before, working conditions are not the be-all and end-all of a job. Moreover, some companies do very well in the department of art, architecture, and community consciousness. Businessmen have been among the leaders in numerous urban renewal projects—Pittsburgh, St. Louis, and Philadelphia are examples—and many companies have rejected otherwise ideal plant locations for the sole reason that the community resources were inferior; they knew full well that their key people would balk at living there. My only purpose in bringing up this point again is to stress that "little things" weigh heavily. If corporations are paying more attention to them, this is largely a reflection of need for highly able technical personnel. There is a direct carry-over to the rest of the work force. Deere and Company, Signode Corporation, and Container Corporation of America are among the companies which will bear witness to the fact that production and office workers, as well as denizens of the laboratory, respond with enthusiasm to tasteful, handsome surroundings.

Dealing with a mixed bag of personal drives and expectations, corporations now tend toward an ever broader band of incentive offerings. Whether the spectrum is as yet broad enough remains to be seen. The record is spotty from company to company, and if some have been remiss in liberalizing their thinking, others are wondering whether they have gone too far too fast. Even a relative short exposure to the idea of sabbaticals, for example, suggests that there are large numbers of people who want no part of it. If sabbaticals are made mandatory and used as a device for sharing the work, they can hardly be termed an incentive, and one would expect the net result to be more negative than positive.

There is an alternative. Corporations can move toward an incentive system in which the choices are made not by the employer but by the employee individually. Rather than impose a single parcel of pay and benefits on the entire corporate work force, it may be possible to show the employee multiple alternatives, and let him pick the ones that mean the most to him. At least one major corporation, Mobil, is now offering such options for part of its benefits package. Other companies are watching the experiment closely, for they are thinking of going this route themselves. The mechanical and administrative problems, which once seemed insuperable, have been eased by improvements in technology—computers can handle the bookkeeping—and the idea can now be tested on its merits.

If at this point corporations appear to be hesitant about what to try next, it is because they too are groping for answers in an area where the questions have changed rapidly and solutions are far from self-evident. Someone still has to mind the store. However a company may wish to honor employees' wishes, people cannot wander into work at odd hours of the morning, and attend only to such chores as happen to catch their fancy. Hours and benefits must display rhyme and reason, reflecting the realities of production schedules and mill costs, not forgetting that customers, suppliers, and stockholders also have a stake in the corporate output.

If there is to be a useful colloquy between individual and organization, each must be able to assume a degree of maturity and candor on the part of the other. On the corporate side, the offerings must mean something, and not merely be a new label on an old package. The phony title, which claims for a man a distinction that honesty does not allow him to claim for himself; the benefit an employee does not want or cannot use, and which he regards as no gain at all; the new job which is advertised to him as weighty and challenging, but which the employee knows to be within the range of an adolescent's skill—these are not incentives but façades.

As for the party of the second part, the individual in this contract, he too must operate on rational grounds. Managers are not mind readers, endowed with extrasensory receivers tuned to the wave length of unspoken ambitions. If the individual cannot air his wishes and grievances openly, if he insists upon protesting one condition when it is actually another that bothers him, there can be no productive communication. If some elements of his work are monotonous, he must be mature enough to realize that this is likely to be the case in any occupation. Ninety per cent of any job is routine. What makes a job worth doing is not freedom from monotony, but the feeling that an individual contribution is made, by a man working at or near the top of his talents.

Conceding that difficulties continue to complicate life in an organized society, granting that the corporation is the locus of as many of them as any other type of institution, it is worth our while to weigh the pros and cons of life in large organizations, and to reflect on the approach suggested by the learned professor mentioned at the beginning of this chapter. The problems of the individual in the organization are not so much corporate as societal, and in the effort to devise solutions, we can only ask that companies meet the employee half way.

THE CORPORATION IN SOCIETY

As an institution of service to society, the business corporation has in some ways succeeded not wisely but too well. Its feats of production and distribution, so remarkable by past standards, are today so familiar as to be taken for granted. It is as though the full dinner pail had forever been assured, and there were no trick at all to providing economic service to a society of more than 200 million people, mostly prosperous. Other yardsticks are requested, and when they are applied, the corporation is often ruled deficient, and sometimes claimed to be irrelevant or hostile to the American dream. Beyond the humdrum process of buying, selling, and making, business is held to have marginal or negative utility, if indeed the question of its contribution comes up at all.

This is a sorry state of affairs. To leave it at this suggests that big business units are at best necessary evils, tolerated by a nation grown so soft and fat that it lacks the will and energy to set matters right. At worst, the big corporations are presumed to be oligopolies of such power that opposition is futile. "I am the King," and in our time "I" is short for Incorporated. The Establishment: long may it reign.

Resting in the middle, half way between the extremes, is the charge that big business is a social anachronism. Its leaders are too preoccupied with profit, and too insular, to understand or respond with any sensitivity to the racial and urban crises that threaten to dismember the American social structure. Corporate spokesmen pay lip service to equality. They agree that cities have problems. But they do not put their money and muscle where their mouth is. If America is to follow its better nature, and build the truly open society of its dreams, the job will have to be done without much help from the business gentry living behind the gates of suburban estates.

Neither the corporation nor society can afford to proceed on this basis, or needs to. The objective of the contemporary business organization—the only objective it can legitimately expect a free society to honor—is to make a profit by performing useful functions effectively and responsibly. The key words there are "useful" and "responsibly." Both have social as well as economic loading, as increasing numbers of corporate executives are aware. Companies which operate within the confines set by society may prosper. Those which transcend the boundaries, or ignore the responsibilities which society reasonably assigns to them, will be brought to heel in courts of law, or be so stigmatized by public opinion that they will be unable to keep their people or their profits.

Corporations have plenty of faults, and some of them are duly noted here. But perfection is not the claim. The only claim made—the rationale for the large corporation as it exists today—is that it is the best instrument yet devised to permit men as individuals to render certain kinds of contributions to man in the plural. Those contributions are limited but important for, in addition to its productive prowess, the corporation is an important agent in the advancement of science, the predominant agent for the application of science, and a focal point for the generation of much of the wealth underwriting educational, cultural, and defense programs. A big company, in sum, is much more than an economic convenience for its stockholders. From the broader point of view, it can be an extraordinarily useful social device. It is an invention put to good use and, not at all tangentially, its activities are more securely under society's control today than ever before.

A great many people obviously do not look at it that way. Even the corporation's best friends sometimes damn it with the faintness of their praise. Aging defenders of the faith, struggling to their feet from the depths of their club chairs, mutter tired clichés about "people's capitalism" and "free enterprise," and the dangers of "creeping socialism." With friends like these, who needs enemies?

Enterprise is patently not free; as everyone can plainly see, it is circumscribed on all sides by legislation and social custom. By and large it is a good thing for business that this is so, for the business community as much as the public has benefited from social control. As one example, the principal of antitrust law, if not all of the interpretations courts place on it, favors men of commerce more directly than anyone else. Monopolies and cartels, after all, give advantage only to the scattered few who come out on top; for the rest of the business world, the prospective competitors and suppliers, monopoly spells reduced profits or extinction.

"People's capitalism"? This raises a point to which I will return a little later. At the moment, let it only be said that the words strain credulity. The 24 million people who are direct owners of corporate stock do not quite make a quorum. Does 10 or 12 per cent of the population add up to "people's capitalism"?

As for "creeping socialism," that discussion could consume a volume of its own. It is not worth it. The anguished protests and platitudes mostly miss the point. There are overriding reasons why government is so active in what businessmen used to regard as the sanctity of the private sector. One, noted before, is the overt abuses of some companies, and the anguished howls of their victims (which, for example, brought about the regulation of public utilities and led to our basic antitrust legislation, the Sherman Act of 1890 and the Clayton Act of 1914). A second reason has been the failure or inability of the private sector to undertake projects the public has held necessary (e.g., unemployment compensation and other compulsory social insurance programs, inaugurated at a time when private programs were all but nonexistent).

Let us not beat a dead horse. There are more timely

issues being brought to the forum, not by the old folk but by the young. In their own way, the youngsters manage to dodge the clichés and make the basic question clear: Where does big business fit in American society?

"Business is for the birds"

A spate of recent surveys, supplemented by interviews, with college students, corporate recruiters, and university staff members, suggest some intriguing answers. In making career choices, young graduates leaned to jobs in teaching, academic research, and public agencies. They said they wanted to serve mankind, not make money. I would be the last to protest their idealism. Rather, as a member of a generation roundly scorched for its supposed materialism, I would raise a bronze statue to the dedicated young, and give it residence on the Mall in Washington in permanent view of critics present and future. However, for this essay, it is important to note the view of the young toward commerce.

"Business," as one told *The Wall Street Journal,* "is for the birds."

Business is an intellectual Siberia; company men have no values beyond the superficial. A parroting of views familiar to the campus, perhaps; but another thought emerged by implication. Public service and private gain were discussed as mutually exclusive. Business versus service. To choose one is to deny the other. A Stanford graduate came closest to putting it in explicit terms. As he saw it, his classmates found in commerce a code appealing to the kind of man "whose first responsibility is not his fellow man but his company's profits."

Other spokesmen have been less polite. The student movement of the mid 1960s, which flashed to the world's attention with the Berkeley crisis in 1964, had adopted two years earlier a statement of guiding principles. In this credo, the Port Huron Statement of the Students for a Democratic Society, appear phrases reminiscent of the days of the Wobblies and Eugene V. Debs: ". . . the irresponsible power of military and business interests"; [a nation] "manipulated by economic and political opponents of change"; ". . . obvious oligopoly and other forms of minority rule defy real individual initiative or popular control."

One can dismiss these reactions if he wishes. There has long been an anti-business streak in rebellious youth—"Wild-eyed visionaries," their fathers say, "who never met a payroll"—and some of the radical spokesmen are wild-eyed indeed. Many of the reports from campuses make no pretense of offering a balanced cross-section. They have come from selected schools, and have been light on science majors, engineers, and business-school graduates. When those groups are included in the sampling, student animosity toward business appears less formidable, and the worst that can be said is that students are indifferent to corporate careers and do not wish to become involved. Moreover, the students who are particularly hostile to commerce may have had a dose of history strong on tales of corporate insularity, arrogance, and Babbittry. If so, corporations have no one to blame but themselves. In the past some of them presented a face only a stockholder could love, and professors have long memories.

One could dismiss the problem, then, but at a cost. Whether the rejection of commerce is torrid or tepid, it is expressed not by the least educated of the groups in society, but by the most educated. It is not a cry wrung from underprivileged masses yearning to be fed, nor is it merely the product of oratory by street-corner Marxists. It is instead a point of view found among sons and daughters of middle- and upper-income families. Among them are many of the brightest and most idealistic young people in the nation. (It is worth noting that the radical student movement of the sixties, like the radical labor movement of the thirties, has drawn some articulate and sharp-minded leaders, along with the great unwashed.) Quick-minded and otherwise, shaggy or well groomed, committed or merely opportunistic, these young people come from the quarter of the population which has been most exposed to the world of ideas and which, in all likelihood, will produce a disproportionate share of the political and social leaders of the future. What they think makes a difference, and even a moderation of their opinions, which may come with time, leaves but a grudging feeling of acceptance of a major social institution.

The condemnation of the corporation is by no means the exclusive property of student radicals. In a paper presented to a subcommittee of the U. S. Senate in May 1965, it is alleged that society defaults on its duty to steer technology toward the public interest, and instead "turns the job over to great monopolistic corporations." The problem, we are told, is to get control out of the hands of "irresponsible power-seekers," "private monopolists and militarists," so that the community can direct progress toward "life-promoting or humanistic ends," and "maintain an open, competitive society."

This is no echo of the students' manifesto, but the statement of a professor of economics at the University of Illinois. His dark interpretation of the American scene, far from being singular, is an entrenched conviction in various parts of the academic and intellectual community. Similar conclusions appear again and again in the literature of the humanities and social sciences, sometimes put less vitriolically but still leading to the conclusion: commerce *versus* service.

What is "versus" doing there? Surely there is a narrowness of vision as to what constitutes public service. On the basis of the words, which are all we have to judge by, any service of genuine merit directed to the public's interest ought to qualify. Thus, give praise to those who bind man's wounds and ease his pain. But is there to be no honor for those who manufacture and develop the medicine to save lives? People in big corporations do that sort of work.

To teach a child is a noble calling; I know of none higher. But is it no public service to clothe him against the elements, to help provide the food he will eat, to make a toy for his pleasure, or to print a book for him to read? Corporations do those jobs.

To train the high school dropout for useful work, to remove him from the street corner and the welfare rolls, is a major goal of numerous state and federal programs. Is there then less merit in similar programs sponsored by profit-making companies—many of which do this at their own expense, with skills developed through decades of vocational training?

We send food and medical aid abroad, to people threatened by starvation and pellagra and malaria. Yet the man who works at a corporate laboratory, developing soil nutrients and weed killers that may add 10 per cent to the grain yield of hungry countries—is that man's work to be scorned by virtue of its sponsorship? His labors may even be called ominous, for there are those who say that this chemical meddling with nature's delicate balance will be the death of us all. But "nature's balance" is maintained by survival of the fittest, with population control by starvation. Is this to be our ethic?

It is a fine thing to open a man's mind through the arts. Is it then contrary to the public interest to open the vistas of geography by providing equipment for transportation, or to expand the range of eye and voice through communications? These are missions at which corporations have proved highly adept. Communications, as a matter of fact, is the business of the biggest corporation in the world, AT&T.

But, it is protested, businessmen work for profit. So they do, and in varying measure so do professors of economics, doctors of internal medicine, and surrogate judges (often, with better-than-average yield; the income of doctors is among the highest of any occupational group in the nation, and the ante for top-ranked professors, as of this writing, has climbed over $30,000 per year in certain universities and disciplines).

There is a difference. To the man of commerce, profit constitutes the visible measure of organizational performance; to the professional man, the educator, the "public servant," financial gain is secondary and non-institutional. It is only a passport to a satisfactory living standard. To use this as the dividing line, though, leads to absurdity. It implies a two-class society with a neat separation of profit-seekers and public servants, and with all altruism resting in hearts uncorrupted by commerce. It also splits the population somewhat unevenly, inasmuch as a heavy majority of the labor force earns its keep in profit-bent organizations. Thinking of that comment by the young man from Stanford, are we seriously to believe that all those people, and especially the ones in positions of highest corporate authority, live in such a moral vacuum that they put company profits above any ethical commitment, and succumb to a raw materialism from which other (better) men are immune? We are drifting into nonsense.

Moreover, if we pursue this policy of apartheid to its logical conclusion, we encounter the impossible. Where are we to put all the institutions which display the not-for-profit banner, but which were founded and financed by people who stooped to the nasty business of buying and building and selling? Duke University, for instance, or Stanford. How about the Sloan-Kettering Institute, which is automotive money all the way, or Rockefeller Institute (now University), that splendid bioscientific by-product of black gold? What are we going to do with Harvard, founded to educate young men chiefly for the ministry, a private, not-for-profit institution but one whose endowment now totals more than one billion dollars? Where is the money? A large chunk of it is invested in the stocks of corporations which, Harvard prays, will earn profits and mail the dividends to Cambridge, Mass.

Plainly, the profit-nonprofit division gets us nowhere, except to prove in still another way that this is, indeed, an interdependent society. This perhaps is what the young generation finds most bothersome. As they say, it is all one big ball of wax—corporations, universities, government—rolled into an undifferentiated mass. The point they miss is that there is differentiation and, equally important, that there is a system of checks and balances among these institutions. There is interdependence, yes, but there is also plurality. In the current mixture, with the voices of educators, scientists, labor leaders, military men, government figures, civil rights leaders, and business executives all having an effect on public policies, the American society is probably more pluralistic, in the political sense, than it has been at any time in the past.

The Measure of Utility

How, then, do we distinguish and assess the particular contribution of the private corporation? What is its "social utility"? The phrase has a nice ring to it, bespeaking dedication to timeless and honored goals, but unfortunately it is another of those phrases utterly lacking in precision. It means, as Lewis Carroll put the point, just exactly what one wants it to mean; no more, no less. Very well, let us try to construct our own framework for definition.

If the large corporation is to be adjudged useful, it must meet several stringent qualifications. By its own admission it exists to make and do things. As a first qualification, then, it ought to make and do them acceptably well. If its products and services cannot meet minimum standards, the institution scores zero on the "utility" scale.

Further, to conform to the Western world's interpretation of freedom, the public must be offered choices in economic as well as political affairs—genuine choices, not Hobson's variety. The market must offer alternatives, more than one of which is capable of filling a buyer's needs. Otherwise, no matter how many producers there are, the economy is not open but shut, and not competitive in any real sense. Plurality of economic choice, then, must be a qualification.

Accountability is also to be measured. Who holds the reins? This too is fundamental. Corporations could make useful products in abundance and variety, with appealing efficiency and, at the moment, a proper regard for the niceties of behavior. However, each of these arguments—

efficiency, the promise of prosperity—can and has been used to rationalize the rise of monopolies and cartels. Once the public lets go of economic authority, it is only a matter of time until people become the victims instead of the beneficiaries of their economic system. Who is in charge here?

Fourth, as a way of restating the other three qualifications, the net contribution of the corporation must be positive. With all side spurs and tangents counted in, the resultant vector must be in a direction the majority of the public wants to go. Otherwise, we are in a wagon with the horses pulling crooked.

More qualifications could be added, but these will serve. They put "social utility" into terms that can be discussed, and provide room for specific questions. Think of the trinkets and trivia peddled today. Sample one week's worth of prime-time network television programming. Is this what one calls meeting a standard of public acceptability? How pluralistic is an economy in which a few corporations loom so much larger than the rest? Do the big ones call the shots for the millions of smaller companies and their customers? How much actual choice does a consumer have, with the minions of advertising working to the corporate account, molding his psyche from infancy to old age? To what extent are corporations accountable when some of them are large enough to finance their own growth with retained earnings, and their ownership is so dispersed that few stockholders can make an impression on corporate decisions? Net and overall, is the profit motive the best we can do, or would we be better served by an ideology more inclined to "things that really count"?

Who Says What Counts?

Let us first clean up, or at least rough up, the usual terminology. The profit system is a device, not an ideology. Because it has made many men rich and some companies large, it finds partisans to defend its goodness. Because some men have used it greedily or criminally, it draws charges of immorality. Yet the profit motive lacks an inherent moral connotation. It is ethically neuter.

The profit motive serves as an incentive to the most cynical and grasping of men, and to the most humane and generous. It has found use in republics, monarchies, and socialistic states. In recent years, it has been invoked in parts of the Soviet economy as a spur to greater output, apparently on the theory that the capitalists, for all their imputed decadence, may have stumbled across one or two thoughts worth borrowing.

The profit motive probably will not serve the Russians very well, for it is doubtful that Soviet planners are willing to make a necessary sacrifice, and give up their own authority in the marketplace. Walter Lippmann, in *The Good Society*, laid out the prerequisites.[1] The kind of economy that flourishes in modern times, he said, requires a government operating through an orderly process of law, rather than by arbitrary fiat. The consumer's freedom of choice is essential, and cannot be supplanted by the decrees of planners. As Lippmann shrewdly cautioned, the more elaborate the economic structure, the more vital the element of free consumer choice; complex societies are less susceptible than simple ones to the wise ministrations of central planners. The Russian economy is elaborate and growing more so, and planners there have had ample opportunity to study Lippmann's thesis: *The Good Society* was published in 1937. Whether they will heed his words is another matter.

Whatever the outcome there, in more open and competitive economies such as our own, the profit motive has proved marvelously appropriate as a traffic control center. It functions with dispatch and flexibility, steering commercial organizations into some ventures and away from others, dispensing goods and services rapidly, favoring those agile enough to adapt to changing market demands, penalizing those too stubborn or too slow to change with the times.

It is not always kind and it is rarely forgiving. Countless mom-and-pop food stores have failed because they were in the wrong place at the wrong time. A freeway cut them off, or A&P moved in next door. Other companies large as well as small have slipped from view because they wanted to sell buggy whips to a world that roared off behind a V-8 engine. But to the consumer, who is supposed to be the beneficiary of all this commercial scrambling, the profit motive has shown that it can turn the resources of a nation to his needs, his moods, and even his whims. If this is not one of the "things that really count," our protestations about popular rule are badly awry.

I think it was Plato who first pointed out that democracy is the worst possible way to run things, unless one considers the other ways. This applies as much to economics as to politics. Were the world led by truly wise and perfect men and populated only by selfless citizens, we could dispense with profit and the whole market system surrounding it, and consign all authority to the sages. There would be no question about what to produce or how much to charge or what standards of taste and quality to follow. Solon of the Marketplace would decide and at a stroke sweep away the trivial and the useless and the inartistic.

There are candidates for the job. All manner of men, some no doubt driven by selfless and sincere motives, are prepared to change the existing system, either by crowning themselves Lord High Arbiters of the Marketplace, or by selecting others to perform the same function as agents of the national government. I applaud their intentions but deplore their means. Even if the care of the commissar should prove tender and loving, his decisions may not be any wiser or farsighted than yours or mine. All things equal, and in keeping with Mr. Lippmann's counsel, we do well to let the public make its own decisions with as few intermediaries and as little censorship as possible.

This is hardly an original argument. Plato, be it noted, was careful to place his philosopher-kings in the mythical Republic. He did not confuse them with the actual rulers of Athens (of whose decisions he frequently disapproved). After twenty-five centuries of waiting for a utopia to materialize, with numerous and tragic experiments with non-popular rule, we can safely accept Plato's conclusion. The alternative to *vox populi* is the surrender of power to rulers equally as fallible as their subjects.

Inasmuch as *populi*, in America, speak with many separate voices, it is certain that no standard of taste and utility will prevail unchallenged. Unavoidably, the bazaars of commerce will offer the gaudy with the graceful, the shabby with the superior. There will be gimcrackery as long as one man can be found who will make it, and a second who will buy it. Cast-iron burros and ceramic flamingos will desecrate lawn and garden. Some houses will be "ticky-tacky" and some will be shamefully ostentatious. Custom cars will bleat through chrome tailpipes. Cosmetological marvels will do wonders for aging faces. Soap opera and "Grand Old Opry" will go on doing wonders to our minds. The Boob Tube will talk to boobs and anyone else who will listen.

Those reared to quieter and more refined tastes find this appalling. Often it is appalling. Therefore, people who care about the public weal should redouble their efforts to elevate our tastes and level of learning. More power to them. This is what critics and teachers are for. It is vital, though, that they persuade and not compel, teach and not indoctrinate. For the principle at stake here is far more important than the problem. The frivolous indulgences, the toys and tiger tails, are harmless departures representing a tiny portion of the national economic effort. It is overzealous to amputate an arm to cure a hangnail.

Then, too, the keepers of the cultural grail, though rarely in doubt, have in the past occasionally proved to be in error. Country music, folk songs, and early jazz once drew disapproving glances in all the best circles, only to draw applause later as "native art forms." Laurel and Hardy movies, having debased the tastes of one generation, have been revived by the next for presentation in palaces of culture, with people of impressive artistic credentials offering learned praise. It is only a matter of time until some roadside purveyor of concrete donkeys is discovered to be the Grandma Moses of the sculpture circuit. In a country that in a few decades went from Cubism and Art Nouveau to Op Art and Happenings, and then revived Tiffany's gaudy lampshades, whom would we appoint to draft the equivalent of a Pure Food and Drug Law for the mind? Who is to separate Camp from what counts?

The Forces of Restraint

Is there to be no restraint at all, then? Of course there is. It already exists in the form of laws and customs which proscribe many forms of misbehavior in the marketplace. The right to compete implies no license to deceive or endanger the public, as is made clear by a vast body of legislation and judicial interpretation. One would also hazard a guess that, in the future, unless the business community does a better job of policing its own ranks, and finds ways to restrain the half truths, distortions, and stratagems of some of its members, there will be more laws and decrees than there are right now, enforced not only by slaps on the wrist (cease and desist orders) but possibly by jail sentences and surely by public ridicule. The price-fixing case in the electrical industry indicates the power of that ridicule. Several years after the court handed down its sentences, long after the financial claims and settlements had moved to the back pages of the newspapers, college students continued to taunt corporate visitors and recruiters with memories of the scandal.

The primary restraining order, however, comes not from a courtroom, but from the consumer. He buys or he does not buy, and he runs his own court of appeals. This, more than the corpus of law, is the force that guides the market.

Companies strain hard at the arts of persuasion and sometimes make so much noise about it that they fail to hear the customer's quiet voice speaking. Businesses large and small persuade, cajole, pester, and tease. They adorn their wares, decorate their stores, knock on doors, put on fashion shows, offer trading stamps, survey patterns of population and earning power, consult psychologists, put up billboards, sponsor parades, pour billions of dollars into television and newspaper advertising, and fly Santa Claus to the supermarket by helicopter not long after the first of November. Yet the consumer may yawn and turn away, and often does.

The size of a business organization or the amount of static it generates lends no overwhelming advantage and gives no exemption from competitive factors. Bigness makes companies more visible and raises the stakes in the game, but this can be a mixed blessing. The Ford Motor Company, to drag out a much used example, lost several hundred million dollars in its failure with the Edsel. Ford's size and voluminous advertising budget went for naught at a time when consumers shifted their mental gears and (as the Volkswagen people were suggesting) decided to think a little smaller. The Edsel debacle was hardly a singular incident. Chrysler had a similar flop with its Airflow sedan in the 1930s, and almost any large company, in the privacy of its executive suite, will admit to crushing defeats along with its proud victories in the marketplace. (Incidentally, years later some GE engineers, playing with a device that simulates a wind tunnel, put models of many cars to an aerodynamic test and discovered that the old Chrysler was a superior piece of engineering design. Chrysler's only trouble with the Airflow was that the public was not buying aerodynamics.)

The consumer has little immediate reason to care about the dimensions of the companies serving him. As a wayfaring motorist, he is unconcerned with the fact that Howard Johnson is a millionaire with a large yacht, or that Holiday Inns have multiplied into the hundreds. What the traveler wants to know is whether the hamburgers are tasty and the rooms are clean. Or, to put it in the feminine gender—where two-thirds of the nation's buying power is focused—the lady of the house is the last to care whether the company that makes Frigidaires is big or small. If the refrigerator stops working, she is wholly unimpressed by the fact that General Motors has assets of more than $13 billion and boasts more than thirty vice presidents unless, of course, one of the veeps happens to be in the neighborhood and is handy with a wrench.

She can well afford this independent attitude, for she and her family are no longer stranded in a market of minimal choice. The limitations of geography and technology, and the vicissitudes of weather no longer dictate a seasonal and uncertain offering on the store counter. As recently as a century ago, the thinness of population in most areas produced in effect a succession of local monopolies, small firms relatively immune to the intrusion of competitors purveying fuel, building materials, farm equipment, and other goods equally basic to life. Enterprise in those days enjoyed more freedom than its customers, for in many small and relatively isolated communities, the vendors on the spot commanded the lion's share of the consumer's dollar.

Today's merchant takes his customers less for granted. Food comes fresh, canned, frozen, dried, condensed, powdered, boxed, fortified, or precooked, in approximately the same variety in Cheyenne as in Baltimore, and with little reference to the seasons. If American tableware fails to suit the fancy, the store will stock Swedish modern, knowing full well that the customer can always find it in the store across the street, pick it out of the Sears' catalog, or order from Stockholm direct.

To wood and brick as building materials have been added steel, aluminum, glass, cement, and, most recently, a selection of plastic products, available from competing vendors. To wool, cotton, silk, and linen, the time-honored fabric materials, have been added rayon, acetate, nylon, polyesters, acrylics, and polypropylenes, all of twentieth-century origin, each multiplying the buyer's options.

A further form of competition has emerged to magnify consumer choice, and it is a direct product of prosperity. A typical family can meet its minimal needs of food, clothing, housing, and transportation with about one-half of its spendable income. The other half it is free to dispense as it pleases. The money may be used to make a down payment on a second car, to embellish the wardrobe, to panel the game room, to finance a trip to Yosemite, or to build the savings account. The modern corporation, which once spent its time worrying about line-for-line competitors, now finds that strangers have crashed the party. With Ford, Chrysler, and General Motors, the foot soldiers of the showroom floor spear at each other's customers with one hand, and with the other try to shield themselves from flank attacks by travel agents, boat sellers, and dispensers of hi-fi equipment. This makes life difficult for the man of commerce; he never knows whether his product is competing with an encyclopedia or an outboard motorboat. But the consumer likes the arrangement.

The Pluralistic Market

The vector of commerce is away from monopoly toward pluralism, and producers and sellers must respond in kind. U. S. Steel can no longer afford to think of itself as a company in the ferrous metals business alone; it is in the business of making structural and decorative materials, and as such must cope with firms offering wood laminates, non-ferrous metals, and other construction substitutes. By the same token, Standard Oil of New Jersey is not simply a gasoline maker but a producer of portable energy and a dealer in dozens of materials derived from petroleum sources. In this broader context, it can hardly number its competitors; the total is certainly in the thousands.

The size of an individual company no longer serves as a measure of concentration, nor does it minimize the number of other entrants. The larger and more profitable its markets, the more likely a big company is to draw new competitors. In 1902 U. S. Steel accounted for two-thirds of domestic ingot production. As of 1964 the same company accounted for less than one-quarter of the ingot production. Du Pont has long been the largest single chemical manufacturer in the world, yet it accounts for less than 8 per cent of the sales of the U.S. chemical industry, and in dozens of individual product lines it has for years been outpaced by smaller rivals. Du Pont has a minimum of fifteen major competitors each in fibers, plastics, industrial chemicals, coated fabrics, photographic products, pigments, and explosives. In a few high-volume products, such as paint and antifreeze, the competitors are numbered by the hundreds, and Du Pont is far from the largest contender.

New competitors dive into the chemical industry each year, undeterred by the fact that Du Pont, Dow, Monsanto, and Union Carbide are big and well established. The number of firms in the chemical industry climbs with each census of business, and at last report had reached twelve thousand.

The pattern is not the same in all industries. In some, the price of buying in is so staggering that a few large firms hold the fort. Auto making is a case in point. However, even for them there is no security in size, as Studebaker, Packard, and Kaiser can testify. Then, too, some enterprising foreigners have found or created their own holes in the U.S. market—MG, VW, Volvo, and Mercedes, for instance.

With the changeable currents of commerce, any company can be bypassed, or swept over the falls. How often this happens is suggested by a listing of the one hundred largest companies in manufacturing. The first such list was made for the year World War I ended. Of the one hundred companies then on the list, less than one-half can claim continuous membership in the "hundred largest" club. One can make no claims at all; it has gone out of business. A number of others fell from the list because their products became obsolete, or because they could not or would not adapt to changing market conditions.[2]

The biology of the business world is at times confusing. The relationship between large and small firms is not that of shark and minnow; instead, it is symbiotic, with each depending on the other. For the most part, large corporations do not compete with small ones; they meet rivals of their own size. Smaller organizations, competing against each other, are more often than not the customers of the big corporation, and if there is one thing businessmen understand, it is that you do not eat your customers.

There is also the matter of subcontracting, an especially vigorous practice in industries which can divide their products into components and farm them out to specialty producers. The aircraft industry is the classic example. Lockheed several years ago won a $1 billion contract for a transport plane, and to prove a point kept track of its disbursements through the chain of sub- and sub-sub contracts, out to the fifth generation. The company found that $620 million of the prime contract had traveled to a total of six thousand companies in the fifty states and Canada.[3] Sub and double-sub has become the rule of life in many large corporations, not only because Uncle Sam encourages it on federal projects such as aircraft development, but because smaller firms often provide special talents prime contractors lack, or cannot match in cost. Subcontractors speak a language purchasing agents understand, and this in part explains the fact that the number of small and medium-sized businesses in the United States is at an all-time high.

This incidentally is one of the areas where some self-policing by business is in order. With no implication that this in any way applies to the Lockheed example, it is clear that a big corporation may be far more solicitous of its customers than its subcontractors. It is one thing for the contractor to make the most favorable purchase he can, and another for him to use size and leverage to squeeze suppliers and subcontractors, some of whom are so specialized that they have no other place to sell their wares. This does not appear to be a widespread problem. The conditions for abuse do not exist in many industries, and salesmen with whom I have discussed the question say they have encountered only scattered cases of it in all of their contacts in industry. Yet it can happen and on occasion does, and an angry congressman fortified by chapter-and-verse evidence could quite literally bring the

House down on corporations trying to use thumb screws on their smaller neighbors.

"Administered prices"? "Monopoly"? There are segments of the market where these exist, where competition deliberately is limited or eliminated, and prices are administered in the most overt way. Airlines and railroads, municipal bus companies, and public utilities supplying telephone and electrical service fall into this category. These are special cases, with the "administering" done by public agencies, and with the number and type of competitors controlled to avoid an otherwise chaotic situation.

There are also instances in which corporations have run afoul of antitrust laws, guidelines on mergers, and other strictures intended to keep the market open and competitive. These too are special cases, some reflecting deliberate violations of law, some springing from changing interpretations in a body of law so complex that few people anywhere profess fully to understand it. Innocent or otherwise, transgressions are ancillary to the main point. The question is whether the large corporation, operating within the bounds of jurisprudence, yet retains a power in the market that transcends effective control. If such a power exists it has been well hidden from public and corporate view. Judging by the conditions of the market, the large corporation is a welcome and useful participant in the most competitive and pluralistic economy yet known.

The Owner's Eye?

There is one area and one only in which experience points to a problem of broad public concern that is yet unresolved. This is the problem of ownership participation. Corporate stock has been dispersed so broadly that in many large companies no individual stockholder, or close-knit group of owners, retains an effective voice in management. There is a touch of irony in this, and a loss to the companies involved. Whether we intended this to happen or not, it has come about because the base of capitalism has broadened so notably. The result for many companies has been a dilution of ownership interest, and little if any participation.

In the aggregate the majority still rules, but stockholders rarely meet in the aggregate. They are scattered all over the nation. They vote, if at all, by proxy, and most of them know so little about the details of the business that they could not offer helpful counsel if they wanted to. If a business is being badly or even dishonestly managed, the owners may be the last to learn the truth. Knowing, they may still feel helpless. A stockholder of modest means undertakes the labors of Hercules when he tries to solicit proxies for an assault on the management citadel. It can be done and has been, but several recent cases suggest that it takes five to ten years for a reform movement to gain momentum. In that much time, a precarious business situation can deteriorate into disaster. Unless a sense of responsibility and participation travels with ownership, the "people's capitalism" mentioned earlier in this chapter takes on overtones of owner anarchy.

A far healthier situation is to have a band of interested owners looking over management's shoulder, qualified to pass judgment on performance, and representing too much voting strength to be ignored. This is especially effective if the owners look upon the corporation as an enduring investment, to be maintained generation after generation. For such men provide a perspective not always found in the hired manager. The investor who is looking fifty years ahead, in the hope of building something for his grandchildren, is perhaps not so likely to act on short-range expediency and ignore problems that someone else can worry about "after I retire." His own interest dictates an approach closely attuned to society's objectives, for only through such a careful matching can the organization hope to prosper long-term. The professional manager, for all his acumen and diligence, rarely shares this perspective and commitment.

The typical stockholder, for his part, is likely to display a still more transient view. Despite the worshipful tone used to describe him in various brochures, as often as not he is in for a quick buck, and out again when the federal timetable lets him report his winnings at capital gains tax rates. He goes where the action is. This may be good fun —speculation is after all a game—but it makes no contribution whatsoever to the corporation, and adds nothing creative to the economy. It is merely horse swapping at an auction market.

There are exceptions, of course. Among investors (as distinguished from speculators) there are men who have worked diligently to enhance the stock in their portfolios or their customers'—for frequently such men are themselves bankers, investment counselors, or brokers. Consider as an example the investment banker Sidney Weinberg, senior partner of Goldman, Sachs & Company. In a business career of more than fifty years he was a director of more than three dozen firms, and an active rather than a passive one.

On the corporate side, there are still many companies in which the principal owners run the organization or direct the men who do. Du Pont is such a company. Polaroid and Xerox are younger examples. In such organizations, whether the founding family retains a strong minority interest or an absolute majority of the voting stock, one still finds men who look upon the ownership function with an almost puritanical sense of duty. But how many such men are there? By and large, as far as big corporations are concerned, the owner-manager, the man with a personal and permanent commitment to the company, is a vanishing American.

This is no apologia for inherited wealth, nor a plea for primogeniture. It is but an acknowledgment of an existing condition. The leveling process that flattened the wallets of one generation and bit into the inheritance of the next also muted the voice of the owner-manager. It remains to be seen whether an acceptable substitute can be found.

Thus far the alternatives tested have been found wanting. Institutional investors holding large blocks of corporate stock are sometimes encouraged to exercise more leverage in corporate affairs. These investors—the mutual funds, investment banks and trust companies, insurance companies, and pension funds—represent large numbers of individuals, but their opportunities to make an effective contribution are sharply limited. Their members are indirect owners, two steps removed from the corporations in which they have invested, and it is not always clear what course the managers of these portfolios are best advised to follow. Harvard, moving back to that example, might want its investment banker to move in one direction, while another client, perhaps a private estate, might have different objectives in mind. Moreover, depending on the relationships among companies, managers with funds to invest have to think twice before committing large sums in another company. The government frowns on such involvements, and in some cases prohibits them altogether.

One notable case, which was in and out of the newspapers for more than a decade, was the ownership that Du Pont held in General Motors common stock. That investment dated from 1917, with Du Pont holding a large minority position and taking an active role in the review of GM performance. As a result of antitrust action, as finally adjudicated by the U. S. Supreme Court, Du Pont was obliged to shed itself of the GM stock and give up its seats on the GM board. There was no evidence that competition had been reduced, or that there had been wrongdoing in any way—the district court in fact specifically found otherwise—but the Supreme Court's conclusion nonetheless was that such an intercompany interest was not a good idea for the future. Thus, that group of interested owners no longer is permitted to look over GM's shoulder, to advise and review management performance.

How great is the loss? Perhaps considerable, though it is not possible to attach a figure to it. One can only cite a reaction, which came not from Du Pont but from General Motors, in the form of a comment from Alfred P. Sloan, Jr., a central figure in GM for half a century. He alluded to the years when his company was struggling to find its footing, and when a number of Du Pont representatives were close at hand, including Pierre S. du Pont, Walter S. Carpenter, Jr., and John J. Raskob. In Sloan's opinion, "No one deserves more credit for the success of General Motors than that group of men from Du Pont who helped us."[4]

General Motors is big and strong now, and the big fellows are supposed to be able to take care of themselves in the hard, cruel world. But a basic point remains. The interested and informed stockholder, whose watchful participation has been of immeasurable importance in the growth of enterprise, is a force in fewer companies, and effective substitutes are hard to find, a fact which should trouble business leaders as much as anyone else. The consumer has not suffered directly—his freedom of choice remains unimpaired—but the corporate stockholders and employees ultimately may suffer, and in the long run the public also may. What is at stake here is not the legal question of accountability. Management is clearly accountable to the owners of the corporate assets. What is not clear is how those owners, dispersed so broadly, can in any effective way either assist or control the corporate activity, and whether "professional managers" as a general rule will operate as responsibly and effectively without benefit of "the owner's eye."

A Technical Quartet

At the beginning of this chapter the corporation was billed as a leading light in science and technology. The point deserves expansion, for here too the commercial organization has a public contribution to make. The private corporation fits in a special way into the matrix of science and engineering in the United States. Its contribution is essential and is in some respects unique.

We in the United States have for some years been able to boast the largest and most affluent technical establishment in the world. In round numbers, we have about 1.5 million scientists and engineers. Two-thirds of them are employed in industry. Funds to support research and development have been increasing every year, and of the total (more than $25 billion per year at last report) two-thirds is spent in industry.

The quality of the nation's technical output, which in the long run counts for more than the quantity, is uncommonly high. Among scientists themselves (who are really the only ones qualified to hold an opinion here) the United States is the acknowledged leader in several branches of science, and ranks with the best in almost any discipline. Much the same is true in engineering.

Money and manpower do not alone account for this. Smaller nations also can excel in science. Sweden, Great Britain, and West Germany are examples, and none of them has a population one-third as great as that of the United States.

Nor does an explanation lie in the political structure. Freedom may make a difference, but not enough to keep the Chinese from gaining nuclear power potential, or the Russians from demonstrating a talent for space shots.

Once upon a time, in one of our more jingoistic moods, we Americans sold ourselves the idea that heaven had blessed this nation with superior technical talents. That fable, which could cause a good deal more mischief if taken seriously today, should by now have been laid safely to rest. We have home-grown some impressive talent, but many of our most distinguished practitioners of science came here as immigrants, and do not belong to America even educationally. Einstein, Fermi, von Neumann, and Bethe, to name a few of the lions of physics and mathematics alone, were born and trained in Europe. One can play the same game in biology and other sciences.

Where the United States has had an advantage is in the structure of the technical establishment, and in its ability to generate and apply new knowledge. The technical effort in twentieth-century America has been predicated not on one or two types of sponsor but on four, producing diversity on a scale that no other nation has quite been able to match.

Within this quartet of sponsors—government, private foundations, the academic community, and private industry—there have been multiple incentives and alternative outlets to creativity. There has been little effort to allocate formal responsibilities, but in practice there has been a gentleman's agreement about the division of labor. Everyone in the quartet does not try to sing all parts.

Universities and private foundations have focused largely on explorations of fundamental nature, the first in conjunction with the teaching function, the second in a more independent and self-contained fashion.

Government has provided support for research on problems that reach beyond the resources of individual laboratories—public health, national defense, oceanographic and meteorological research, and agricultural problems calling for broad control measures.

Private industry, and notably the large corporation, has seen its primary job as one of translation and application, turning fundamental discovery into products of widespread utility, and utilizing technology to enhance efficiency. (It is no coincidence that in the past two decades industrial output has climbed at approximately the same rate as the number of scientists and engineers in industry.)

The division is not as neat today as it once was. Corporations perform about one-fourth of all basic research, on the premise that they will derive eventual benefit, and with the result that they help replenish the fount of knowledge as well as draw from it. Some universities have hordes of technical people working on government or industry contracts that have little or no scientific content, and little if any connection with the educational process. Government has extended its support into a host of disciplines and projects, overlapping and sometimes preempting the academic community on one side and industry on the other. Much of what passes for research is, in the words of a former assistant secretary for defense, "cutting tin and pouring concrete."

The dividing lines, though, are still visible. The four types of sponsoring organizations retain a difference of purpose and outlook. Each has its own yardsticks for the selection of projects; each dangles different incentives before the eyes of the technical man. There is a versatility and vigor that could not be retained in a structure more monolithic. If a project is inappropriate to one form of organization, it may hope to find support in another. If the directors in one agency are blind to an exciting new proposal, there is at least a chance that better vision will prevail elsewhere.

The efforts of these agencies are mutually reinforcing. University laboratories could no more dispense with the apparatus supplied by industry than industry could do without the fundamental theory developed by basic research. Private research foundations, though modest in scale (they account for only about 1 per cent of research and development expenditures) and something of an anachronism in the age of "big science," continue to make contributions to knowledge wholly beyond the proportions of their buildings and budgets.

"Spin Off"

Federal programs pointed toward military and space applications have produced "spin off" into the civilian sector of the economy. By the same token and in even more dramatic fashion, industrial research pointed toward commercial markets has supplied countless inventions and developments essential to defense. In their development of plastics, high-temperature metals and ceramics, computer technology, fuels and lubricants, insulating materials, communications apparatus, recording equipment, and other "hardware," corporate laboratories have provided key components of military equipment, very often funding the research with their own money. Whether such companies are "defense centered" or not, their accrued technology is indispensable to national security. Tangentially, it may also be noted that corporations pay about $40 billion per year in federal income taxes, which is not at all irrelevant to the financing of defense.

There is another form of "spin off," commonly overlooked but perhaps capable of wide application to national advantage. This is the use of business management's methods and systems in areas of governmental and public need. No one is suggesting that we try to run the country the way Boeing runs an airframe plant. However, preliminary trials at least suggest the possibility that some of the techniques developed by private corporations can be helpful in untangling the snarls that confront public agencies.

The state of California, for example, has turned to companies in the aerospace industry for aid in analyzing the monumental problems that confront that fast-growing urban area. Why the aerospace industry? Surely these companies claim no special wisdom in such areas as urban transportation or crime control. The reason is that such commercial organizations have access to special techniques and tools for the analysis of complex systems. What is loosely called operations research or systems analysis is now quite common in industry, and it could be an approach useful elsewhere, in government as in commerce, to attack all sorts of problems from block-blight to highway planning. The Space-General Corporation in 1965 did a study for California on control of crime and delinquency. The study mapped out areas of high population density, low income, high dropout rates, and high incidence of crime, and reported that all of these intersected in one area—Watts. The study did nothing to save Watts, which was ripped by riots late that summer, but it offered the hope that similar studies could bolster preventative programs, if put forth early enough.

Lockheed turned to computerized information handling systems as a tool for improving the flow of information among various levels and agencies of government. Its report on California government suggests savings that could run more than $100 million per year.

North American Rockwell assessed California's transportation problems and, with the aid of a mathematical model of the state's economy, produced a forecast of the state's transportation needs for the rest of the century.

In a television special, David Brinkley and NBC's news department turned their attention to the crushing problems U.S. congressmen face in obtaining accurate, timely information without inundation. The program noted that senators and representatives are often forced by the limits of human endurance to act with inadequate analysis. There is no way at present for them to digest all the materials relevant to their decisions. In preparing the program, NBC asked The Arthur D. Little Company to search out possible solutions. The management consultants pointed to big business, and suggested that Congress explore some of the corporation's techniques for collating and analyzing information. To film one example, NBC took its cameras into the chart room where Du Pont executives measure the state of the corporate health, and described the system used there—a system devised in the 1920s, since refined, and now used in many corporations.

Government units, let it be said again, cannot be run like corporate divisions. None of the studies mentioned here has yet produced any dramatic change, not alone because of governmental inertia and changing administrations, but because politics is complicated by more than statistics and State House personalities. However, there is no reason why government cannot borrow more liberally from the experience of industry. "Spin off" of this sort is there for the taking.

Genie: Friend or Foe?

Technology is dangerous. All of this meddling with molecules and life forces creates new problems and accentuates old ones. It brings change with no guarantee of progress. It forces readjustment of the educational process, of the production and distribution system, and of patterns of life and work. It abolishes jobs as well as creates them.

It could kill us all. As we hardly need be reminded in these days of nuclear proliferation and chemical-biological warfare, extermination is entirely possible for the occupants of Spacecraft Earth. Kurt Vonnegut, Jr., a novelist whose sharp wit never masks the depth of his affection for mankind, is one of many who have suggested that the terrors of technology outweigh the good. As he said in one book review, "Thoughtful young people aren't enthusiastic about careers in science anymore, I'm told. Does anybody who got past junior high school want to guess why?"

Yet without science there is no advance. Knowledge in any form is potentially disruptive, and a scientist cannot be told to pursue only "safe" projects any more than a philosopher can be told to think only harmless thoughts.

As astronomer Fred Hoyle says:

> The situation is that scientists produce science, and you must not expect them to produce anything else. If you do not like what they produce, then have no science. This, in fact, was the decision made in Italy after the time of Galileo. . . . The decision plunged Italy into centuries of unnecessary poverty, and perhaps for this reason the experiment is not likely to be repeated.[5]

Hoyle's point is, if anything, more pertinent to our century than to Galileo's. Despite the gains registered in the interim, there is as much work to be done now as then, and much of it depends for its accomplishment on science and engineering. The rising aspirations of the world's population, not to mention the increase in total numbers, require an uninhibited expansion of our technical capabilities.

To renege on this would in effect be to resign from civilization. Domestically the consequences would be bad enough; internationally, they are unthinkable. Technical advance remains an absolute prerequisite of new employment opportunities and economic expansion, to wealthy and poor countries alike. In a world where more than half are hungry, knowing pain and limitless want, anything less than a maximum effort would be an act of gross inhumanity.

The question, then, is not whether we ought to have technology, but how best to stimulate it, apply it, and above all control its consequences. Here as in the economic arena, the approach that is most productive is the pluralistic one, with a maximum of diversity among sponsoring organizations, as much latitude for the creative individual as can be mustered, and a much stronger degree of citizen participation in decisions about the dissemination and application of technology.

It may be that only scientists and engineers are qualified to pass on the technical merits of research and development projects. But they are no better equipped than the rest of us to set the priorities for society. In asking how technology is to be used, we move out of the realm of "is-is not" questions, into the subjective world of "ought-ought not." There, no single class of men, whether they be scientists or novelists, qualifies for sovereignty.

There must be choice. If all technology were to find its way to a single sponsor, we would in fact have a technocracy. Some fear we are not far from it now, in view of the rising proportion of research and development that is funded by the federal government. I am not that pessimistic, chiefly because the other and private agencies, independent of federal control, are doing more and better research than ever before.

Universities, though pressed by financial need to seek government support for research, yet retain their liberty of spirit. It appears to be growing, not waning, as academicians live up to their conscience and come to grips with essential questions about the mission of the scholar. The doctrine of "publish or perish" may drive some university scientists to pursue almost any project as long as they can get a paper out of it—as D. S. Greenberg so neatly puts it, "As long as you're up, get me a grant"—but many other faculty members, at cost to their own budgets, refuse to play the game that way. The university and society are the stronger for their presence.

The other large-scale presence on the scene is the corporation. Here too, government is sometimes the customer, but by no means always. Private corporations continue to make vital technical contributions, unduplicated elsewhere, at their own expense. If there is a trend to be seen here, it is toward more and better research under private sponsorship. Companies, like universities, have found that it does not pay to skew science and engineering too far in any one direction, especially when it places them at the mercy of changeable men in Washington.

Robert W. Austin, a professor of business administration and a director of a number of corporations, is one of many who have argued persuasively that the private corporation has a responsibility to fill not only in the creation of technology, but also in alleviating its social impact. Business organizations have willingly unleashed their technological innovations, but as Austin points out, they have been in no hurry to claim responsibility for all of the results, or to do much about the side effects.[6] I agree with his contention that unless big business voluntarily expands its role here, other segments of society will have to move in. Big government is the obvious candidate.

Acknowledging that Austin is right about the past, change for the better is to be noted in the present. My observation suggests that corporations are trying to anticipate the impact and side effects of processes and inventions on employees and on the general public. More important, many companies are taking action to prevent or alleviate problems. Pollution control is one example. Here is an issue of tremendous social consequence, and one on which action is imperative. The corporate response has been spotty. Some companies have played ostrich; some have dragged their feet, stalling expenditures as long as possible—both courses which invite further federal and state intervention, now forthcoming. It is significant, though, that other business organizations, of their own volition, began decades ago to put brains and money to work on problems of air and water pollution. Their research and control programs long antedate the present public clamor, and have provided much of the information and equipment that now make better control possible. Gains are not acquired cheaply. In the chemical industry alone, investment in pollution abatement and control facilities has long since passed the half-billion-dollar mark, and the research and operating expenditures top $100 million per year. The numbers are going up rapidly, under the pressure of new and more stringent laws.

Industry is not the sole or principal source of pollution. Community sewage, motor vehicle exhaust, and other sources are involved. Yet significantly, engineers and advisers from large corporations have been among the leaders in analyzing urban pollution conditions and in proposing solutions. This type of assistance, uncompensated and often unpublicized, is but a supplement to the corporation's basic responsibility to mind its own smoke stack; but it is one more sign of a changing sense of corporate duty.

In a totally different area, but one equally responsive to Professor Austin's point, corporations are increasingly looking ahead to the impact technical change will have on employees. Chapter 8 talked about the individual and retraining programs, but there is more to it than that. There is, if you will, a social side. An industrial plant is a major source of income to a small or medium-sized city. If the plant shuts down, the whole community suffers. Technology makes plants obsolete, and shuts some of them. What is the corporation's response?

Again, there are all shades to the answer. Some companies lay off the work force and walk away. Others do what they can to ease the blow. But what is notable here are the cases which could easily escape outside notice, because no crisis was allowed to materialize. The plant shut down, but the community felt no blow because there was none.

An example is an industrial plant at Old Hickory, Tennessee, near Nashville. Opened in 1925, the plant is still going strong, but it is not the same plant it was in 1925 or 1955. The owner, Du Pont, first made rayon there, later added cellophane, and still later added a series of other products. The rayon plant shut down in 1961. Cellophane disappeared from the site in 1964. Had it not been for the introduction of new products, two of which went in as cellophane went out, the shutdown of those initial products would have left the Old Hickory plant as cold as a tombstone. The key item here was foresight. Several years before the cellophane unit phased out, Du Pont saw the handwriting on the wall and began to look for other products that could go into Old Hickory. Planning and retraining made it possible to move 449 employees into entirely new jobs. As far as most people in the Nashville area are concerned, life at the plant has gone on with scarcely a ripple. Its paychecks and purchases say prosperity louder than ever.

This is a wholly unconfirmed suspicion, but for the benefit of the young man from Stanford let me add my own belief that Du Pont could have squeezed a bit more profit out of one or two of those newer products by producing them at other locations. I have not seen the detailed cost studies, but on the basis of surface evidence it appears that the men who made the decisions were trying to do more than maximize short-run profits. They were considering the corporation's relationship to long-service employees, and to the community. (Of course, one can respond to this by saying that this policy, followed long-range, *is* the way to maximize profits, an argument with which I would agree.)

Outside the Mainstream

What about the people who have not been able to get into the industrial work force, the blacks, the Mexican-Americans, the Puerto Ricans, and others so long excluded by prejudice and poverty of background? What is the corporation's response?

Here again, no general answer serves, and the usual disclaimers apply. Some corporate leaders, determined themselves to uphold the status quo or fearful of redneck reactions on their plants, have done little or nothing to hire Negroes for other than menial jobs. Pressed by civil rights laws and the cold questions of compliance officials, they try to take refuge in tokenism, and point to a few "showcase Negroes." The convenient word in their vocabulary is "qualified."

"But no other qualified Negroes applied," they say.

Other corporate executives have acknowledged the seriousness of the national problem and have moved decisively to do something about it. They have gone beyond mere compliance with the letter of the law, into what they call "affirmative action" programs to identify, recruit, train, and upgrade Negroes and members of other minority groups.

They have quietly dropped employment prerequisites that effectively froze out many ghetto residents—the high school diploma and the blemish-free police record, for instance. They have changed screening and placement tests which once were loaded with cultural bias, modifying the tests to make them nondiscriminatory and then testing these tests against on-the-job performance, to assure that they are predictive as well as fair. Training programs once intended only to impart craft skills have been expanded to include remedial schooling in the Three R's.

Euphemisms about "following local customs" have been replaced by no-nonsense orders from top management imposing nondiscriminatory standards throughout the corporation. White Citizens Councils, calling on company officials to see if they can find a wink behind the policies, have been politely received and sent away unsatisfied. No wink.

The corporate outreach has gone far past the factory gates. Corporations have helped launch and support school-based programs to lift disadvantaged young men and women to levels where they can qualify for skilled jobs. Potential dropouts have been steered back toward the mainstream through programs such as Upward Bound, designed not only to keep young people in high school, but also to prepare them for college. Upward Bound, now a national program, began with encouragement and money from a private corporation.

In some cases, instead of bringing ghetto residents to the industrial plant, the plant has gone to the ghetto. Western Electric, for example, has opened a plant in a slum area in New Jersey, and staffed it almost entirely with men and women who five years earlier would have been called "unemployable." IBM has a similar operation in the Bedford-Stuyvesant area of New York.

In other instances, a buddy system has been created to help new employees make the transition to industrial life. As the program is set up in one of the auto companies, the "buddy" is available off the job as well as on. Many of the newcomers have never held a steady job in their lives; they show up for work the first day but not the second, at which point the "buddy" shows up at the man's house to find out why. It is a one-on-one situation, but not a supervisor-subordinate one. The "buddy" is not the new man's boss, and if the new man is black, so is his "buddy."

Business leaders are not inclined to be boastful about these programs, and they have no reason to be. They know as well as anyone else that if thousands of people are being helped, hundreds of thousands of others remain untouched. Business can claim no singular credit for what has been accomplished. Foundations, church and civic groups, and government have been equally involved, and there is the realization that the corporation, like other institutions, was late in coming to the scene. The element of self-interest, the fact of government compulsion, and the scale of the job that remains to be done, all call for humility instead of self-proud rhetoric.

Many of the programs that have been launched may not float for long, and businessmen know it. Some programs have already foundered, or proved misguided. Government-funded slum clearance projects, for example, have torn down more low-income housing than they have built. Instead of solving the slum problem, they have moved it to new neighborhoods.

As another example, industry's efforts to set up branch plants in the ghetto have often met with resistance from the very people the plants hoped to employ. What is wanted, black spokesmen have said, is black-owned and black-run enterprises, not whitey's charity.

At a 1968 meeting sponsored by the National Association of Manufacturers, a young black leader from New York unloaded these remarks on his white, well-heeled audience:

> "You say we don't know how to run our own businesses yet; but in this city alone we have started a whole string of small enterprises, and we haven't had one of them fail yet. How many of you corporation executives can match that record?
>
> "You say we don't have the trained leadership we need. Yet I come before you with an M.B.A. from Harvard, and I can put together a management staff all with college degrees, including Master's and Ph.D.'s, all black—a good many of them clerking at the Post Office at the moment.
>
> "You say you want to help, yet we have asked for your money, either in loans or equity capital, and we haven't seen a cent of it yet. Every penny we have put in our businesses has been black money.
>
> "You say you'll invest in us if we let you run the show. We think you've been running it too long."

Perhaps it is significant that the audience was neither stunned nor offended. In the clusters of conversation after the meeting broke up, the common remark was "Maybe he's right." Such an attitude, to say the least, is not in keeping with the more venerable traditions of the NAM.

Times have changed and so have businessmen. Perhaps it is not too much to hope that the changes have come in time. Business leaders have always understood that neither they nor their organizations could survive in a crumbling economic structure. They are seeing, too, that they cannot survive in a crumbling social structure.

In Cash and Kind

It is not always easy to draw a line neatly separating a company's business from the community's. With a fair amount of arm twisting, corporations are asked to give money to schools, sponsor public service programs on television, back museums and orchestras, buy collections of modern art, join in movements to reform architecture or preserve wildlife, lend executives and consultants to Washington, put their muscle behind open-housing legislation, and in general inspire employees to good works in their home towns.

"Enlightened self-interest" is a popular criterion, but not always a clear one. Short of stripping the corporate treasury, where do you stop? A good case can be made for support of education, not as a gift but as an investment. Corporations currently donate $250 million per year (not counting tax support) to educational institutions, and in view of the mounting needs of colleges and universities perhaps that sum should be doubled. Why not do the same for secondary and elementary schools, which are no less important to the long-range manpower problem?

What about museums and libraries? Is not the quality of our cultural life every bit as important as the quantity of engineers and scientists we turn out? Some choices have to be made, and admittedly they are often arbitrary. There is, though, one solid buttress holding up the wall. Business has a limited mandate from society and it is in everyone's interest to keep it that way.

The bulk of the community contribution is and should be and must be personal, not corporate. A private company's major job, in the interest of its employees and the community as well as the stockholders, is to fulfill its economic role. If its executives and owners wish to make major contributions to society well removed from the economic mission, they are invited by the tax laws to set up organizations parallel to the Ford Foundation, and make philanthropy their principal business. A company can ignore a certain amount of the "government work" that goes on in its interior, but to cloud the basic purpose is bad business, and bad for society.

Desperate as we may be for donations to worthy public projects, fat as the corporate treasury may look from the outside, we must hesitate before loading more responsibilities on the corporation. To reverse the old saying, with responsibility goes authority, and authority carries power. It would be a long step backward for corporations to tell people—employees or otherwise—whether they ought to vote or whether the town should float another bond issue for another new school. If men and women fall short in the duties of citizenship, it is doubtful that the commercial organization, gifted largely in the manufacture and distribution of goods, is the appropriate agency to sponsor corrective action. People in corporations often have training that can contribute to community decisions. The community should not hesitate to call on them. But the corporation by itself has no special competence in such matters, except as dictated by the statistics of its employment roll.

(As a passing point, anyone looking for a subject for his Ph.D. thesis in sociology will find fascinating possibilities in the "government" jobs that are handled in corporations. Unbudgeted and often unpublicized, they comprise a substantial but as yet unmeasured contribution to the community. Some of them are indeed government work. There is a daily parade of businessmen going through National Airport and Union Station, on their way to conferences with Washington officials who seek their advice. Being knowledgeable about these matters, the government men often start at the top of the executive ladder, ask for the president or vice president, and obtain his help for free. The rest is "government work" of the other kind—free mimeograph service for the local boys' club, free time for a division head to chair the Community Fund drive, free service from an accountant in setting up the books for a new neighborhood college.

(As part of the research exercise, a doctoral candidate might try to estimate the number of civic and community organizations that would collapse if corporation employees suddenly suspended all their "unauthorized" office work. The thesis might also comment, in suitable academic prose, on the contention still popular in some academic quarters that businessmen are too busy making a buck to care about the rest of the world.)

Corporations are often and correctly accused of failing to lead in social reform. It is said that they follow public sentiment, usually several paces to the rear. This is true and it leaves us with problems, especially in communities lacking in other leadership. But is it wise on that basis to lift authority for social change from public hands, and assign it to corporate management? The luck of the draw gives some communities businessmen-citizens of the caliber of Joseph Wilson of the Xerox Corporation and David Rockefeller of the Chase Manhattan Bank; but it produces other executives less notably qualified for community leadership, and likely to make social problems worse rather than better.

It is correctly said that corporations in manufacturing are failing to provide the additional millions of employment opportunities for Americans joining the work force, and that employment is increasing mostly in the services sector of the economy. This is true not only for the present, but also is indicative of a trend that is part and parcel of our economic history. From 1870 on, the services (trade, finance, real estate, teaching, insurance, etc.) have been catching up with the goods-producing activities (mining, manufacturing, construction, etc.). The curves touched about 1955, and on a head-count basis we are now a service economy; less than half the work force is employed in goods-producing jobs.[7]

This is the highest compliment to American industry. Through the process of industrialization and by the application of technology, we have made agriculture and manufacturing so proficient that we have gained a leverage in manpower of almost six to one: 30 million people providing food and other material goods for themselves and more than 170 million others. What a monumental accomplishment, in a world that so recently had 90 per cent of its population locked into agriculture alone. What wealth and talent this gives us to meet other needs and wants.

The quota system does not apply here. There is no "right" number of people who ought to be working in big corporations or little ones, in the goods sector or in services. The objective is to make maximum use of the resources and talents available.

It is also said that big industrial corporations are not coming to grips with the "problem" of leisure. This too is correct. As an instrument for the furtherance of "the leisure society" and the misplaced ethic behind it, a manufacturing corporation is a colossal failure. It was invented not as a substitute for work but as a device for getting work done. The danger today is not that we will debase ourselves with excess spare time, but that as a nation we will turn away from work as a viable ethic in life, and repeat the pattern of decay and dissolution that was the history of earlier societies.

Until the world has a surplus of everything else, in goods and services alike, it will not have a genuine surplus of leisure. What ought to concern us is not overabundance but the still desperate shortage of time, physical resources, and brainpower to do the work that needs to be done to keep man alive and civilization in one piece. It is in this effort that the corporation, as a tool of productive accomplishment, can display the most impressive talents.

The primary (though not singular) social responsibility of the corporation is to do what it knows how to do best. To amend President Coolidge's unfortunate statement, the first business of business is business. Only if it fulfills that charter can it go on to meet the broader responsibility implied by a statement Theodore Sorensen made to a group of industrial leaders: "The business of business is America."[8]

As an agency of production responsive to the approval and censure of the society that gives it permission to survive; as a center for the advancement of technology; and as a focal point for a broad range of talents, the corporation affords a mechanism to multiply the effectiveness of individual effort. As a purveyor of products and services and as a force for the expansion of the pluralistic economy, the private corporation is an instrument, and perhaps the key instrument, for the generation of such wealth that for the first time in history it may economically be feasible to dream of a civilization that no longer needs, in the words of Jacques Barzun, "to suppress half of mankind to refine part of the other half."[9]

Some years ago a Swiss economist, William Rappard, attempted to isolate the factors that accounted for America's unmatched prosperity. He concluded that there were four: mass production; a passion for productivity; the spirit of competition; and the application of science to everyday economic needs.[10] The large corporation and its band of workers have been uniquely involved in all four.

Man incorporate, for all his imperfections and failings, is an uncommonly useful man.

NOTES

Chapter 1. INTRODUCTION

1. Notable evidence along this line has come from Harvard's David C. McClelland, who with a number of colleagues has found strong correlations between the performance of various societies and the attitudes and entrepreneurial spirit of the people. See his *The Achieving Society* (New York: 1961).

2. It should be noted that much of the indignation about "guaranteed income" and the so-called "negative income tax" has centered on proposals no one has made. Spokesmen such as Robert Theobald and Milton Friedman did not recommend putting everyone on the dole. They merely proposed that, where other measures have failed, the government step in to raise the level of income for a family to some minimal level. Also, some of the proposals are fashioned in such a way as to retain an incentive to work, which is by no means true of all existing welfare programs.

3. Borzoi (Knopf) edition (New York: 1945), vol. 2, p. 114.

4. Here as elsewhere, economic and census data have been drawn primarily from publications of the U. S. Department of Commerce, notably *Historical Statistics* and *Statistical Abstracts*, and from the numerous publications of the National Industrial Conference Board.

5. The opinions of youth are notably mercurial, giving survey data about them a short half-life. Still, what amounts to a trend cannot be ignored. Particularly in the past decade, studies by Gallup, Louis Harris, Opinion Research Corporation, and others have been remarkably consistent in reporting youthful doubt and disdain of the commercial facet of the workaday world, based largely on the belief that commerce has only material rewards to offer.

6. See Edith Hamilton's citation, *The Echo of Greece* (New York: 1957), p. 25.

7. Georges Friedmann, *The Anatomy of Work*, trans. by Wyatt Rawson (New York: 1961), pp. 158–159.

8. I am indebted for this gem to T. S. Ashton, who quotes it in "The Treatment of Capitalism by Historians," in *Capitalism and the Historians*, ed. by F. A. Hayek (Chicago: 1954), pp. 33–63.

Chapter 2. THE INSTITUTIONAL HERITAGE

1. No attempt will be made here to offer a critical bibliography of economic history. However, selected works that bear upon the themes developed in this chapter should be mentioned. An excellent one-volume survey is Robert L. Heilbroner's *The Making of Economic Society* (Englewood Cliffs, N.J.: 1962). Other works on which I have drawn include:

Miriam Beard, *A History of Business* (Ann Arbor, Mich.: 1962 [1928]).

G. F. Renard, *Life and Work in Prehistoric Times* (London: 1929).

Gustave Glotz, *Ancient Greece at Work* (London: 1926).

Greek Economics, ed. and trans. by M. L. W. Laistner (London: 1923).

George M. Calhoun, *The Business Life of Ancient Athens* (Chicago: 1926).

Robert S. Hoyt, *Europe in the Middle Ages* (New York: 1957).

M. L. W. Laistner, *The Intellectual Heritage of the Early Middle Ages*, ed. by C. G. Starr (Ithaca, N.Y.: 1957).

———, *Thought and Letters in Western Europe* (Ithaca, N.Y.: 1957).

G. Renard and G. Weulersse, *Life and Work in Modern Europe* (London: 1926).

Max Weber, *The Protestant Ethic and the Spirit of Capitalism*, trans. by Talcott Parsons (Glencoe, Ill.: 1948).

Tom B. Jones, *Ancient Civilization* (Chicago: 1960).

Mikhail Rostovtsev, *The Social and Economic History of the Hellenistic World* (New York: 1941, 3 vols.).

Joseph R. Strayer and Dana C. Munro, *The Middle Ages: 395–1500* (New York: 1959, 4th ed.).

Prosper Boissonnade, *Life and Work in Medieval Europe,* trans.
by Eileen Power (London: 1927).

Economic Organization and Politics in the Middle Ages, ed. by
M. M. Poston et al. (Cambridge: 1963).

R. H. Tawney, *Religion and the Rise of Capitalism* (New
York: 1942 [1926]).

2. *Cyropaedia,* trans. by Walter Miller (London: 1914), VII
ii 5–6.

3. *The Histories,* trans. by A. de Sélincourt (Baltimore:
1954), p. 132.

4. Georges Weulersse, *Le Mouvement Physiocratique en
France de 1756 à 1770* (Paris, 1910), vol. 2, p. 396.

5. Population estimates are drawn from *Atlas of World History,* ed. by R. R. Palmer (Chicago: 1957).

6. Cited in *Life and Work in Modern Europe,* pp. 373–374.

7. J. E. T. Rogers, *Six Centuries of Work and Wages* (New
York: undated volume published about 1884), p. 555.

Chapter 3. THE ROLE OF TECHNOLOGY

1. Though the history of technology is drawing increasing
attention from scholars, there are as yet few books which attempt to integrate technology into social and economic history.
Science, engineering, and invention are well documented as
individual entities, and there have been many attempts to explore the intellectual and social ramifications of science, but a
general argument of the type presented in this chapter must be
developed mostly from more narrowly focused works. Books
which have been helpful here include these:

Charles Singer et al., *A History of Technology* (London: 1954–
1958, 5 vols.), by all odds the most comprehensive current
work.

Abbott Payson Usher, *A History of Mechanical Invention*
(Cambridge, Mass.: 1954 [1929]).

James Kip Finch, *Engineering and Western Civilization* (New
York: 1951).

Lynn White, Jr., *Medieval Technology and Social Change* (Oxford: 1961).

H. Butterfield, *The Origins of Modern Science: 1300–1800*
(New York: 1957).

Charles C. Gillespie, *The Edge of Objectivity* (Princeton: 1960).

Alfred R. Hall, *The Scientific Revolution: 1500–1800* (New York: 1954).

Alexandre Koyre, *From the Closed World to the Infinite Universe* (Baltimore: 1957), p. 314.

Arthur O. Lovejoy, *The Great Chain of Being* (Cambridge, Mass.: 1936).

A. Wolf, *A History of Science, Technology, and Philosophy in the 16th and 17th Centuries* (New York: 1950), and his companion volume on the eighteenth century (1952).

2. The citation is from Adriano Tilgher's *Work: What It Has Meant to Man Through the Ages,* trans. by Dorothy Canfield Fisher (New York: 1931), a book on which I have drawn both in this chapter and in the next.

3. For both, see *Daedalus* (Summer 1965, vol. 94, no. 3).

4. The vineyards and olive groves were laid waste during the Peloponnesian War (431–404 B.C.), and thereafter a greater portion of the city's wealth had to be raised through sea trade and domestic manufacture of products for export, much in the manner of Phoenicia.

5. Useful references for this period are Gustave Glotz's *Ancient Greece at Work* (London: 1926); George M. Calhoun's *The Business Life of Ancient Athens* (Chicago: 1926); and *Greek Economics,* ed. and trans. by M. L. W. Laistner (London: 1923).

6. Trans-Mediterranean passages were made by at least 1400 B.C., and the Phoenicians are known to have sailed out of the Mediterranean as far as England; they are believed to have circumnavigated Africa. But these were extraordinary feats, far from routine.

7. Two textbooks provide a quick introduction to economic life in this period: Robert S. Hoyt's *Europe in the Middle Ages* (New York: 1957); and C. Harold King's *A History of Civilization* (New York: 1956).

8. *Republic* III: 406.

Chapter 4. THE ETHIC OF WORK

1. Ancient literature is so liberally sprinkled with such aphorisms that a listing quickly becomes laborious. Many examples

will be found in Plato. Hesiod's *The Works and Days,* trans. by Richard Lattimore (Ann Arbor, Mich.: 1959), contains even more. The Peripatetic quotation is from *Oeconomica* I: vi, 3, published with *The Works of Aristotle* (London: 1903–1931).

2. Economic histories often describe the ways in which people have made a living, but few scholars have attempted to uncover and record the attitudes toward labor prevalent in different times and places. Among the books and articles that have dealt with the ethic of work, these three are particularly pertinent, together with McClelland, Tawney, and Tilgher, *op. cit.:*

A. T. Geoghegan, *Attitudes Toward Labor in Early Christianity and Ancient Cultures* (Washington, D.C.: 1945).

Ernst Troeltsch, *The Social Teaching of the Christian Churches,* trans. by Olive Wyon (New York: 1949 [1931]).

R. Mondolfo, "The Greek Attitude to Manual Labour," in *Past and Present* (Oxford: 1954), vol. VI, pp. 1–5.

Chapter 5. THE ETHIC OF COMMERCE

1. Cited by Daniel Bell in "Notes on Work," in *Encounter* (June 1954, vol. 2, no. 6), p. 15.

2. An excellent if biased introduction to the rise of nineteenth-century socialism is available in Edmund Wilson's *To the Finland Station* (New York: 1940). Other references for this chapter, in addition to the economic works cited for previous chapters, are:

Morris Ginsberg, *The Idea of Progress* (Methuen, Mass.: 1952).

Man, Work, and Society, ed. by Sigmund Nosow and William H. Form (New York: 1962).

Henri Pirenne, *A History of Europe,* trans. by Bernard Miall (Garden City, N.Y.: 1956, 2 vols.).

H. M. Robertson, *Aspects of the Rise of Economic Individualism* (Cambridge, England: 1933).

Adam B. Ulam, *The Unfinished Revolution* (New York: 1960).

Chapter 6. AN AMERICAN SYNTHESIS

1. *Of Plymouth Plantation,* ed. by Samuel Eliot Morison (New York: 1952).

2. The comments of the more prominent Americans need no elaboration here. However, Lucy Larcom and William Manning deserve special note. Manning's essay, completed in 1798, provides a quaint but revealing insight into popular attitudes of the time. The current edition was published in 1922 by The Manning Association, Billerica, Massachusetts. Miss Larcom was but one of a number of mill girls who together wrote and published a periodical, *The Lowell Offering,* in the 1840s. Selections from it will be found in *Mind Amongst the Spindles* (Boston: 1845); and a brief description of life and work at Lowell will be found in Edmund Fuller's *Tinkers and Genius* (New York: 1955), pp. 176–190.

3. A boundless collection of such songs may be found in the New York Public Library's music department, and I am indebted to the librarians there for the titles cited.

4. In addition to *Historical Statistics, op. cit.,* these references apply to Chapter 6:

The Diary and Autobiography of John Adams, ed. by L. H. Butterfield (Cambridge, Mass.: 1961).

Howard I. Chapelle, *The History of American Sailing Ships* (New York: 1935).

Katherine Coman, *Industrial History of the United States* (New York: 1911).

Foster Rhea Dulles, *The United States Since 1865* (Ann Arbor, Mich.: 1959), published jointly with a companion volume by Michael Kraus, *The United States to 1865.*

Harold Underwood Faulkner, *American Economic History* (New York: 1960).

H. J. Habbakuk, *American and British Technology in the 19th Century* (Cambridge, England: 1962).

Courtney R. Hall, *History of American Industrial Science* (New York: 1954).

Brooke Hindle, *The Pursuit of Science in Revolutionary America* (Chapel Hill, N.C.: 1954).

John Jewkes et al., *The Sources of Invention* (London: 1958).

Richard Ketchum, *The Pioneer Spirit* (New York: 1954).

John W. Oliver, *History of American Technology* (New York: 1956).

John B. Rae, "The 'Know-How' Tradition: Technology in American History," in *Technology and Culture* (Spring 1960, vol. 1, no. 2), pp. 139–150.

Ross M. Robertson, *History of the American Economy* (New York: 1955).

Arthur Meier Schlesinger, *Paths to the Present* (New York: 1949).

John W. Ward, *Andrew Jackson: Symbol for an Age* (New York: 1955).

Mitchell Wilson, *American Science and Invention* (New York: 1960).

Chapter 7. CORPORATE BAEDEKER

1. This is not to say, of course, that all academicians and critics interested in the corporation are spectators with no more than secondhand insight. One prominent trend of recent years is the drawing together of campus and corporation, and many faculty members, especially but not exclusively within business schools, can claim close exposure to corporate activities through consultantships, directorships, or previous employment.

Even among this group, though, the absence of continuing, day-to-day contact with the corporate interior leaves gaps of information, and invites the perpetuation of stereotyped views.

2. Here as in several other places in this chapter, figures are used which are subject to annual change. However, statistics are given only where the order of magnitude is what counts most, and where year-to-year change does not alter the general point being made.

3. I question, too, whether they ever were as much like tin soldiers as they have been portrayed. For some reason, students and critics of the industrial economy have been inordinately fond of studying the automobile assembly line and/or textile manufacture. Both have long involved large numbers of redundant, low-skill tasks. However, such working conditions were and are far from universal.

4. Gardner uses the term in the title of a stimulating article in *Harper's* (October 1965).

5. A thoughtful discussion of this danger is offered by Philip Abelson, who argues that, at least within research groups, dissension can be especially destructive, with personality clashes turning attention away from creative effort. See "Group Activity and Creativity in Science," in *Daedalus* (Summer 1965, vol. 94, no. 3), pp. 603–614.

Chapter 8. THE MANDATE OF MANAGEMENT

1. As much as any single factor, this may account for mis-understanding of the management process in large corporations. As Edward S. Mason has pointed out in the introduction to *The Corporation in Modern Society* (Cambridge, Mass.: 1959), it is all too easy to create a situation in which those who know don't tell, and those who tell don't know.

The more readable popular works frequently present as typical management activities which seem remote or foreign to the insider's experience, and, as a more serious failing, do not deal with intriguing general problems that can be seen there. Vance Packard's *The Pyramid Climbers* (New York: 1962), and William H. Whyte, Jr.'s *The Organization Man* (New York: 1956) are examples of otherwise useful books (both say much that is true and needs to be said) marred by this lack of deeper insight.

Introspective business leaders who might make notable con-tributions to the understanding of the management process have only occasionally risen to the challenge. There are few memoirs of opinion (or management philosophy, if you will) to set along-side Crawford H. Greenewalt's *The Uncommon Man* (New York: 1959). Even such prominent works as Alfred P. Sloan, Jr.'s *My Years with General Motors* (Garden City, N.Y.: 1964) are largely pro forma accounts of what happened, and do not supply the perspective and evaluation of personal factors their authors could have provided. In my view, Ernest Dale's chapter on GM in *The Great Organizers* (New York: 1960), pp. 71–111, gives a better feeling for the subtleties and root problems of management than Sloan's more detailed treatment.

Among scholarly treatises which attempt to deal with funda-mentals, as contrasted with specific administrative functions (e.g., control) or "How To" books, these four might be cited, plus Dale's book:

Peter Drucker, *The Concept of the Corporation* (New York: 1946).
——, *Managing for Results* (New York: 1964).
Rensis Likert, *New Patterns of Management* (New York: 1961).
Wilbert E. Moore, *The Conduct of the Corporation* (New York: 1962), a sometimes angry but pertinent view.

2. For discussions of this see William H. Read, "The Decline of the Hierarchy in Industrial Organizations," in *Business Horizons* (Fall 1965, vol. 8, no. 3), pp. 71–75; R. L. Simpson, "Vertical and Horizontal Communications in Formal Organizations," in *Administrative Science Quarterly* (1959, vol. 4), pp. 188–196.

3. Cited by Daniel Bell, *Work and Its Discontents* (Boston: 1956), p. 7.

4. Meany made this point in an address before the National Industrial Conference Board, New York City, September 19, 1966.

Chapter 9. THE INDIVIDUAL IN THE ORGANIZATION

1. For one such argument see psychologist Harry Levinson's "Anger, Guilt, and Executive Action," in IBM's *Think* (March–April 1964).

2. Robert Blauner, *Alienation and Freedom: The Factory Worker and His Industry* (Chicago: 1964).

3. "The Human Side of Automation," in *Business Horizons* (Spring 1960).

4. Polly Redford, "Small Rebellion in Miami," in *Harper's* (February 1964).

5. Dr. Argyris recounted this episode at a conference at Cornell University, August 11, 1961. I do not know whether he has included it in his published works.

6. François Mauriac, *The Viper's Tangle* (New York: 1960 [1947]), p. 60.

7. *The Concept of the Corporation* (New York: 1946), p. 152.

8. *Harper's* (December 1946), pp. 391–392. For other and later illustrations, see *Men at Work*, ed. by W. F. Whyte (Homewood, Ill.: 1961); *The Making of Economic Society; Man, Work, and Society;* and *The Anatomy of Work*.

Chapter 10. THE CORPORATION IN SOCIETY

1. Walter Lippmann, *An Inquiry into the Principles of the Good Society* (Boston: 1937).

2. A. D. H. Kaplan made this study for the Brookings Institu-

tion beginning in 1947. It was first published under the title *Big Enterprise in a Competitive System* (Washington, D.C.: 1954) and was revised and updated, under the same title, in 1964. Other data in this section are from corporation annual reports and from the Manufacturing Chemists Association, Washington, D.C.

3. *The Wall Street Journal* (November 18, 1965).

4. A. P. Sloan, Jr., to author, personal interview, August 10, 1959.

5. Fred Hoyle, *Of Men and Galaxies* (Seattle: 1964).

6. "Responsibility for Social Change," in *Harvard Business Review* (July–August 1965), pp. 45–52.

7. The statistics of this make fascinating reading, and can be found in many of the publications of the U. S. Department of Commerce. One convenient summary and analysis is offered by Victor R. Fuchs of the National Bureau of Economic Research, published as an Occasional Paper of the Bureau, and also available in *The Journal of Business* (University of Chicago: October 1965), pp. 344–373.

8. Speaking before a conference sponsored by the National Industrial Conference Board, New York City, April 18, 1966.

9. Jacques Barzun, *God's Country and Mine* (Boston: 1954), p. 191.

10. *The Secret of American Prosperity* (New York: 1955).

INDEX

ANCHOR BOOKS